Education and Girls on the Autism Spectrum

Education and Girls on the Autism Spectrum

Developing an Integrated Approach

EDITED BY JUDITH HEBRON
AND CAROLINE BOND

Jessica Kingsley *Publishers*
London and Philadelphia

First published in 2019
by Jessica Kingsley Publishers
73 Collier Street
London N1 9BE, UK
and
400 Market Street, Suite 400
Philadelphia, PA 19106, USA

www.jkp.com

Library of Congress Cataloging in Publication Data
A CIP catalog record for this book is available from the Library of Congress

British Library Cataloguing in Publication Data
A CIP catalogue record for this book is available from the British Library

ISBN 978 1 78592 460 6
eISBN 978 1 78450 837 1

Printed and bound in Great Britain

Contents

Acknowledgements

The editors wish to thank all of the chapter authors for their time and willingness to contribute to this book, often combining writing with very busy professional or student schedules. We are also grateful to the many autistic girls and young women who have contributed to the book either directly or indirectly. Without your generous participation and sharing of experiences, this book would not have been possible. Finally, thank you to Mandy Toothill for helping us to produce the diagram for the Bronfenbrenner framework that guides the organisation of the book.

Introduction

Caroline Bond and Judith Hebron

Autistic girls have been described as 'twice excluded' (Shefcyk 2015, p.132) and 'research orphans' (Bazelon 2007, p.1). Gender differences between autistic girls and boys are increasingly acknowledged as resulting in girls being less likely to be identified as autistic (Krahn and Fenton 2012), and even when they are identified, autism research has tended to focus predominantly on boys. This exclusion of girls from the autism literature also means that school staff may not be aware of the needs of autistic girls, potentially resulting in under-recognition and a lack of appropriate support (Morewood 2018; Moyse and Porter 2015). Although research focusing on the specific needs of autistic girls remains in its infancy, awareness of the need to recognise and support girls in education has been growing (Nasen 2016). This book aims to draw together personal experiences, professional expertise and research in order to promote improved identification, understanding of needs, and appropriate support for autistic girls in education.

Although the predominant medical term is 'autism spectrum disorder' (ASD) (American Psychiatric Association (APA) 2013) many autistic people challenge the concept of autism as a disorder or deficit and instead view it as a neurological difference which provides them with unique strengths as well as differences. Given that for some people autism is an essential aspect of their identity, they may refer to themselves as autistic rather than as a person with autism

(Milton 2012), while others prefer alternative terms, such as 'autism spectrum condition'. However, there remains a lack of agreement in relation to autism terminology (Kenny *et al.* 2016), and Gernsbacher (2017) advocates the use of identity-first language in order to reduce stigma. For these reasons we have chosen not to adopt a standard terminology for this book, with individual chapter authors using their own preferred terms. Having consulted with autistic chapter authors we have adopted the term 'autistic' for the introduction and conclusion of the book.

This introductory chapter provides an overview of the field. It begins with a brief history of autism and diagnosis, looking at how our knowledge and understanding of it has developed. Alongside this, we explore how our awareness of the needs of autistic girls and women has increased, particularly through the writing and advocacy work of key women who are themselves autistic. We then focus more specifically on autism education and research, and the representation of autistic girls within this research. Finally, an integrated approach is proposed in order to draw together the many systems impacting upon autistic girls during their education. This integrated approach is then adopted as the organising structure for the chapters of the book.

A brief history of autism

When autism was first described by Leo Kanner and Hans Asperger in the 1940s they were writing mainly about males. Asperger's patients were all boys and Kanner's were predominantly boys. Alongside this focus, Kanner's view that autism was very rare and characterised by a profound lack of affective contact and elaborate repetitive behaviour further shaped diagnostic systems (Silberman 2015). This resulted in a narrow definition of autism, low prevalence rates and limited research on educational approaches.

It was only in 1979, when Lorna Wing and Judith Gould published their Camberwell study, that the concept of autism began to broaden. Wing and Gould (1979) not only looked at how prevalent autism was among children and young people with Kanner's early childhood autism profile, but they also identified a wider group of children and young people who did not fully meet Kanner's criteria. This wider group had a triad of difficulties characterised by differences in social communication, social interaction and social imagination, together with restricted activities or interests. In a further broadening of criteria in 1981, Lorna Wing (1981) also drew the English-speaking world's attention to the work of Hans Asperger by highlighting that individuals vary in relation to the triad of difficulties, with individuals who demonstrate good verbal abilities and socially aloof behaviour considered similar to some of the young people identified by Asperger in his 1944 study. Wing and Gould proposed that there was an autism spectrum which encompassed a wide range of individual profiles across the dimensions of the triad of difficulties (Wing and Gould 1979). The work of Wing and Gould subsequently formed the basis of a revised version of the *Diagnostic and Statistical Manual of Mental Disorders III-Revised* (APA 1987) which was based around this triad of impairments.

The most recent manual, the *Diagnostic and Statistical Manual 5* (*DSM-5*) (APA 2013), represents a substantial revision of autism diagnostic criteria and now includes just two overarching criteria for an autism spectrum diagnosis: (1) social communication and social interaction deficits, and (2) restricted, repetitive patterns of behaviours or interests. Social communication and social interaction difficulties may include deficits in social-emotional reciprocity or non-verbal communication and/or difficulties making and maintaining social relationships. These social difficulties will vary substantially between autistic people but might be evident through difficulty interpreting their own or other people's emotions, difficulties responding to social cues such as when to take turns in a conversation, or difficulty forming friendships. Restricted and repetitive behaviour may include stereotyped motor movements, lack of flexibility, restricted interests and under- or over-sensitivity to sensory input. Again, behaviour difficulties will vary substantially between individuals but could include preference for particular routines such as eating at a particular time, having narrow or unusual interests such as finding out everything they can about a particular celebrity, collecting lamp post numbers, or being very sensitive to particular sounds such as a school bell.

Although Wing did not differentiate Asperger syndrome as a separate diagnostic category from autism, Asperger syndrome and high-functioning autism did become distinct categories in the diagnostic systems in the 1990s. However, the most recent version of the *DSM-5* (APA 2013) attempts to integrate the different terms, such as 'childhood autism' or 'Asperger syndrome', under one umbrella term: autism spectrum disorder. This overarching label allows for differences in language development or degrees of learning difficulty to be captured using descriptors, rather than through more specific labels (such as high-functioning autism, pervasive developmental disorder or childhood autism) as was the case in previous diagnostic manuals. However, these changes have not been without controversy, especially as those people meeting criteria for an Asperger syndrome diagnosis now receive the broader autism spectrum diagnosis, which some perceive as too broad to accurately describe their needs. This expansion of the autism spectrum has also meant that diagnoses are now much more common, with estimated prevalence rates of 1.7 per cent among the primary-school-age population in the UK (Russell *et al.* 2014).

Autism and personal experience

Although autism prevalence rates of four boys to one girl have often been cited (Fombonne 2009), one of the first people to write and present about their experience of having a diagnosis of autism was a woman, Temple Grandin. Her first book, *Emergence: Labeled Autistic* (Grandin and Scariano 1986), played an important part in breaking down the stigma surrounding autism. The writing and experiences of other female authors such as Donna Williams, Claire

Sainsbury, Ros Blackburn and others have also continued to provide an important counter-balance to medical and academic discourses: 'right from the start, from the time someone came up with the word "autism", the condition has been judged from the outside, by its appearances, and not from the inside according to how it is experienced' (Williams 1996, p.14).

Autistic women have been influential in the development of autism advocacy groups and have helped to raise awareness of less-researched features of autism, such as the importance of sensory sensitivities and the significant impact these have on their lives: 'One of my sensory problems was hearing sensitivity, where certain loud noises such as a school bell hurt my ears. It sounded like a dentist's drill going through my ears' (Grandin 2015).

Many autistic adults have particularly welcomed the inclusion of sensory factors in the current *DSM-5* (APA 2013) criteria. The significant impact of these difficulties in education settings was further developed by Donna Williams:

> There are many things that people with autism seek to avoid: external control, disorder, chaos, noise, bright light, touch, involvement, being affected emotionally, being looked at or made to look. Unfortunately, most educational environments are all about these very things. (Williams 1996, p.284)

These personal experiences of autism have been crucial in advancing our understanding and have also challenged the way autism is defined and researched. As highlighted by Donna Williams, personal experiences of autism may not easily fit with medical definitions and there continues to be much debate about terminology surrounding autism.

Autism research, like diagnosis, has historically been dominated by a medical and scientific approach. This focus has meant that research funding has tended to be directed towards understanding the biology and causes of autism and less funding has been directed towards interventions, services and social issues (Pellicano, Dinsmore and Charman 2013). Pellicano *et al.* (2013) undertook a survey of research-funding priorities identified by adults with autism, parents, professionals and researchers: their analysis found that these stakeholders wanted research priorities to be services such as post-diagnostic support, interventions and awareness-raising (such as community awareness-raising and autism awareness training). These research findings provide strong evidence that training for those working in education and interventions for autistic children and young people need to be key priorities.

Diagnosing autistic girls

In parallel with the wider field of autism research, the limited research relating to autistic girls has tended to focus on prevalence, diagnosis and how autism presents in girls. It is interesting that although Kanner's and Asperger's research focused predominantly on boys, they both observed potential gender disparities. Furthermore, Wing (1981) suggested that presentation in girls may be subtler – and therefore missed – due to compensatory mechanisms, leading to what has become known as the 'camouflage hypothesis'. However, these observations were not explored in more depth until relatively recently. Krahn and Fenton (2012) argue that viewing autism through a 'masculine lens' (p.95) such as Baron-Cohen's 'extreme male brain theory of autism' (2002) has contributed to the exclusion of girls as a specific group in autism research. Recent studies indicate that the male to female gender ratio in autism might be 5:2 (Kim *et al.* 2011), which is closer than previously thought. Rates of diagnosis also vary across the autism spectrum, and historically girls have been more likely to be diagnosed if they have additional learning needs, and less so if they are higher functioning (Lai *et al.* 2015). This presents a challenge for schools as there are therefore likely to be many girls in mainstream education who are not diagnosed or receiving appropriate support.

There is also growing evidence of a female phenotype in autism (Mandy *et al.* 2012). Compared to autistic boys, autistic girls tend to show more desire to interact with others and may often be perceived as 'just shy'. They have a tendency to imitate others, mask or camouflage their social interaction difficulties, and develop compensatory strategies. Autistic girls may also have one or two close friends. At primary school they may be looked after by peers but they may be bullied at high school. They are also likely to have better linguistic skills and greater imagination than boys, with their restricted interests tending to involve people or animals, such as celebrities or horses, rather than objects. Additionally, autistic girls tend to be perfectionists, controlling in their interactions with peers and demand avoidant. They may also have episodes of eating problems (Lai *et al.* 2015).

Although the broad autism spectrum criteria within the *DSM-5* (APA 2013) are not gender-specific, Lai *et al.* (2015) point out that at the narrower end of symptomology there may be more subtle gender differences, as indicated above. Narrower symptoms include behavioural characteristics such as use of eye contact and restricted interests, with these symptoms forming the basis of many assessment tools, such as the Autism Diagnostic Interview – Revised (Lord, Rutter and LeCouter 1994). However, by focusing on these narrower symptoms where there are more gender differences, assessment tools and processes may be more biased towards a male presentation of autism. For instance, the Autism Diagnostic Observation Schedule (ADOS) (Lord *et al.* 2002), which is viewed as a 'gold standard' instrument, was developed with mainly male cases (Koenig and Tsatsanis 2005), and so may not pick up on features more specific to females. Several studies have also found that girls meet diagnostic criteria for autism in different ways to boys (e.g. Lai *et al.* 2015). Duvekot *et al.* (2017) found that scores for restricted interests and repetitive behaviour are predictive of an autism diagnosis in boys but not in girls, while sensory symptoms are equally predictive for boys and girls.

There is some debate about how co-occurring conditions contribute to diagnosis in boys and girls. Some studies indicate boys are more likely to demonstrate co-occurring externalising behaviour such as aggression and hyperactivity while girls show more internalising symptoms (Mandy *et al.* 2012). Where girls are reported to have additional emotional and behavioural problems this may increase the likelihood of diagnosis (Duvekot *et al.* 2017). These differences in mean levels of symptomatology and patterns of symptoms suggest that current observational and parent-report measures may not be accurately capturing the subtler presentation of autism in girls (Duvekot *et al.* 2017; Little *et al.* 2017). It is acknowledged in the *DSM-5* that if girls do not have additional learning or language difficulties their social communication needs may not be identified as these may present in less obvious ways compared to autistic boys (APA 2013). There is some evidence to support this, as Mazurek *et al.* (2017) found in a comparison of *DSM-IV* (APA 1994) and *DSM-5* (APA 2013) diagnoses that older girls with stronger cognitive abilities were less likely to be diagnosed using the *DSM-5*. Some initial attempts have also been made to develop measures which are more sensitive to autism in females, such as the Autism Spectrum Screening Questionnaire – Revised Extended Version (Kopp and Gillberg 2011). A lack of research on gender role factors that may influence expression of autism in girls also means that the interaction between development and environment over time is unclear, making it difficult to know what a 'typical' female presentation might be at a particular age.

Parents have also reported subtle differences between boys and girls (Mademtzi *et al.* 2018). Although social interaction, co-occurring anxiety and inappropriate sexual behaviour have been identified in the literature as challenges for boys as well as girls, gender-specific difficulties have also been noted. These include difficulties socialising with other girls, puberty, problems accessing intervention due to late diagnosis, and sexual vulnerability. Studies have also focused on professionals' awareness of gender differences in autism. Hillier, Young and Weber (2014) found among a sample of high-functioning boys and high-functioning girls assessed for autism spectrum difficulties that teachers and clinicians reported a female autism profile of milder social impairments and subthreshold restrictive and repetitive behaviours. Teachers reported substantially fewer concerns about girls overall and less externalising behaviour than boys, potentially leading to girls being perceived as less impaired in a school setting. A further study by Jamison *et al.* (2017) focused specifically on clinicians who were involved in diagnosis. They found that 70 per cent of clinicians reported noticing more sex-related differences in core symptoms. Open-ended responses indicated that perceived differences were particularly in the area of repetitive behaviour and less so in social communication features. Fifty-four per cent of clinicians also noted gender differences in secondary symptoms, such as sensory and emotional difficulties. These differences in presentation between girls and boys were particularly evident during school-age and adolescent periods, indicating that these might be key periods of vulnerability for autistic girls.

These differences in diagnostic criteria and presentation pose challenges as girls are more likely to be under-diagnosed, diagnosed later than boys or missed entirely (Lai *et al.* 2015). It is interesting to note that a number of women writing about autism, such as Sarah Hendrickx, Clare Sainsbury and Gunilla Gerland, were themselves not diagnosed until they were teenagers or adults. Late or misdiagnoses are often reported (Jones 2001; Kanfizer, Davies and Collins 2017) and can have a profound effect on educational experiences and adult outcomes. Currently the average age for boys to receive a diagnosis of ASD in the UK is 67.27 months whereas for girls it is 72.05 months (Brett *et al.* 2016). Possible reasons for these gender differences in diagnosis include girls being less likely to present with 'classical autism', gender-biased interpretations of their behaviour, and diagnostic overshadowing where girls are more likely to be diagnosed with secondary conditions such as depression rather than autism. These factors mean that girls are less likely to be identified by schools and referred onto more specialist services such as Child and Adolescent Mental Health Services or educational psychology.

Autism and education research

In the UK, as in many other countries, there has been a gradual move away from segregated education provision for children and young people with special educational needs. The inclusion movement of the 1980s and the Salamanca Statement (UNESCO 1994) emphasised the importance of children with special educational needs being educated alongside their peers. However, given the diverse needs of autistic children and young people, there has been gradual recognition internationally of the need for a continuum of educational provision from mainstream schools through to mainstream schools with resource provision and special schools (Bond and Hebron 2016). Although many autistic pupils are educated in mainstream settings and benefit both socially and academically from these experiences, there are also many young autistic people who struggle with the demands of mainstream and are at risk of increased anxiety or exclusion. Academically able young people whose autism is less obvious may find school more challenging as they get older, especially navigating the social and organisational complexities of mainstream high school (White *et al.* 2007). Experiences of bullying and reduced social acceptance are also likely to negatively affect emotional wellbeing and educational attainment (Ambitious about Autism 2013).

Autism research in education has sought to identify ways of improving the educational experiences of autistic children and young people and has tended to focus on three main areas. These are educational interventions, good practice, and educational experiences of autistic children and young people. Although there are many autism interventions, some of which are developing an evidence base in schools, Simpson, Mundschenk and Heflin (2011) argue that this area of research remains in its infancy. Kasari and Smith (2013) point out that consideration of the perspectives and needs of autistic children and young people and their families and schools has received limited attention in intervention research, making it difficult to bridge the gap between research and practice. A second area of research has focused on good practice and has identified aspects of this common to education settings across the continuum of provision (Bond and Hebron 2016). These include whole-school factors (e.g. ethos and leadership), classroom approaches (e.g. differentiation), autism-specific adaptations, peer understanding, and collaborative working between pupils, school staff, families and external professionals. Although this research is useful, embedding these approaches in schools takes time and many teachers still report that they have not had sufficient training to enable them to effectively support autistic children and young people (Segall and Campbell 2012). The third area relates to experiences of education: this has particularly highlighted the needs and concerns of academically able young people in mainstream education (McLaughlin and Rafferty 2014) and confirms the importance of a number of factors identified in the good practice literature, such as teachers providing structure and promoting positive peer relationships (Hebron and Bond 2017).

Although these three areas are useful in informing our knowledge of how to support autistic children and young people in education generally, the research has focused on all-male or mixed samples with small numbers of girls. This means that to date there is limited information about autistic girls' experiences of education, and little research on interventions or good practice which are so important for their success in education. However, a small but growing number of studies are now being published in these areas.

Autistic girls and education research

Although most autism and education research has not focused specifically on girls, researchers have recently begun to explore gender differences in social interaction at school. Dean *et al.* (2014)

found that primary-aged autistic boys and girls were similar to their classmates in preferring to socialise with the same gender, but autistic boys and girls were more similar to each other in their levels of social acceptance and social exclusion. Autistic boys were more likely to be excluded by their peers than autistic girls, while girls had a greater tendency to be overlooked than autistic boys. More recently Dean, Harwood and Kasari (2017) observed 7–8-year-old boys and girls to provide evidence for the camouflage hypothesis. While autistic boys were more likely to play alone, girls were harder to identify as they masked their social difficulties by staying close to peers and moving in and out of activities. From both of these studies, Dean *et al.* (2017) argue that gender needs to be considered when designing interventions. As girls' relationships are more language based, they are likely to need interventions focusing on the quality of their social interactions. An ethnographic study by Moyse and Porter (2015) also identified similar masking of difficulties in the classroom, leading to teachers potentially underestimating girls' difficulties.

A study of gender differences in social relationships in adolescence among pupils attending special schools also found some subtle gender differences (Sedgewick *et al.* 2016). Autistic girls showed similar social motivation to non-autistic girls, but autistic boys showed less. Although autistic girls were very similar to non-autistic girls in many social dimensions, autistic girls did report more aggression in their relationships than non-autistic girls. The authors attributed this to autistic girls having more difficulty reading subtle social signals. It would be interesting to see if similar patterns are identified among autistic girls attending mainstream schools.

Several studies have also used interviews to explore the experiences of autistic girls. Cridland *et al.* (2014) explored the experiences of a small sample of autistic girls and their mothers during adolescence. The study confirmed a number of broad challenges, such as late diagnosis, being 'surrounded' by boys, the complexity of adolescent female relationships, and managing puberty. Specifically in relation to high school, positives identified included the structure and range of subjects studied, while negatives included classwork demands, making friends, the larger environment, lack of staff knowledge about autism, and transition between multiple teachers. A larger study by Honeybourne (2015) involved interviews with 67 autistic women and girls regarding their experiences of school. Reported difficulties included feelings of isolation and loneliness as a consequence of friendship difficulties and feeling misunderstood. These studies also highlight the importance of devising strategies to help autistic girls navigate social relationships and develop the social skills necessary to manage such experiences. A recent blog (Morewood 2018) also highlights how late diagnosis and hidden mental health difficulties can have severe consequences for girls in high school and how co-produced outcomes can have an important role in addressing girls' needs.

In relation to intervention it is promising to note that studies are beginning to look at differential effects of interventions. For instance, McMahon, Vismara and Solomon (2013) found evidence that a social skills intervention had differential effects by age and gender. In relation to gender, although girls interacted more than boys at the beginning of the intervention there were still positive outcomes for both boys and girls. A small number of studies have also evaluated interventions specifically targeting girls. As peer awareness has been found to support inclusion, Ranson and Byrne (2014) investigated the effects of an anti-stigma programme on girls' attitudes and behavioural intentions towards autistic peers and found mixed outcomes. They concluded that further research is needed in this area. More recently Jamison and Schuttler (2017) have provided a positive evaluation of a social skills intervention developed specifically to meet the needs of autistic girls. Although these studies are promising, investigating differential intervention effects or interventions specifically for girls is a relatively new area in autism research which requires further study.

Developing an integrated approach

Bronfenbrenner's bio-ecosystemic model (2005) is a well-known framework which has been applied generally to the needs of autistic children and young people (Humphrey *et al.* 2015). We propose that this model is a useful and pragmatic way of representing current understanding of the experiences of autistic girls. The model helps to capture the dynamic interactions between systems such as autism diagnostic processes and school systems and how these factors shape the experiences of girls in education over time. This model (see Figure I.1) is adopted as the organising framework for this book.

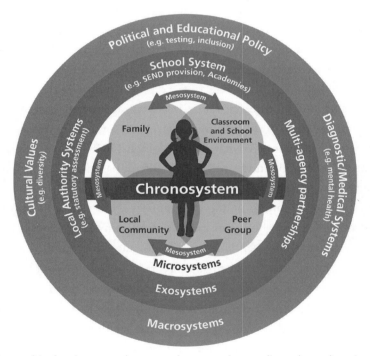

Figure I.1 An integrated approach to understanding the educational experiences of autistic girls (adapted from Bronfenbrenner 2005)

In the first part of the book we place the perspectives of autistic girls and their families at the centre. In Chapter 1, Rachael Salter, a young autistic woman, describes her experience of mainstream education, illustrating how microsystems such as the family, school and peer group interact and change over time. In Chapter 2 Elizabeth Critchley and her mother, Sarah-Jane, describe their experiences of navigating diagnostic and educational systems, showing how the family systems interact with exosystem factors such as support professionals, and how macrosystems such as diagnostic criteria can be experienced both negatively and positively.

The second part of the book moves onto focusing more specifically upon education systems across the age range. In Chapter 3, Lynn McCann, a specialist teacher, describes how autistic girls present in early years and primary education and provides some practical strategies for teachers. In Chapter 4 Judith Hebron describes how transition can present many challenges for autistic girls in negotiating changes at the mesosystem and exosystem levels. Two case studies illustrate the complexity of transition systems and experiences. In Chapter 5 Gareth Morewood, Carla Tomlinson and Caroline Bond focus on one inclusive mainstream secondary school which has adopted a systemic 'saturation' approach to meet the needs of all autistic pupils. How this model is being further developed to support autistic girls specifically is described. In the final chapter of this section, Sarah Wild provides unique insights into meeting the needs of girls attending the only residential school specifically for autistic girls in the UK. Key areas of mental health and staying safe are particular foci in this chapter.

In the final part of the book the focus shifts to how support professionals (i.e. those involved in specialist intervention and diagnosis) can develop effective multi-agency partnerships with schools to enable them to effectively meet the needs of autistic girls. In Chapter 7 Christopher Gillberg considers challenges at the macrosystem level. He outlines the challenges for psychiatrists in diagnosing autism in girls and emphasises the importance of developing a complete profile which includes assessment of overlapping neurodevelopmental disorders and mental health needs. This is followed by Judy Eaton's chapter looking at the mental health challenges experienced by autistic girls, drawing on her experience as a clinical psychologist. Implications for schools and specific educational difficulties such as school refusal are also discussed. In Chapter 9, Alexandra Sturrock and Etienne Goldsack provide a detailed account of the language and communication needs of autistic girls and how these can be supported in school, which is complemented by Etienne's unique insights as an autistic woman and speech and language therapist. This part concludes with Siobhan O'Hagan and Caroline Bond's chapter discussing how educational psychologists can support schools in identifying and better understanding the needs of autistic girls. Although there is limited evidence for interventions specifically for girls, the chapter highlights the importance of working collaboratively across systems and the development of individualised plans.

In the concluding chapter we draw together the themes from the various chapters to provide a synthesis of our current knowledge and understanding of autistic girls. We revisit Bronfenbrenner's model in order to provide an integrated picture of our current knowledge and identify challenges and facilitators at various levels. In concluding the book, we also identify promising avenues for future research and practice to enable a supportive and inclusive educational experience for autistic girls.

References

Ambitious about Autism (2013) *Schools Report 2013: Are Schools Delivering for Children and Young People with Autism?* Accessed on 3/1/19 at www. ambitiousaboutautism.org.uk/sites/default/files/Schools_Report_2013.pdf

American Psychiatric Association (1987) *Diagnostic and Statistical Manual of Mental Disorders: DSM-III-Revised* (3rd edn). Washington, DC: American Psychiatric Press.

American Psychiatric Association (1994) *Diagnostic and Statistical Manual of Mental Disorders: DSM-IV* (4th edn). Washington, DC: Amercian Psychiatric Press.

American Psychiatric Association (2013) *Diagnostic and Statistical Manual of Mental Disorders: DSM-5* (5th edn). Washington, DC: American Psychiatric Publishing.

Baron-Cohen, S. (2002) 'The extreme male brain theory of autism.' *Trends in Cognitive Sciences, 6,* 6, 248–254.

Bazelon, E. (2007) 'What autistic girls are made of.' *The New York Times*. Accessed on 24/10/17 at www.nytimes.com/2007/08/05/magazine/05autism-t.html?page wanted=1&_&_r=0

Bond, C. and Hebron, J. (2016) 'Developing mainstream resource provision for pupils with autism spectrum disorder: Staff perceptions and satisfaction.' *European Journal of Special Needs Education*, 31, 2, 250–263.

Brett, D., Warnell, F., McConachie, H. and Parr, J. R. (2016) 'Factors affecting age at ASD diagnosis in UK: No evidence that diagnosis age has decreased between 2004 and 2014.' *Journal of Autism and Developmental Disorders*, 46, 6, 1974–1984.

Bronfenbrenner, U. (2005) *Making Human Beings Human: Bioecological Perspectives on Human Development*. London: Sage Publications.

Cridland, E. K., Jones, S. C., Caputi, P. and Magee, C. A. (2014) 'Being a girl in a boys' world: Investigating the experiences of girls with autism spectrum disorders during adolescence.' *Journal of Autism and Developmental Disorders*, 44, 1261–1274.

Dean, M., Harwood, R. and Kasari, C. (2017) 'The art of camouflage: Gender differences in the social behaviors of girls and boys with autism spectrum disorder.' *Autism*, 2, 6, 679–689.

Dean, M., Kasari, C., Shih, W., Frankel, F. *et al.* (2014) 'The peer relationships of girls with ASD at school: Comparison of boys and girls with and without ASD.' *Journal of Child Psychology and Psychiatry*, 55, 1218–1225.

Duvekot, J., van der Ende, J., Verhulst, F. C., Slappendel, G. *et al.* (2017) 'Factors influencing the probability of a diagnosis of autism spectrum disorder in girls versus boys.' *Autism*, 2, 6, 646–658.

Fombonne, E. (2009) 'Epidemiology of pervasive developmental disorders.' *Pediatric Research*, 65, 6, 591–598.

Gernsbacher, M. A. (2017) 'Editorial perspective: The use of person-first language in scholarly writing may accentuate stigma.' *Journal of Child Psychology and Psychiatry*, 58, 7, 359–361.

Grandin, T. (2015) 'Thinking the way animals do: Unique insights from a person with a singular understanding.' Accessed 22/10/17 at www.grandin.com/references/thinking.animals.html

Grandin, T. and Scariano, M. (1986) *Emergence: Labeled Autistic*. Novato, CA: Arena Press.

Hebron, J. and Bond, C. (2017) 'Developing mainstream resource provision for pupils with autism spectrum disorder: Parent and pupil perceptions.' *European Journal of Special Needs Education*, 32, 4, 556–571.

Hillier, R. M., Young, R. L. and Weber, N. (2014) 'Sex differences in autism spectrum disorder based on DSM-5 criteria: Evidence from clinician and teacher reporting.' *Journal of Abnormal Child Psychology*, 42, 1381–1393.

Honeybourne, V. (2015) 'Girls on the autism spectrum in the classroom: Hidden difficulties and how to help.' *Good Autism Practice Journal*, 16, 11–20.

Humphrey, N., Bond, C., Hebron, J., Symes, W. and Morewood, G. (2015) 'Key Perspectives and Themes in Autism Education.' In N. Humphrey (ed.) *Autism and Education*, Volume 1. London; Sage.

Jamison, R., Bishop, S. L., Huerta, M. and Halladay, A. K. (2017) 'The clinician perspective on sex differences in autism spectrum disorders.' *Autism, 21*, 6, 772–794.

Jamison, T. R. and Schuttler, J. O. (2017) 'Overview and preliminary evidence for a social skills and self-care curriculum for adolescent females with autism: The girls night out model.' *Journal of Autism and Developmental Disorders, 47*, 110–125.

Jones, G. (2001) 'Giving the diagnosis to the young person with Asperger syndrome or high functioning autism: Issues and strategies.' *Good Autism Practice, 2*, 2, 65–75.

Kanfizer, L., Davies, F. and Collins, S. (2017) '"I was just so different": The experiences of women diagnosed with an autism spectrum disorder in adulthood in relation to gender and social relationships.' *Autism, 21*, 6, 661–669.

Kasari, C. and Smith, T. (2013) 'Interventions in schools for children with autism spectrum disorder: Methods and recommendations.' *Autism, 17*, 3, 254–267.

Kenny, L., Hattersley, C., Molins, B., Buckley, C., Povey, C. and Pellicano, E. (2016) 'Which terms should we use to describe autism? Perspectives from the UK autism community.' *Autism, 20*, 4, 442–462.

Kim, Y. S., Leventhal, B. L., Koh, Y. J., Fombonne, E. *et al.* (2011) 'Prevalence of autism spectrum disorders in a total population sample.' *American Journal of Psychiatry, 168*, 9, 904–912.

Koenig, K. and Tsatsanis, K. (2005) 'Pervasive Developmental Disorders in Girls.' In D. Bell, S. Foster and E. J. Mash (eds) *Handbook of Behavioral and Emotional Problems in Girls* (pp. 211–237). New York: Plenum Publishers.

Kopp, S. and Gillberg, C. (2011) 'The Autism Spectrum Screening Questionnaire (ASSQ)-Revised Extended Version (ASSQREV): An instrument for better capturing the autism phenotype in girls? A preliminary study involving 191 clinical cases and community controls.' *Research in Developmental Disabilities, 32*, 2875–2888.

Krahn, T. M. and Fenton, A. (2012) 'The extreme male brain theory of autism and the potential adverse effects for boys and girls with autism.' *Journal of Bioethical Inquiry, 9*, 1, 93–103.

Lai, M. C., Lombardo, M. V., Auyeung, B., Chakrabarti, B. and Baron-Cohen, S. (2015) 'Sex/gender differences and autism: Setting the scene for future research.' *Journal of the American Academy of Child and Adolescent Psychiatry, 54*, 1, 11–24.

Little, L. M, Wallisch, A. M, Salley, B. and Jamison, R. (2017) 'Do early caregiver concerns differ for girls with autism spectrum disorders?' *Autism, 21*, 6, 729–732.

Lord, C., Rutter, M., DiLavore, P. C. and Risi, S. (2002) *Autism Diagnostic Observation Schedule Manual.* Los Angeles, CA: Western Psychological Services.

Lord, C., Rutter, M. and LeCouter, A. (1994) 'Autism Diagnostic Interview – Revised: A revised version of a diagnostic interview for caregivers of individuals with possible pervasive developmental disorders.' *Journal of Autism and Developmental Disorders, 24*, 5, 659–685.

Mademtzi, M., Singh, P., Shic, F. and Koenig, K. (2018) 'Challenges of females with autism: A parental perspective.' *Journal of Autism and Developmental Disorders, 48*, 1301–1310.

Mandy, W., Chilvers, R., Chowdhury, U., Salter, G., Seigal, A. and Skuse, D. (2012) 'Sex differences in autism spectrum disorder: Evidence from a large sample of children and adolescents.' *Journal of Autism and Developmental Disorders, 42*, 7, 1304–1313.

Mazurek, M. O., Lu, F., Symecko, H., Butter, E. *et al.* (2017) 'A prospective study of the concordance of DSM-IV and DSM-5 diagnostic criteria for autism spectrum disorder.' *Journal of Autism and Developmental Disorders*, 47, 2783–2794.

McLaughlin, S. and Rafferty, H. (2014) 'Me and "It": Seven young people given a diagnosis of Asperger's syndrome.' *Educational and Child Psychology, 32*, 1, 63–78.

McMahon, C., Vismara, L. A. and Solomon, M. (2013) 'Measuring changes in social behavior during a social skills intervention for higher-functioning children and adolescents with autism spectrum disorder.' *Journal of Autism and Developmental Disorders, 43*, 1843–1856.

Milton, D. E. M. (2012) 'On the ontological status of autism: The "double empathy problem".' *Disability and Society, 27*, 6, 883–887.

Morewood, G. (2018) 'From high achiever to school refuser.' Optimus Education. Accessed on 10/04/18 at http://blog.optimus-education.com/high-achiever-school-refuser

Moyse, R. and Porter, J. (2015) 'The experience of the hidden curriculum for autistic girls at mainstream primary schools.' *European Journal of Special Needs Education, 30*, 187–201.

Nasen (National Association of Special Educational Needs) (2016) *Girls and Autism: Flying Under the Radar.* Tamworth: Nasen.

Pellicano, L., Dinsmore, A. and Charman, T. (2013) *A Future Made Together: Shaping Autism Research in the UK.* London: Institute of Education.

Ranson, N. J. and Byrne, M. K. (2014) 'Promoting peer acceptance of females with higher-functioning autism in a mainstream education setting: A replication and extension of the effects of an anti-stigma program.' *Journal of Autism and Developmental Disorders, 44*, 2278–2796.

Russell, G., Rodgers, L. R., Ukoumunne, O. C. and Ford, T. (2014) 'Prevalence of parent-reported ASD and ADHD in the UK: Findings from the Millennium Cohort Study.' *Journal of Autism and Developmental Disorders, 44*, 1, 31–40.

Sedgewick, F., Hill, V., Yates, R., Pickering, L. and Pellicano, L. (2016) 'Gender differences in the social motivation and friendship experiences of autistic and non-autistic adults.' *Journal of Autism and Developmental Disorders, 46*, 1297–1306.

Segall, M. J. and Campbell, J. M. (2012) 'Factors relating to education professionals' classroom practices for the inclusion of students with autism spectrum disorders.' *Research in Autism Spectrum Disorders, 6,* 3, 1156–1167.

Shefcyk, A. (2015) 'Count us in: Addressing gender disparities in autism research.' *Autism, 19,* 2, 131–132.

Silberman, S. (2015) *The Legacy of Autism and How to Think Smarter About People Who Think Differently.* London: Allen and Unwin.

Simpson, R. L., Mundschenk, N. A. and Heflin, J. L. (2011) 'Issues, policies, and recommendations for improving the education of learners with autism spectrum disorders.' *Journal of Disability Policy Studies, 22,* 1, 3–17.

UNESCO (United Nations Education Scientific and Cultural Organisation) (1994) *The Salamanca Statement and Framework Action on Special Needs Education.* Paris: UNESCO.

White, S.W., Scahill, L., Klin, A., Koenig, K. and Volkmar, F.R. (2007) Educational Placements and Service Use Patterns in Individuals with Autism Spectrum Disorders. *Journal of Autism and Developmental Disorders, 37,* 1403–1412.

Williams, D. (1996) *Autism: An Inside-Out Approach.* London: Jessica Kingsley Publishers.

Wing, L. (1981) 'Sex ratios in early childhood autism and related conditions.' *Psychiatry Research, 5,* 2, 129–137.

Wing, L. and Gould, J. (1979) 'Severe impairments of social interaction and associated abnormalities in children: Epidemiology and classification.' *Journal of Autism and Developmental Disorders, 9,* 11–29.

PART 1

Personal Perspectives

CHAPTER 1

Education as a Girl with Asperger's Syndrome

A First-Hand Perspective

Rachael Salter

Introduction: A little bit about me

At around age seven I was on holiday in Scotland with my family and my parents bought me a new pair of walking boots. I had heard that you needed to 'wear in' new boots so I asked how far I would need to walk in them to wear them in. Jokingly, my dad told me that if I walked around the edge of the car park of the bed and breakfast 50 times they would be worn in. A little while later, my parents found me, boots on, walking around the car park as close to the edge as possible. This is the moment that my mum became 100 per cent sure I had Asperger's syndrome (AS), although I didn't get a diagnosis until a few years later.

My name is Rachael Salter and I am a 23-year-old postgraduate student. I was born in Aberdeen in October 1994 and hold diagnoses of AS, obsessive compulsive disorder (OCD) and Ehler's-Danlos syndrome (EDS) hypermobility type (a rare, multi-systemic connective tissue disorder). I come from a quite large family; I am the second child of four. I have one brother, who is two years older than me, and identical twin sisters, who are two years younger. My father is a software developer and chief information officer for a company producing marine navigational software, and my mother is a university lecturer and programme director.

I attended nursery school in Scotland until 1999, when my family moved to England, where I attended primary school, secondary school and sixth form. I was in mainstream school throughout all of my compulsory education. I graduated from the University of Keele in 2017 with a first-class honours degree in music and have recently competed an MA in the applied psychology of music. In September 2018 I began an MA Social Research (Interdisciplinary) at the University of Leeds, and I am currently researching the impact and role of music on the lives of young people on the autism spectrum. In September I hope to begin teacher training.

My parents had suspected I had AS from when I was a toddler and this was confirmed when I received my diagnosis at age 11. I have always struggled with anxiety and various aspects of social interaction. Getting a diagnosis of AS helped me in many ways, boosting my confidence and allowing me to understand why I think and behave in a different way to other people. From nursery school to the present day, AS has had a massive impact on my experience of education. I am writing this chapter in the hope that I can provide the reader with a better understanding of what it is like to be a girl on the autistic spectrum going through the education system. In this chapter, I will discuss the mannerisms and characteristics I displayed that led to my diagnosis of AS and how these have developed as I have grown and matured. I will also discuss how various situations, attitudes and behaviours have affected me and my ability to learn and how the types of support I needed changed as I moved though the education system. Although this chapter will focus on my own unique experiences, there are parallels with the experiences of many young girls with AS going through the education system.

Early years and primary education

My parents, when looking in retrospect, believe that I showed behaviours indicative of AS from just a few weeks old. I have often been told how, during my first few weeks, I would not stop crying. My parents had tried everything they could think of to get me to stop but nothing worked until my gran suggested they put my hood up; I was asleep within minutes. From then on, whenever I was upset or anxious they would put my hood up, or put a hat on me, and I would quickly calm down, often falling asleep. This is a coping mechanism I still use. When I'm tired, ill or feeling anxious I put up my hood or wear a hat and it helps me keep calm. It is difficult to explain why this helps me; it is almost as though it is a metaphorical barrier to the world and the things that make me feel uncomfortable.

Another indicator that I was on the spectrum was the names I gave my toys when I was younger. I still have three toys that I have had since I was a baby: a stuffed clown, a large rag doll, and a small rag doll. These are, quite logically, called Clownie, Big Doll and Little Doll, respectively. Throughout my childhood all of my toys have had similarly logical, unimaginative names. They tended to be named after the animal/thing they are or something related, such as Santa Bear, a bear in a Santa costume.

I had what could be seen as obsessions from a very young age, starting when I was about two years old. I was given a toy tape player with a tape of 'Twinkle, Twinkle Little Star' in it. I would carry this tape player everywhere, playing the song over and over again, and quickly learnt how to sing it. Most of my peers could not sing at this age, let alone teach themselves a song by ear. Music is an obsession that developed as I got older and is a fundamental part of my adult life. I also became obsessed with numbers from a young age: I remember doing times tables and number puzzles with my parents for fun when we were out on family walks. As I grew I started to get tired quickly when we did things as a family, which we now know is due to my EDS. As I tired I would become anxious and struggle to socialise with my siblings, so my parents would do times tables or list prime numbers with me to keep me enjoying myself.

When I was younger I didn't often play with other children and I still usually prefer to do things on my own. I attended the nursery at primary school and at the first parents' evening, I was described by my teacher as a bright and engaged pupil who tended to play alongside the other children rather than with them. I don't remember too much about my time at nursery school, but I expect this description is accurate. I have always been happy to be around other people and not interact with them. In fact, as I am writing this I am sitting in the quite busy Old Bar in Leeds University Union at a table on my own and have been for several hours. One thing I do remember about nursery school was our visit to the library; I don't remember anything about it except that I was wearing my favourite purple coat with hearts on it, and I was very excited.

I have been told that, well before I could read, my parents would often find me in the bookcase (yes, in it!) with the books on the floor around me. I would be sitting with a book on my lap, looking at the pages as if I was reading it. I do not know what I got out of this but once I learned to read my interest in books only increased. At primary school there was a reading scheme designed to take even the most talented readers until at least Year 5 to finish. I had finished the scheme by the end of Year 2, and by the time I left to go to secondary school I had moved on to books which many teenagers and even some adults struggle with, such as *The Lord of the Rings* and *To Kill a Mockingbird*. I have loved reading for as long as I can remember and often have multiple books on the go at a time.

If I enjoy a book I will become obsessed by it and read it multiple times back to back; I did this with the Harry Potter series. I was introduced to Harry Potter by my parents when I was six or seven years old. Every evening, one of them would sit with me on my bed and read a chapter to me while I followed the words. It was not too long before I was reading them on my own. I have read each Harry

Potter book at least eight times so far. I think I became obsessed with Harry Potter as I related to Hermione; she loved books, just had a small group of friends, and was very logical, just like me.

I attended local infant and junior schools and throughout primary education I liked going to school, just like Hermione Granger. I have always enjoyed learning and being challenged, and when I came across a subject or topic that interested me I would find out everything I could about it. This proved to be both an advantage and a disadvantage at school. When I began studying a subject that I was interested in, I would be focused in class and would progress quickly, often excelling. However, once I had reached a certain level I found that I was not being challenged by the curriculum and would become bored and easily distracted in class. This can be demonstrated by comparing my Year 2 SATs (standardised assessment tasks) results with the teacher comments on my Year 2 report. I achieved the top mark in my class for Reading and Comprehension and the second highest mark in my class for Maths in my SATs. However, while acknowledging the excellent standards achieved across subjects, she also commented on how I could achieve more if I was able to focus fully on classroom tasks.

I think that if there had been more challenging tasks available to me in these subjects I would have been much more focused and therefore performed to a higher standard in class.

Although I generally liked going to school there were periods of time when I found it very difficult, and more often than not this was because of my relationships with my peers. In infant school no one really minded if I didn't want to play with them and wanted to read or do something alone instead, but as we got older they began to notice that I was different. Unfortunately, this led to bullying. I was very good at not letting other people get to me, and to be honest I didn't always understand that they were making fun of me, but there was one particular period in Year 4 during which I struggled to cope. I have never had a large number of close friends, and so when my best friend started to bully me I didn't realise what was happening. Although I didn't have a diagnosis of OCD at this point, Anne[1] had worked out that certain things would cause me to get very anxious and even have panic attacks, so she would do these things. This went on for several months until I began missing school because of my anxiety and my parents persuaded me to tell them what was happening. My parents reported this to the school and I remember us all going for a meeting with the head teacher, my class teacher, Anne and her parents. During this meeting, it came out that Anne's older sibling had been bullying her and so she had been taking it out on me. It was agreed that we would be moved so that we sat at different tables during class and that, at least for a few weeks, we would be kept separate at break time. Additionally, the other two girls in my class that I got on with were told about it and asked to make sure I was okay at break and lunch times. Eventually, as the situation with her sibling was sorted out, Anne and I became friends again and we were friends throughout secondary school; however our friendship was never as strong as it had been before the bullying started.

I had my final assessment and was diagnosed with AS on 9 June 2006 when I was 11 years old, and I remember parts of the day well. I was one of a team representing my junior school at a 'young engineers' competition. My parents collected me halfway through the last task. They took me to a specialist children's centre where, following conversations with me and my parents, a doctor gave me the diagnosis. Though I didn't really understand the diagnosis at the time, I remember feeling relieved; I already knew that I was different to my peers and having this diagnosis meant I could start to understand why. My diagnosis boosted my confidence and gave me a better understanding of how my mind works, but the way it helped me the most was by helping me understand how my typically developing (TD) peers thought. Through being able to recognise

---

1 Names and identifying information have been changed throughout the chapter.

which of my characteristics are 'different' I began to understand why TD people act and react to things differently to me, particularly in social situations. This understanding then allowed me to begin to teach myself the social and communication skills that I did not naturally develop.

Secondary education

My transition to secondary school was quite stressful, though I think I coped with it a lot better having had a diagnosis than I would have done without one. I remember that, before the school year started, I visited the secondary school on a couple of occasions with my mum and we were shown around, along with another young man with AS with whom I later became, and am still, good friends. During these visits we were given a tour of the school, introduced to our form tutors and were shown a specific room we could go to if we needed some time out. While at secondary school I was given a 'care card' which allowed me to leave class, or come inside at break time, and go to this room if I became overwhelmed and needed some time alone. I remember being very anxious about starting a new school and meeting a lot of new people in the lead-up to starting Year 7, and visiting beforehand really helped. The visit gave me some level of familiarity with the staff and my surroundings and so, on my first day, I wasn't overwhelmed by new things. The experience was still stressful but having that familiarity and knowing there was somewhere that I could escape to if I needed it gave me the confidence to go and make an effort with my new classmates. Another thing the school did which helped make the transition easier was to make sure I was in the same form as one of my best friends from primary school.

Overall, my transition into secondary school went quite smoothly and I didn't really have any issues in school until later in the year. These issues arose when I began having lessons with one particular teacher, Mr A, who didn't understand my AS, and I don't think made any attempt to. There were many incidents that caused me to become very anxious in Mr A's classes. On one occasion, Mr A had copied a fact from the text book onto the board incorrectly and, as I had the text book in front of me, I noticed the mistake. I was sitting in front of his desk so I got his attention and pointed out the mistake, to which he responded something along the lines of 'I'm the teacher, not you, don't be so cheeky.' So not only did I have to sit for the rest of the lesson knowing that the fact on the board was incorrect, I was upset about being told off unfairly. Another, more serious, incident happened a while later when I was having a bad day with my anxiety anyway and was being bullied by some of the 'popular' girls in my year. One of these girls, Betty, would find it funny to hide my things and watch me get anxious about not knowing where they were. On this particular day Betty had taken my pencil case, which was where I kept my care card which allowed me to leave class. I was becoming more and more anxious, when Mr A decided to tell me off for not having a pen. When I tried to explain that this was because Betty had taken my pencil case, Mr A told me to stop making excuses. At this point I told Mr A that I needed to leave class and that my care card was in the pencil case which had been hidden; however, Mr A told me that I couldn't leave without showing it to him and that I needed to stop making a fuss. I didn't actually need to show my care card to Mr A as it was on my record, a fact which he knew but I didn't understand at the time as I had not been specifically told. I ended up having a panic attack in class. Following this incident, I was told I could just get up and leave without telling the teacher if I needed to. Luckily, Mr A was an anomaly and most of the other teachers I had at secondary school at least tried to understand and make adaptions for me, even if they got it wrong sometimes.

I found that there were many differences between primary and secondary school and one of the biggest was the amount of homework. There was, obviously, a lot more homework in secondary school, but I liked this. At secondary school, the school day finished at 3pm, and we didn't eat dinner until around 7.30pm when both Mum and

Dad were back from work. This left me with most of the afternoon and evening with no set routine, so I would do my homework and then do my oboe practice, which would take up a few hours. This was my routine for at least the first few years of secondary school, but as I got older I found I was more comfortable with not having a regular routine.

My love of reading was strongly encouraged throughout primary school, but when I got to secondary school I found there was very little support or encouragement for reading outside the set curriculum. When we studied a book in English we would read the book as a class. This caused me problems as I was a quick reader and would get very frustrated by the slow pace, and so in these lessons I would sit at the back of the classroom and either read ahead or, if I had already finished the book, read a different book entirely. Unfortunately, this meant that if the teacher asked me to read a section aloud I would not know where in the book to read from. In these instances, the teacher would often assume that I was not paying attention as I did not want to do the reading, and so I would get in trouble. In reality I had already done the reading, usually several times over. This happened in Year 11 when we studied *To Kill a Mockingbird* for GCSE. As I mentioned above, I first read this book when in primary school and had read it many times by the time I was studying for my GCSEs, so I became bored very quickly when we read it as a class. The teacher taking these lessons, Mr B, had not taught me previously, and there were several instances where he told me off for 'not paying attention' when we were reading, which would make me anxious and upset as I felt I had done nothing wrong. Eventually my mum got in contact with Mr B and explained the situation. After this, I was allowed to read anything I wanted while they were reading in class so long as I put my book away when we were doing other things. Once he understood my condition and the situation, Mr B very quickly became one of my favourite teachers. He would give me extra challenges when I found the work easy, so I wouldn't become bored, and he also adapted assignments when I struggled with them. One example of this was when we were set the task of writing a short story. The original assignment was to create a character, which we had to describe in detail, and write an adventure based on that character. I was struggling to imagine a character with enough detail, so Mr B allowed me to use a secondary character from an existing book. I chose the character Brom from the Inheritance series and thoroughly enjoyed writing a story about how he became a dragon rider.

One of the biggest challenges I faced during my time at secondary school was the effect of my social anxiety. I don't cope very well in crowds or noisy situations so break time and lunchtime were a problem, especially if I was tired. There were a couple of things that I did that helped with this. During Key Stage 3 I joined the book club and the junior choir, both small clubs that met at lunchtime. These clubs meant that for two lunchtimes a week I could be inside, away from the people and noise, and I could be doing something I enjoyed such as reading or singing. During the other three lunchtimes, I would go to the school pond with my two friends, Cara and Dani. The school pond was in a courtyard in the science block, which you could only access through the technician's office. Usually, students weren't allowed into the pond courtyard unless they were there for a science lesson, but it was arranged that Cara, Dani and I could spend our lunches there so I had a space away from the noise and the rest of the students. We would weed and help the technician to plant up the pots and planters. As I got older, I made a bigger group of friends and became better at managing in a busy, noisy situation and so needed to go to the pond courtyard at lunch less and less.

I believe the improvement in my ability to cope in social situations is largely due to my involvement in musical performance ensembles. I began playing the piano at a very young age and then joined a recorder ensemble at the local music centre at the age of nine. I started to learn to play the oboe in the spring of 2006, just before I started at secondary school, and quickly advanced; by the time I was in Year 9 I had a distinction at Grade 5. I was involved in a number of local ensembles throughout my time at secondary school and I began playing with the county youth wind band in 2010. I soon became the principal oboist and had the amazing opportunity of playing with them in Japan in 2013. I also played first oboe with a European youth orchestra in 2012. Playing with these groups meant that I was socialising with quite large groups of my peers on a regular basis at rehearsals, and the situation allowed me to do so without the usual anxiety. I knew that I could talk to the other members of the group about something I was interested in (music) without seeming like someone with a slightly weird obsession. Additionally, the rehearsal setting meant that the socialising was in a structured setting and each individual had their own, distinct role. The social skills that I learnt during these rehearsals were skills that I could then use in a non-musical setting and helped me become much better at coping in those situations. I also found that being involved with musical performance ensembles improved my ability to focus on a task without getting distracted when other things are going on around me, something that is very useful in education! My own experience of this has motivated me to research the possibility of musical performance and training being used to help others with high-functioning autism spectrum conditions (ASC) to succeed in mainstream education at undergraduate and master's level.

Music has always been one of my favourite subjects as I find both playing and listening to music helps me to manage my AS and cope with certain situations. If I am in a situation where there are lots of people I don't know, on a busy train for instance, I use listening to music as a kind of barrier to the world, in a similar way to how I use hoods and hats. Additionally, I find that playing music helps me to express, understand and process my emotions, and in particular helps me to 'escape' if I am feeling overwhelmed. I also enjoyed art lessons at school for similar reasons. I normally enjoyed maths and the sciences too; however I often found that the work wasn't challenging enough and so would get bored easily. In these subjects, the teacher had a massive impact on whether or not I enjoyed the class. For example, in Year 10 I had two maths teachers. I would always look forward to one teacher's lessons as they would set the work for the class and then, when I finished that work, they would set me further challenges which built on what we were doing. These exercises were often from the A level syllabus. On the other hand, when I had finished the set work in the other teacher's class she would just set more of the same problems, meaning I often ended up doing the same thing over 50 times in the same lesson. The subjects that I didn't enjoy tended to be those which I had little interest in, such as religious education and geography, or those where I would have to work with others, such as PE.

When I first started taking exams I loved them. I liked the fact that we each had our own space, there would always be some challenging questions, and no one was allowed to talk so there weren't lots of distracting sensory stimuli. This showed in my GCSE results, although my health began going downhill and I was quite ill during my Year 11 exams. Nevertheless, I still achieved four A*s, five As and two Bs. Unfortunately, my health continued declining throughout sixth form, and by the time I finished my A levels I hated exams. I was prepared for my GCSEs so had very little anxiety surrounding them; however my health had meant I had missed nearly 50 per cent of school throughout sixth form and despite my best efforts, I could not catch up. As I did not feel prepared for my A level exams, I would become very anxious in the lead-up to one. This anxiety would then trigger a migraine and I would either miss out on even more preparation time, making me more anxious, or have to sit the exam with a migraine, which I did on several occasions. Following some tutoring, resits, emergency surgery, an extra year and a lot of incredibly hard work, I still managed to come out the other side with four A levels, but the grades (BDDE) were markedly lower than the four A*s I was initially predicted.

Throughout my A levels I struggled in a number of ways but the two biggest challenges I faced were my own self-confidence (or lack of!) and other people's attitudes. When I am tired or not feeling well my AS traits become more obvious. Because of my health problems I was often tired or not feeling well while I was in sixth form and my situation had one of two effects on the people around me. There were some people whose attitudes only created more barriers to my education. One example of this happened at the end of a class at the start of Year 13. When I had sat my AS exam in this subject at the end of Year 12 I was so ill that I was rushed into hospital in the afternoon so, unsurprisingly, I failed the exam. Normally this would have meant that I wouldn't be able to continue the subject but because of the situation I was allowed. At the end of the first lesson back my teacher called me to the front of the class, and with the classroom door open, told me that I shouldn't be in the class, as I wasn't clever enough and needed to work harder. This obviously upset me a lot and, although action was taken by the school once my mum had reported the incident, it massively knocked my already low confidence.

A second example of people's attitudes creating barriers was on my Year 12 report in a different subject, which reads 'she needs to improve her attendance to maximise progress and achievement'. This comment would have been appropriate for someone who was skipping school, but as I was in and out of hospital, was having around three migraines a week and would often attend school with a migraine, this comment just caused undue distress and anxiety.

On the other hand, most people were understanding and supportive. My head of sixth form fell into this group and I will always remember one of the things he said to me. I had been having a particularly difficult time and my mum and I had gone to see him to talk about any further adjustments that needed to be made in school. I was very upset and anxious during this meeting and he said to me, 'I can see you coming back here in three years' time and telling me that you are graduating with a first-class degree.' Knowing he believed in me boosted my confidence and made me determined to prove him right. I did, and going back to school to tell him was one of the best feelings I have ever felt.

Higher education

As my health had affected my A level results, I was unable to go to my original first-choice university and got my place at Keele University through clearing. Although I now know I did incredibly well considering my circumstances, at the time this massively knocked my confidence. I began university life with very little self-confidence and a lot of anxiety. I am very glad that I ended up where I did, though, because the support I was given was incredible.

Before I started my degree, I was invited to stay at the university alongside other students with support needs for a weekend which was hosted by Disability and Dyslexia Support (DDS). During the weekend we stayed in university halls, had tours of campus, our departments and the halls we would be living in, met older students and had the opportunity to talk to a DDS staff member about the individual support being put in place. Once I started I was provided with a specialist mentor with whom I met once or twice a week. I was provided with an en-suite bedroom, and eventually a single-occupancy flat, as sharing a bathroom and kitchen with others was causing me anxiety, and multiple adjustments were put in place for my academic work. There was also a group which met weekly to which all students with ASC were invited. Additionally, information was made readily available about counselling, advice, study skills and other support services at the university. I very quickly settled at Keele and had the support I needed to succeed. I am very happy I did my BA at Keele as the support they offered provided me with the skills and knowledge I need to succeed at postgraduate study at a much larger university where there is less support available. I also do not believe I would have achieved a first-class honours in my undergraduate degree if I had attended a different university.

For the first year of my undergraduate degree I studied maths and music, dropping maths at the end of my first year. The departments and teaching styles were very different in each department. In maths we had 'examples classes' in which there would be around 15–20 people and we would discuss the content of the week's lectures and try some problems. I quite enjoyed these classes as the problems were always challenging and the small class size meant it never became too overwhelming. You also quickly became comfortable around everyone in the group. The maths lectures, on the other hand, would involve nearly 200 students and could be very overwhelming. I found that it helped if I sat near the front and at the end of the row so I could leave the lecture theatre for a few minutes if I got anxious. In contrast, there were only 21 students in the year doing music, so even the biggest lecture group was quite small. Most of the lectures and seminars in music were held in classrooms, rather than big lecture theatres, which I felt much more comfortable in. Due to the nature of the subject, there was also a much wider range of teaching and assessment styles in music than in maths. All the assessments in maths were exams, which I find very distressing. Although I had a separate room for all of my exams, I would still get very anxious in the lead-up to them. The assessments in music were generally coursework based or recital based, which was less stressful as I felt less time pressure and could produce multiple drafts. The musical performance modules were assessed through a recital, but I was more comfortable doing these than sit-down exams as recitals involve playing an instrument so I could lose myself in the performance.

At university I was involved with a number of music performance societies and held several committee positions. Through these societies I met a wide range of people from all over the university with a shared interest in music. All of my closest friends from university are people I met though these societies, rather than my course or accommodation. Unfortunately, I ended up having to step back from two of my committee positions due to being the victim of cyberbullying. I eventually decided to step down as chair of, and stop playing in, one band for the rest of the year as it was affecting my mental health. I reported the bullying to the university and the student was banned from student union societies. Despite this, I returned to the band in my final year and found being involved in societies very enjoyable.

Summary

Overall I feel I have been very lucky with the support offered to me throughout my education. While some of the biggest barriers to education I have faced have been due to the attitudes of both teachers and peers, the support and understanding I received from most of my teachers, peers and my family have been invaluable in enabling me to succeed in education. In particular, encouragement of my love of reading and my involvement in music gave me the confidence and social skills I needed to cope in both education and other areas of life. In my opinion, I owe my success in education, at least in part to the people and institutions that supported me and helped me to learn the skills that I did not develop naturally.

CHAPTER 2

Growing Up and Taking Charge

Personal Perspectives from an Autistic Woman and Her Mother

Sarah-Jane Critchley (mother) and
Elizabeth Critchley (autistic woman)

As a parent, I have one really important job to do, which is to get my children alive and functioning safely into adulthood. You wouldn't think it would be so hard but given the shockingly high rates of mental illness and suicide in autistic people with average or above average intelligence, it is by no means guaranteed. There is a real art to balancing the risk of catastrophe with an ability to build a sense of resilience and trust in your children's ability to figure things out for themselves eventually. Brought up in a farming family who were literally very down to earth, I am the opposite of a neurotically anxious parent and yet I share the anxieties of any parent whose child is really struggling. In spite of that, I feel a deep and abiding love and respect for the young people that they are and have to trust that they will carve their own path in the future given the right support.

Navigating the education system over time

There was a time when I thought the biggest challenge we might face would be what grades our children would get, or whether they would fall in love and have children of their own. I thought we might fall out when they became teenagers or that they might go in for rebellion big time in a way that I never did. Our reality has been very different to that experience. Whilst their peers have moved through the life stages at a more or less steady pace (with the odd little blip on the way), the progress our children make is very much on their own path, to their own timescales and in their own way. The biggest single challenge has not been them, or any issues that they have faced, but the clash of priorities between their wellbeing and the educational and healthcare systems within which we operate.

The scale of the challenge

As with many children, Elizabeth had all of the usual childhood ailments and diseases but ramped up to a higher level. We should have known early on that our life as a family would be anything but straightforward as she was a very colicky baby and didn't sleep well at all. At six months, she was admitted into hospital and moved by ambulance across the site in the early hours of the morning for an emergency scan of her lungs. It turned out to be a severe respiratory tract infection which was successfully treated with intravenous antibiotics. When she recovered some days later, she learned to sit up in the hospital's play area. She smiled, babbled, talked and giggled (early and often) and sang. She turned over, crawled, stood and walked later than other babies we knew of the same age, but still well within developmental milestones.

Our delightful girl would always respond to physical touch, loved being tickled and would make everyone else around her smile. She adored her picture books and was always deeply absorbed in whatever she was doing. As she grew older, the stories we read became longer and more detailed, and she loved listening to them. I was working full-time from the time she was eight months old, so much of her daytime was spent fully occupied at nursery.

It was her nursery who were the first to identify that she was developing differently to her peers. She would escape from the 'music lesson' which involved lots of cacophonous banging and stay in the toilets singing to herself, listening to the bathroom acoustics. They said that she wasn't 'accessing the curriculum' because she hid under the table and would play alongside, rather than with, other children and they were worried about how she would cope in Reception when she went to 'big school'.

Over her lifetime we have worked with a huge range of professionals, diagnosticians and educational staff, each of whom looked at her abilities through their own lens. Over time, they produced a long and detailed list of things that she could not do, but very little detail on what her strengths were. Her physical coordination was poor, and she was diagnosed with dyspraxia at the age of three. The ongoing impact on us as a family of receiving report after report detailing her flaws was that we began to feel as if we were under siege. I find it utterly understandable that parents in similar positions become reactive and combative when the only feedback they ever get is negative. Her independence and social skills lagged behind those of her peers at the same time as we were seeing a brilliant, original mind at work. The massive abilities, interests and passions we saw were not demonstrated in writing or recognised at school and yet her intelligence was obvious to anyone who talked to her.

As a parent, to continually receive negative messages about your child because they do not happen to conform to a very narrow definition of 'normal' can cause huge stress. This does not mean that we were blind to her many issues, but it is notable that of the 19 groups of professionals listed in Table 2.1, the ones who had the most impact and who helped move on our own understanding are those who took the time and the care to see her as a person, rather than a set of criteria which she was not meeting.

Table 2.1 Professionals consulted over the years

Professional seen and phase of education MOT = Moment of Truth	Early years	Primary school	Secondary school
Health visitor	✓		
Nursery school teacher	✓		
Reception teacher	✓		
SENCO[1]	✓	✓	✓
Local authority outreach team	✓	✓	✓
Audiology dept. and ear, nose & throat surgeon	✓		
Community paediatrician	✓	✓	✓
Class teacher		✓	
Gastroenterologist		✓	
CAMHS[2]		✓	
Educational psychologist		✓	
Occupational therapist		✓	
Head teacher			✓
School nurse and pastoral team – MOT			✓
Migraine specialist GP team – MOT			✓
Autism diagnostic services – MOT			✓
Osteopath			✓
Psychotherapist			✓
Early help service			✓

[1] Special educational needs coordinator

[2] Child and adolescent mental health services

Of all of the contacts we had with these professionals , it is fair to say that the vast majority were both negative and generally unhelpful in providing support and were motivated by a need to 'normalise' her rather than to 'optimise' her strengths or her ability to function.

Working with professionals

After years of having less than uplifting meetings with a series of professionals who told us things we rarely wanted to know and just raised our levels of fear and frustration in terms of trying to provide help and support for our wonderful little girl, it is hard not to be defensive when meeting a new professional. This might be completely understandable, but it is less than helpful, and it is deeply important to approach each meeting in a cooperative frame of mind. We have always been completely open with the professionals that we meet on the grounds that if they are not given the full picture it isn't possible for them to make accurate judgements or to provide what help and support they can.

What unites parents and professionals is a wish to do the best for the young person in front of them. Difficulties arise when professionals don't listen to the information which the parent holds. It is also hard when you know that none of the options on offer will work as they do not meet the needs your young person has. We have consistently tried to approach each meeting with a clear idea of what we would like to happen and a suggestion as to how this might be achieved. This approach is really helpful in getting the support Elizabeth needs.

Moments of truth

In all our lives there are times where a change or an intervention has a profound impact on our future direction, what help we might receive, or our current reality. If we look at each one of the interactions we had with the people listed in Table 2.1, they each had the capacity to have a positive or negative impact and each could view the contact very differently. In order to explain this better, we will discuss three specific sessions in terms of their clinical outcomes and how differently these were seen by Elizabeth as a young person, and by me as her parent.

The first time a teacher at nursery school said that they were worried about Elizabeth we felt as if a bomb had gone off in our lives. This feeling was compounded each and every time someone added another negative label to the list.

Please don't get the impression that we walked into any meeting feeling that the person we were seeing ever intended to do less than their best, nor did we feel that they ever wanted to cause harm. We always approached each interaction as a positive opportunity to learn more about the difficulties Elizabeth was facing and ways to help her. It was always obvious that she was different, and so much less obvious what was the cause of her difficulties and what to do about it. We spent 15 years looking for answers, collecting diagnoses as if we were playing some arcane version of disability bingo with hidden rules, each time getting partial answers and plenty of reasons to increase our worries about her ability to complete school, manage independently or function in the way that 'normal' children might. No parent wants to see their child struggling so much. She has always worked so very differently from children around her that it felt as if she only ever had a peer group of one. We struggled to find any form of help that would unlock the massive potential that we could see in this amazingly impressive young lady. So began the seven-year process of 'Project Elizabeth'. We tried everything we thought might help her to be able to function better, from restricted diets, vitamins and fish oils, through specialist exercises for people with dyspraxia and dyslexia to auditory integration. We did not want her medicated, feeling that if she had to be medicated to cope with the education system it was an indictment of the education system, not a failing in her!

Each new thing we tried was researched to see if it could be harmful (in which case we wouldn't touch it with a barge-pole!) and checked to see whether the evidence suggested for its efficacy could have any substance (although the bar for that was pretty low). We then tried it and monitored the effects to see if it made a difference. Some things helped but given that she was developing and maturing all the time, it was not really possible to disentangle how much progress would have been made simply because she was getting older and learning.

Alongside all the home-based therapies and lots of play-based learning, we put in place plenty of quiet time at home for her. She liked time alone with her books and we liked that she was able to be so self-sufficient, like all our family. We are a pretty independent bunch. An early talker and very independent thinker, we took her to the local National Association for Gifted Children group (now called Potential Plus), and even there I would find her sat on a chair reading Shakespeare. Although she loved the activities and amazing opportunities the group provided, she didn't make friends.

At primary school she spent about five years in a morning movement class for children with coordination and learning difficulties, with no discernible benefit, though her need remained stubbornly visible. In a bid to improve her relations with other children, she was part of a social skills group, Social Circles, where a group of children who found it difficult to work with others would try to learn from other children with exactly the same issues.

School attendance has always been an issue, due to illness, rather than school refusal. Elizabeth had many ear infections, tonsillitis and then severe stomach aches and nausea which ended in a referral to a gastroenterologist. She missed a substantial part of Year 6 and was so poorly on her Year 6 residential school trip that she was nearly sent home with the head teacher.

The summer between primary and secondary school saw a spike in her anxiety at the uncertainty around what her new school would be like. Only now, with the understanding that came with an autism diagnosis, would we be in a position to support that change better. Her autistic brother's transition to secondary was much better as a direct result of that experience, though.

In preparing this chapter, it is really noticeable that all of the moments which we identified as making the greatest difference have come very late. Late diagnosis for autistic girls is very common, especially when they make eye contact and appear to be coping at school. She was referred to the community paediatrician who specialised in attention deficit hyperactivity disorder (ADHD), who diagnosed her with (yes, you guessed it) ADHD. Elizabeth was assessed by the social communications clinic who said that as she was a girl, made eye contact and could take turns in conversation, she could not be autistic, and I agreed with them. At that point in time, ten years ago, the picture we all had of an autistic child was male, with a tendency to line up cars, not talk (let alone fluently and eloquently), unaffectionate and avoiding eye contact. Her profile was far more that of a female 'little professor', but her world was words, characters and stories, not numbers and science, so she was missed and misdiagnosed, as are very many autistic girls.

If she had been less intelligent, engaging and enthusiastic about learning, and keen to be liked by professionals, her difficulties would have been underestimated less. The long-term prognosis for her looked so poor, full of 'she may never...', that we had to disengage from services for the sake of our wellbeing. We were making no progress. It was a very dark time that nearly broke us. Boys with behaviour that challenges were identified and supported more often. We weren't. If we had been supported as family, things might have been very different. The old adage that the apple doesn't fall very far from the tree is absolutely true in our family as very many of us have struggled throughout our lives with one issue or another, which means that where we calibrate 'normal' in our family can be very different from a neurotypical perspective.

Landmark moments – same story, different perspectives

In the section that follows, Elizabeth and I will discuss pivotal moments and interactions from each of our perspectives and identify what made (or could have made) a really positive difference to us.

Introduction from Elizabeth

I am not all autistic kids (I'm not even a kid myself any more as much as I remember being one). I can't tell you what the kid you picked up this book for thinks or even how they think it, for the same reason I cannot give you a geography essay on a country I've never heard of. That said, my maps of myself are detailed and extensive for my own safety. I can tell you what I know, what I saw and what I felt because I did all these things (regardless of those who will tell you I'm incapable of them). I will give you this and hope it is enough.

Here are my landmarks. May they be similar enough to yours to help you.

Best wishes, and good luck.

Elizabeth

Diagnosis Day – Age 17

By the time Elizabeth was 17, she had racked up many separate diagnoses, but none fully explained what she was seeing and experiencing. It is fair to say that as she grew into a thoughtful young lady with an amazing ability to analyse and assess her own behaviour and understanding we began to be convinced that the hotchpotch of diagnoses she had been given in fact added up to autism. We did not need her to have a diagnosis to be loved and supported by us, but her experience at school and getting them to take her difficulties seriously in spite of her lack of attendance through illness proved much harder. I was also very aware (as I was working in the autism sector) that the vast majority of autistic people found that having a diagnosis to explain the profound differences they were experiencing was hugely helpful.

As our understanding of a female presentation grew, it became more and more obvious that her amazing strengths, sensory issues and social difficulties were as a result of her neurology, not a lack of maturity, willingness or learning difficulties. So, we gave her the choice about whether she wanted to pursue a diagnosis. At the time, I had no faith in the local diagnostic service to be able to assess her accurately against a female presentation of autism, so we went privately to the Lorna Wing Centre.

We knew that the day was likely to be stressful, that it was somewhere she had never been before, and the frequency of her migraines (which are exacerbated by stress) meant that we had no idea whether she would be well enough to attend any appointment agreed. At the time we were going, she was experiencing an average of two weeks of utterly debilitating migraines in a month. When the date finally came around, we all set off for Bromley and were greeted in the clinic, which looked like a residential house. We sat at a kitchen table with biscuits whilst the team explained how the process would work. It was without doubt the most thorough, detailed and cross-referenced diagnostic process we have experienced, and yet the least stressful as the psychologists we talked to knew what we were describing and really seemed to 'get it'.

Her developmental and family history was taken and recorded against the Diagnostic Interview for Social and Communication Disorders (DISCO) diagnostic test (Wing *et al.* 2002) for a couple of hours. Whilst we were doing that round the kitchen table, Elizabeth was taken upstairs into another room for the normal battery of psychological tests. Both professionals met up to verbally compare results over lunch whilst we walked into town to grab something to eat. After lunch, they shared their conclusions and gave us lots of opportunities to discuss any questions we had, especially relating to her medications for migraine and which would be most effective to treat both her migraine and her anxiety. From beginning to end, it was the most positive, reassuring and helpful process we have ever experienced. So much so, that I regard it as a shining example of how to conduct those meetings.

Reflects or so assessment and diagnosis

Confused parents often end up waiting in a lot of doctors' offices, teachers' offices and, slightly less, child psychologists' offices – the same tests done time after time which all really boil down to what can you remember, can you look at me, do you understand me, how quick are you, what do you remember? They measure your abilities to relate, to understand, to do and to remember; like knocking at a door and seeing if you know how to answer. I've gone to enough of these offices that I don't remember all that much about them. Nothing really changed. The same child walked in the door and then out an hour later.

The Lorna Wing Centre and my diagnosis were nowhere near daunting to me. Analysis itself was nothing new to me; it was a crucial survival tactic. Analysing people and situations is necessary for me. Without it I do not function on a communicational level (going into detail on that would probably be fun but ultimately pointless). The only vaguely worrying thing about getting a diagnosis for me was the small amount of imposter syndrome that must come with this sort of thing when you have an anxiety disorder.

Having an adult around who knew I was masking – other than my parents – was strangely reassuring. The tests were not different from the many others I've taken, but downstairs my parents were listing off my development history, things that even I forgot I did or do (I still run like an anxious duck). I've done professional analysis – who you are doesn't really come into it. That's far too fluid to write down on a medical sheet. What you are comes in thousands of details. Diagnosis for me was just another detail. Strategically important, internally known. A label I am now allowed to use to get myself what I need.

If there was one thing that has impacted most on Elizabeth, it would be her migraines. At the time we decided to take her to the National Migraine Centre, we had already been seen by our doctors who were suggesting specialist help. The migraine specialist was hugely helpful and very thorough, checking her physical health and wellbeing and her coordination, and ruling out other major neurological problems. By this time, Elizabeth was being sent home poorly by the school nurse regularly and was missing over 30 per cent of her GCSE classes. No painkiller she tried was touching the pain and she was lying flat in a dark room, trying to sleep the pain away. Each morning we would go into her room not knowing if it would be a good day (when she was out of pain) or a bad day (where she couldn't move). We were worried that she might not even be able to make it into the exam room for her GCSEs, never mind take the exam. She even had a migraine on the day of her full-day art practical exam and had to ask permission to take her medication, which she was painting as part of her exam.

Again, the difference was that she was believed and that the help which we were given was targeted towards the pain she had and the fastest possible remission of the pain. She was given a migraine 'first aid kit'. The specialist spoke to her and sought clarification from me, rather than expecting me to speak for her. Once we had done that, Elizabeth began to be able to handle her migraines for herself at school (although this usually meant having to come home).

Migraine management

Often, it's the absence of a professional that makes a difference. The moment I really took agency for myself is tied up in my illness (chronic and aggressive migraines are an illness, not autism, just to make that clear for anyone even slightly confused – trust me

I have both). More of a culmination than anything else. At some point you lose patience and demand help.

Our school nurse was lovely, but she was only one woman looking after more than 300 children; by the time I was 16 I'd learned to stop asking the nurse if I should go home and started simply asking her to call my parents. My gaining management over my illness carried over to how I dealt with my anxiety and then from that onto how I processed other difficulties. It took years of comparing my assumptions to the opinions of others to give me any respect for my own, and more time than that to learn my own boundaries. Everything was easier after that. I had never really given my voice its due weight in negotiations for fear of seeming obnoxious or petty in some way, as if that would make me less deserving of help from the people who were employed to help me.

Strange or sad as it is, I might never have learned my level of self-sufficiency if multiple professionals hadn't failed to really make a dent in the amount of pain I dealt with daily. Motivation in one of its most potent forms.

Assessment for an EHCP rejected – 'Ways Forward' meeting with school and local authority

I decided to apply for an Education, Health and Care Plan (EHCP) for Elizabeth when she had missed over a third of her classes and it became clear that her issues were going to be long term and chronic and her current placement unsuitable. The process of applying for the EHCP quite rightly puts the wishes and needs of the young person at the centre of the process. To do that effectively, Elizabeth and I had to work together to write her 'Appendix A', which is the section that records what is important to the young person and their parent or carer in their EHCP. The process was extremely tiring and stressful for all concerned. For all that she is an amazing writer and incredibly bright, navigating this sort of formal document and understanding what they needed to know in order to understand her needs was not something she was capable of doing without significant support. It took us several sessions over two weeks to capture her wishes and the best evidence to justify the help she needed in order to access education at all. We would do an hour or so and then had to return to it the next day until it was done. Our local authority (LA) key worker told us that it was very thorough indeed.

Unfortunately, the LA turned down our application. Their justification was that the school understood her needs and were able to meet them effectively, which was in fact what it looked like from the submissions that they had received from the school. Neither of those points were in fact accurate. The school had suggested that she was receiving interventions which they did not give to her and which would not have been appropriate in her case. It was not until the LA invited us to a 'Ways Forward' meeting with the school to share the decision not to assess her and agree her provision without a plan that we saw what had been submitted. We had always said that we did not want her to have a plan at all if she could be provided something suitable without one. By this point, the school environment was so stressful for her that she was barely able to attend and the process of attending with the SENCO and deputy head tipped her into a migraine on the day. We had (at the suggestion of the Independent Parent Supporter), prepared a statement from her saying what she wanted and how she felt, which they read out on her behalf. This was incredibly powerful.

Once we (and the LA) had discovered that they had not been providing what they had claimed in their submissions to the LA, her school began to try being really helpful and allowed her to manage her anxiety by choosing when to be in school and when to work elsewhere, and to leave the premises at any time so that she maintained control over her escape route.

Negotiating next steps in education

My parents ended up representing me at the Ways Forward meeting; I had a massive migraine that morning. My parents went in with a written statement from me and my very noticeable absence with all the steel-boned exhaustion of parents fighting for a child in long-term pain.

I heard stories from my father about my mother taking any opposition to pieces like a quiet diplomatic dissection. Self-advocacy is difficult especially when there are other complications like being physically unable to be present, but my opinion was there and counted even without my presence.

My mother is a professional in her own right and having found a solution that we agreed might work was dauntless in getting it. Very few are as lucky as I have been.

In a sense my illness became its own milestone, spanning tens of professionals from many fields – it's hard to remember any that aren't connected with it. Being autistic never once merited so much notice (I test with a high level of intelligence and eloquence; for better or worse no one reads a diagnostic sheet with: autistic, dyspraxic, anxiety-suffering 18-year-old and expects me to be what walks into a room). The anxiety inherent in dealing with a system tailored for neurotypical brains affects everything. Every possible solution for the illness had to be filtered through what was practical for an autistic young woman who operates at high levels of anxiety.

Eventually my mother and I won the resources to take my A levels from home to help me recover, and within weeks of class starting I was getting higher grades than I'd had for nearly five years, with anxiety levels lower than they'd been in ten.

The power of voice and self-advocacy

Some children may not have very strong views about what they want to do, and others most definitely do from the earliest of ages! Having some control is a big part of reducing anxiety and increasing wellbeing. I would suggest that without the ability to create an environment which respects a person's sensory and environmental needs as well as building their strengths, any attempt to enable someone to learn and develop is doomed to failure. Many autistic adults who have been treated with interventions in their childhood designed to 'normalise' and enable them to function seamlessly in a 'neurotypical environment' find that approach to be abusive.

We have tried a number of different approaches to self-advocacy as Elizabeth has got older. We gave her choices from the earliest age, and have always involved her in decision making; but now, as Elizabeth turns into an adult, the emphasis is on providing support for her to advocate for herself, rather than on her behalf.

Dropping out of school to get an education

From a very early age, Elizabeth had asked to be home-schooled, but with a mortgage to pay it wasn't a viable choice for us. Even though I am theoretically able to teach her, our attempts to learn things together with us in a teacher/pupil role were never very successful and were always stressful in the extreme. I also wanted to make sure that her understanding and experience wasn't constrained by my mine. How could I possibly teach her the things I was no good at? Of course, now I understand that there are schemes of work to follow, groups who can provide support and other resources, but you do always get a better understanding from a subject specialist and I deeply honour the work that teachers do, never feeling that I could replace what they do effectively.

What has always worked for both of my children is putting them into an environment where they can discover and explore things on their own. Whilst this is a wonderful way to learn, we felt that the academic side of school was not the only reason to attend. We also wanted them both to learn how to 'rub along' with other people and to learn how to operate as part of society through having a school experience. Without their school experience (which was not all bad by any means), the children would not have benefited from such good all-round teaching, been inspired by the most amazing history teacher who had them re-enacting the Battle of Hastings on the playing field or had the common experience of going to school that most people share. It brought them social experiences and real friendships as well as difficult and traumatic events. The understanding that nothing is all good or all bad is a really important thing for autistic children to realise and helps to show the importance of flexibility of thought. Possibly most importantly, it has given them funny (and sometimes hair-raising) stories to share with each other and to serve as opportunities for analysis and learning with any therapists they have!

I have great sympathy with Ken Robinson's (2010) view of schools as factories for education, as suggested by his TED talk (beautifully illustrated by RSA Animate). My children have never fitted well into any standard mould, so it was highly likely that they would struggle in a mainstream environment. However, nothing in life comes entirely easily and we tried everything we could to make school work for Elizabeth. Eventually though, it became clear that even with the school agreeing to and implementing all of the adjustments for her, it was never going to be enough. She was too poorly to attend any physical setting and utterly unwilling to have a stranger enter her safe space in order to teach her, and the imposition of a teaching assistant to deliver 1:1 teaching for three hours a week was never going to be an adequate amount of teaching to enable her to get the three A levels she was studying. The only form of education that she would be able to access was one that had proper teaching of her studies by a specialist in that subject delivered in a way that was available to her online and recorded so that she could access it when she was well enough to study. Only when we had found for ourselves an online school which would enable her to learn this way was she willing to give up on her mainstream school, and she dropped out.

I researched all of the available providers of online school. Few did A levels and most were set up to transition children back into their mainstream provision. By this stage, I knew that there was no way temporary support would work for her. There was no prospect of her health improving, so the education had to be the best she could access and be for the remainder of her A-level studies. To make sure that she had a place and the security of a school routine for the new academic year, we had to pay for her place ourselves as the LA EHCP process chugged along. If we had not done so, she might have lost another year of education, or have been so far behind that she could not have handled the workload involved in catching up. Eventually, outside the statutory timeframe, and with the support of our local MP, she was given an EHCP that specified the conditions she needed in order to be able to receive an education, which effectively meant online schooling.

When she was able to access her education without leaving her room, it made getting to lessons achievable for her, her attendance rate increased rapidly, and she began to get slowly back into learning. We were extremely fortunate to be able to have one of her school friends living with us for most of her first year in online school who brought the social world of school back for her and helped to reduce her isolation.

Planning for the next life stage

Part of the deal we agreed as a family was that if Elizabeth was going to be studying at home, she needed to get out of the house for a walk every day. Slowly, this is rebuilding her strength and has placed her back into the community again, meeting people she knows in town, buying things in shops and going to the gym two or three times a week. Hard physical exercise is a great way of reducing anxiety and has been a key element in building her wellbeing as we move into her final exams.

Having dropped out of school, we were aware that there was the potential for her to be taking her A levels in a very unfamiliar environment but managed to negotiate her taking an AS level at her old school as an external candidate. Surreally, the process of taking exams for her causes less anxiety than attending school in that all you have to do is turn up, take the exam (which is not a social activity) and then leave without talking to anyone. Given how poorly she still is, we are all delighted to find that she has passed her English literature AS level and will take her full A levels in all three subjects in the summer.

When I wrote my book *A Different Joy* (Critchley 2016) I wanted to break up the text with illustrations, and having a tame artist in the house who was obsessed by drawing, I asked Elizabeth to illustrate each chapter heading. To do that she had to read the book, understand how to take a commission, work out how to work with a very difficult and demanding client, and produce illustrations that said what I wanted to say, and met her own exacting standards in exchange for payment. Whilst the process was not an easy one for either of us, it taught her some key freelancing skills which may well come in handy in the future and she can now legitimately say that she is a published illustrator on her CV.

So, what's next? She would like to go to university to study English literature and creative writing, so we have visited a couple of universities so she can get an idea of how they feel. One visit happened to be where one of her best friends studies and so she was shown round by a friend, rather than a stranger. She can't cope with the uncertainty of not knowing if she has a place to go to university, so she will apply after her results are out. Having been out of school for most of the last three years, she is now practising independent travel and building up her confidence (as well as a more rounded set of subjects) by doing an Access to Higher Education course at our local college in September. It will give her another year to build the experiences she needs to feel more confident in her ability to live away from home.

She is also building on other independence skills such as cooking meals for herself (and sometimes the rest of the family as well), washing and cleaning. It does mean that things are not always done perfectly, but in our house, building those skills is far more important.

I am incredibly proud of how well she has begun the process of understanding how to get the best out of herself, what to adapt to make it work for her, and how to build strengths she will need to function in a world that will not always understand and appreciate her the way that we do. She is an amazingly impressive young lady and I can't wait to see what comes next!

References

Critchley, S.-J. (2016) *A Different Joy: The Parents' Guide to Living Better with Autism, Dyslexia, ADHD and More...* London: WritingscorpInk.

Robinson, K. (2010) Changing education paradigms. TED talk. Accessed on 1/8/18 at www.ted.com/talks/ken_robinson_changing_education_paradigms

Wing, L., Leekam, S. R., Libby, S. J., Gould, J. and Larcombe, M. (2002) 'The Diagnostic Interview for Social and Communication Disorders: Background, inter-rater reliability and clinical use.' *Journal of Child Psychology and Psychiatry, 43,* 3, 307–325.

PART 2

School-Based Approaches

CHAPTER 3

Autistic Girls in the Early Years and Primary School

Lynn McCann

For years I have worked with and supported autistic pupils in schools. As an early years trained teacher who now is an autism specialist consultant, I became very interested in why girls were being diagnosed so much later than boys. When I knew girls who had been diagnosed in the primary years, there had been some behavioural indicators that were obviously different and sometimes challenging enough for a clinician to recognise as autism. However, more common in my experience were girls being diagnosed in their late teenage years and into adulthood.

This chapter will look at the ways we might spot autism in young girls and how they might look different from more typical autistic boys. We will look at two case studies and examine what support and interventions can be put in place in the early and primary school years to enable autistic girls to manage the challenges they face and to be able to develop a healthy self-image before the teenage years arrive.

It seems common that autism is less noticed in girls in the early years and primary school. We know that the diagnostic criteria are male-orientated and many teachers have not had autism training. The wider professional network is largely unaware of the way that autism presents in females. Therefore, the GPs, health visitors and paediatricians that may be asked to look at girls with autistic behaviours may dismiss them because they are judging them on the male criteria.

We know that the core difficulties are the same in male and females on the spectrum, so we need to examine what these look like in the lives of very young girls and how that might be different to the perceptions we have about autism from the majority of writings about boys.

In the early years girls starting nursery or reception class can seem initially very shy and quiet. They can take longer to settle in and attempt to interact with others. We now know that autistic girls are often great imitators. They watch and copy what others are doing. Some girls might focus on favoured activities in the classroom and use these as their 'domain' from which to observe, manage and direct interactions with others. Therefore, teachers don't notice much amiss. They see a child who is taking longer to settle but then seems to be doing okay. They see a child who plays, seemingly sociably and imaginatively. However, girls can have repetitive play and a preference for mechanical or sensory toys just like autistic boys (Harrop, Green and Hudry 2017). In addition, they may also be inclined to play with traditionally female-based toys such as dolls, love to make collections, and engage in role play that follows a script. Play in autistic girls can be 'scene-setting' rather than role play, where the girl is practising social situations so that she can learn what to do (Gould and Ashton-Smith 2011).

Parents of girls diagnosed later in the primary years or secondary school have often said that they knew their daughters were different from an early age. Their own perception that autism was a male condition prevented them from pursuing this further. Young autistic girls who have been referred to health services in the early years are often investigated for sensory, emotional, behavioural or mental health conditions, which have been picked up first. By the time they receive an autism diagnosis they have already been in the health system, some for many years (Fisher Bullivant 2018; Gould and Ashton-Smith 2011). It takes someone who understands the female aspects of autism to piece together these clues.

In the early years and lower primary years autistic girls learn to mask their differences and difficulties. It is not known if they do this consciously or whether it develops as a natural behaviour for them in response to their environment. However, it is common for autistic girls to seem to be coping daily in the classroom but frequently become very distressed or shut down when they are at home. Sleep and eating difficulties often start early but these also can be masked as the girl may quietly go unnoticed to bed or make credible excuses for a limited diet. Often parents are aware of their sleep and food difficulties but do not associate them with autism.

Some very young girls may seem to have a dual personality where they are quiet and compliant at school but difficult and temperamental at home, not because of the home environment, but because that is the safest place to be themselves and let out all the stress of an extremely exhausting day pretending to be like everyone else. Autistic girls often have good verbal ability and even if they use echolalia (repeated phrases they have learned) they are context specific so more difficult to detect. This chatty, surface sociability can look typical; but when listened to properly can show that the young girl is directing, controlling the play and conversation, and unresponsive to the ideas and suggestions of others. The verbal ability, and sometimes superior reading ability of autistic girls in the early years and primary school can mask poor understanding of inference and social context. The common autistic difficulty of taking longer to process verbal instructions can be masked through quietly observing and copying others, telling others what to do (seeming to be 'bossy'), or through subtle excuses or apologies.

Young autistic girls can be engrossed in their preferred activities, therefore missing instructions. They often have good imaginations, sometimes creating vast make-believe worlds, but have difficulty separating fantasy from reality (or just prefer the predictable, comfortable imaginary world to the real world) (Nasen 2016). This can be misinterpreted as imaginative play in the early years. Teachers see a child playing a fantasy role play game with peers in the playground, not realising that it is entirely the construct of one child, and the others are being told what to do and what to say, and never being allowed to contribute to the content of the play. Autistic girls may become frustrated when peers don't enter into their imaginary worlds as intensely as they do.

For others, fiction books are their preferred worlds. A bookish girl is not seen as unusual but it is the intensity that makes it unusual. This has a positive side: a book, its characters and contexts are a good way for an autistic girl to learn about the social 'rules' around her and commit these to memory should she ever find herself in a similar situation. Young autistic girls who are bookworms are often engaged in intense sociological studies.

Autistic girls can be hyper-emotional. This is often because of sensory sensitivities but also an acute sense of other people's emotions. This hyper-empathy does not correlate with the popular understanding of an autistic lack of empathy. This notion is in fact a myth in both boys and girls (Hadjikhani 2014). It is often the communication of their emotional states that autistic children find difficult. Cognitive empathy, understanding the emotions of themselves and others, may be impaired in autistic girls, but affective empathy, recognising and feeling the emotions of others, can be something autistic girls are very affected by (Sucksmith *et al.* 2012). It may only be obvious when the child is crying or extremely distressed that she struggles to process emotions and the emotional states of others. It may easily be misinterpreted as a 'sensitive female trait' rather than the autism spectrum.

Anxiety is often present in the early years and primary school. An anxious young girl may seem shy or quiet and the anxiety may not be noticed. Parents are more likely to see it at home. She may have found many ways to avoid activities and situations that make her anxious by the time she moves into Key Stage 2. Girls are culturally expected to be more sociable than boys, and so an autistic girl may be given more social teaching than a boy might receive, although many of the lessons are subtle and assumed. But even at an early age, girls can be aware that 'reading' social situations and knowing what to do isn't a natural thing for them. The stress of consistently having to work out what to do, watch and copy others and the worry of getting it wrong can develop early on. By the time they reach the pre-teen years, social anxiety is ingrained. Further reading about anxiety and social anxiety is listed at the end of this chapter.

Who does get noticed?

It is often the girls who have more of the male characteristics of autism who get noticed in these early years (Frazier *et al.* 2014). Those who present with challenging behaviour, repetitive behaviours and language delay, often become extremely distressed, are sensory seeking (e.g. girls who don't sit still easily and are on the move much of the time), line up toys, display a lack of interest in social interactions and find it difficult to focus and comply with the teacher's instructions are more likely to be investigated as having special educational needs and, if they are lucky, someone may investigate autism.

In my case studies of two girls, the early signs of autism were missed by parents and teachers and then by clinicians. They were first referred for associated conditions such as anxiety and sensory issues. Happé *et al.* (2012) stated that autistic girls need to have behavioural problems or significant intellectual disability to be noticed.

Girls aren't seen as autistic if they are academically able, mask their social difficulties and save expressing their high levels of distress until home time. If they give eye contact and are compliant, then it can be difficult without more advanced training to notice that this is surface coping and underneath they are struggling with a mass of anxiety, confusion and misunderstandings. Girls also have less obvious restricted and repetitive behaviours (Frazier *et al.* 2014; Happé *et al.* 2012) – one of the main diagnostic criteria in the *DSM-5* (American Psychiatric Association 2013) – leading to the debate that there should be a female version of the diagnostic criteria and a female diagnostic-based assessment. Indeed, in a short section on gender related diagnostic issues, the *DSM-5* (2013) states that autistic girls whose symptoms are more subtle may be missed. Judith Gould and Lorna Wing have developed the Diagnostic Interview for Social and Communication Disorders (DISCO) (Leekam *et al.* 2002) to give a wider perspective on the autistic characteristics of individuals, including more female characteristics. However, this tool is not widely used by clinicians and so young girls continue to be misdiagnosed with learning disabilities or mental health conditions or have their symptoms dismissed entirely.

In my experience, and that of educational psychologists and other clinicians that I know, more autistic girls are noticed between Years 5 and 7. This is because the typically developing girls are starting to enter puberty and developing much more socially complex relationships. It is in these years that young girls start to become competitive with each other and friendships and 'belonging' to certain groups become more important to them. Appearances become very important, encompassing fashion and beauty, fuelled by a massive commercial and celebrity culture. Autistic girls will usually be developing physically as their peers do, but emotionally and socially will seem far younger than their peers. It is the combination of this, along with more sensory sensitivities as the body develops, being aware they are 'different' and being left out of social groups (often accompanied by teasing, mean comments and bullying), that can bring the onset of great anxiety and more severe mental ill health. Anxiety and depression as well as obsessive compulsive disorder (OCD) or severe demand avoidance can become more obvious to teachers. Even if someone begins to realise that this may be autism, it can take more than two years to have that diagnosis confirmed in many areas of the UK. In this context, the importance of early identification, diagnosis and support cannot be emphasised enough.

I will share with you stories of two autistic girls who have had different experiences of being diagnosed and supported as autistic. Their difficulties were noticed but not identified as autism in the early years. The struggles parents had to get doctors, clinicians and teachers to believe the diagnosis are sadly all too common from many testimonies given by autistic women. Names and other identifying details have been changed.

Thea (now aged 10)

Thea's mum knew she was different from when she was a baby, but didn't think it could be autism. She thought she was a strong-willed child. By the time she was midway through the primary years, Thea became really anxious and started to refuse to go to school. She had social communication and friendship difficulties which were not picked up on because the teacher said, 'Girls are complicated.' When the parents approached the school they were made to feel that they were being neurotic and soft with Thea.

Despite being referred to Child and Adolescent Mental Health Services (CAMHS) by the school special educational needs coordinator (SENCO), none of them suspected autism. Thea did not fit the view they had of autism. She did not avoid eye contact, she seemed to have friends and seemed to be able to get on well with the academic work in school. She was only referred to CAMHS because she seemed overly anxious and became difficult to calm when emotional. It was a urology doctor who had known Thea for four years who first suggested autism. The parents then read some of Tony Attwood's work and recognised their daughter immediately.[1]

However, the effort of masking and too little support in school (she had a 1:1 teaching assistant who helped her with reading and writing but not social communication, sensory or emotional regulation), and pressures (i.e. academic, social demands and behaviour expectations) led to Thea developing post-traumatic stress disorder (PTSD). Staff in the school did not understand the difficulties Thea had and because she 'seemed' fine in school they did not see the need to make any further concessions for her. There were no adaptations for her sensory needs and each school day became intolerable, leading to high levels of distress at home: 'She was in sensory, emotional, processing and demand hell and as demands and expectations grew so did her experience of hell. Nobody really picked up on it except where it impacted on her ability to attend school' (Thea's mum). Thea has not been at school for a year but after a time of home-based tutoring support which has developed her self-confidence, she now has a place in a specialist autism spectrum disorder (ASD) school.

Dani (now aged 10)

Dani had sensory issues from an early age and had sleeping and feeding difficulties. She spoke in complex sentences very early on and was reading fluently by the age of three. She was chatty and friendly but she didn't develop reciprocal friendships. She said that other people confused her and she could not cope

---

1 Tony Attwood is a clinical psychologist who has published widely on autism, including *The Complete Guide to Asperger's Syndrome* (2006). See also his website at www.tonyattwood.com.au

if they didn't play by set rules or if games changed. To Dani, things were literal from an early age and if plans changed or people didn't do what they said they would do she would become very distressed and feel she had been lied to. She started to show many signs of anxiety at primary school but it was suggested that she may have OCD or something similar, rather than autism. They said it couldn't be autism because she was sociable and a girl. By this time the lack of understanding and support was making Dani much more anxious each day and threatened to develop into school refusal. Each day going to school felt like torture to her and she was often extremely distressed at home. Staff at the school were reluctant to believe that school might be the cause of this.

However, her parents strongly suspected autism. First, they got her an occupational therapy sensory assessment and approached the local autism team to take it further. Knowing how long a diagnosis can take, the family also sought a private assessment. All the agencies involved, CAMHS, the autism team, speech and language therapist and occupational therapist, eventually agreed an autism diagnosis. This has prompted the school to provide basic autism training for all their staff and more in-depth training for those who work more closely with Dani. They have understood her sensory needs and have made adaptations to the environment and given her a 'sensory diet', which is a regular set of activities to support her sensory needs. Having the diagnosis has helped in the development of strategies and ways of learning that support Dani rather than work against her needs. As Dani's mother stated, 'I want my daughter to grow up knowing she can be and do whatever she wants to without needing to fit in to others' idea of conventional.'

The benefits of an early diagnosis

Spotting autistic girls in the early years in primary classrooms can be of great benefit to them, and it is likely that earlier identification would have helped Thea and Dani. Autism support strategies such as visual timetables, Social Stories™ (Grey 2015; see also https://carolgraysocialstories.com), clear routines and time to process verbal instructions can help them navigate daily routines, changes and the anxiety caused by daily challenges. Addressing sensory needs and teaching self-regulation can start early enough to enable the girl to communicate and manage her sensory needs. Communication and language support can be put in place. This can help her understand what things mean, and about inference and social use of language.

Understanding emotions can be supported, especially ways to manage strong emotions. Part of this is emotional literacy (the ability to understand and express not only one's own feelings but those of others) as well as having key people to talk to who don't dismiss what she is feeling. Learning it is okay to have time out is important as a strategy to manage situations. An academically able girl will also have to deal with high expectations. If she is intelligent, many teachers assume she should be capable and competent in all areas, including emotional intelligence. Understanding the strengths and weaknesses of each child will enable more concessions for areas that they are not so able in.

For parents, being believed that their daughter is autistic is important to them and to their daughter. Seeing her potential and the positives of her skills and talents will boost her self-esteem. The autistic girl needs to grow up knowing she is autistic, and that this explains the way she thinks and experiences the world: not that it is something that will make her 'less' than others and limit her choices in life. Autistic girls and boys have much to contend with as they grow up. Other people's negative opinions, prejudices and wrong assumptions will be added to having to cope with a lack of the right kind of support they need. There remains much to be done to ensure autistic girls have full access to education and a society that makes the necessary accommodations and adjustments for them to thrive.

Recognising autism in the early years and primary – what should a teacher do?

Knowing about autism in girls and recognising a number of signs should not lead to a teacher diagnosing a girl as autistic. It is possible that the difficulties the child is having may be linked to other conditions such as dyslexia, dyspraxia, attention deficit hyperactivity disorder (ADHD), and so on. Children are also deeply affected by external life experiences such as bereavement, family breakdown, abuse and trauma. Autism is a complex condition that can co-exist with other conditions and so a clinical assessment should be done. The class teacher needs to spend some time observing and gathering evidence of their concerns. Observation of the speech, language, social interactions and behaviours of an early years or primary child needs planning and organisation. It may be that a number of staff are able to do short observations. In a classroom, sitting and observing is a real luxury but can be invaluable when getting to really know an autistic child. Then there will be information collected about how the girl manages throughout the school day. Some useful categories to collect information in could be:

- Speech and use of language. Do not assume because a young girl is articulate and chatty that there are no difficulties. Listen carefully. Think about how she responds and understands what is being communicated to her.

- Social communication and interactions in (1) play, (2) adult-directed activities and (3) school routines such as assembly and lunch times. Is the girl really using social skills or is she controlling, copying and finding it difficult to cope with the unpredictable?

- Emotional and sensory reactions. Look for signs of anxiety and the causes of distress. Examine how she moves around the classroom, what she avoids, and if there are places and activities she spends little time in.

- Learning behaviours. She may be academically able but insist on doing things her own way, a perfectionist or have learning difficulties that need further investigation. Check for comprehension and inference understanding. Are things being understood literally?

- Are any intense, rigid or repetitive behaviours seen?

Share with parents/carers and involve them in the collecting of information. Speak to the girl herself to find out what might be difficult for her. Be aware that she may not know that her sensory difficulties are not the norm for everyone else.

The Foundation Stage Profile assessments (statutory assessment of children's attainment at age five) may begin to show an uneven profile of abilities. It is common in autistic children for there to be areas of strength, for example in reading, alongside areas of weakness in an associated area; for example, comprehension. This is termed a 'spiky profile'. Collecting these assessments is an important part of the graduated approach as set out in the SEND (special educational needs and disability) Code of Practice (Department for Education 2013).

At any time, an autism specialist teacher can be consulted to do a more in-depth observation of the child, collate parents' and school evidence, and gather a developmental history. They can supply support advice for the classroom. It may be necessary to commission an educational psychologist to assess further and advise on strategies. Pursuing a diagnosis will depend on the local autism pathway available, and parents should be involved at every stage. Guidelines for autism recognition, referral and diagnosis (NICE 2011/2017) state that there should be a multi-disciplinary team and it is important that they have a good understanding of the presentation of autism in girls. In many areas, the waiting list is two or more years and while the child is on this waiting list, the school need not be waiting to provide support but be working with parents to discover, develop and implement the support the child needs. Autism strategies are developed to provide clarity, structure and a calm environment for the child, and so working to provide the support the child needs can start as soon as the school has a good profile of her needs. The graduated approach (Department for Education 2013) is there to provide this. Assessment is followed by a plan of action, the strategies are put in place and followed consistently, and regular reviews of progress and effectiveness are planned. Once a review has taken place the cycle begins once again with adjustments as necessary. With or without a diagnosis, autism strategies are about good communication and support, and so a child that parents and teaching staff think may be autistic can benefit from some autism strategies whatever the outcome of the assessment.

There are five key areas where support for young autistic girls should be put in place.

1. Support in the environment

Early years and many primary classrooms are too colourful, too busy, too noisy, too messy, too smelly, too much. Primary classrooms tend to be much more decorated than a secondary classroom. As an early years trained teacher myself, I know all about the advice to make a classroom stimulating. However, there is also a movement to make early years classrooms in particular much less stimulating, focusing on a calm and neutral environment instead (Nixon 2017). It is possible to tone down a classroom environment and have clear, neutral spaces where children can just sit and hide away from all the colour, words and pictures that seem to surround every available surface. Plain spaces between displays and a clear wall around the whiteboard can help all children focus better on what is being shown to them on the screen, without lots to distract them on the surrounding wall.

Check that light levels can be adjusted: does she need lower light or to be where there is good light? Ask the girl and her parents, and if possible do a sensory audit with them.

For an autistic girl, a place to sit that belongs to her can be a great help and avoids a lot of anxiety. A named chair, a carpet tile to sit on or a cushion gives her a place that is familiar and predictable. An autistic girl I once supported was refusing to work in some lessons; she wouldn't sit down and paced the back of the classroom becoming more and more distressed. The class teacher could not find a lesson she could consistently join in. I was able to spend time observing her and it showed us that if she had decided to sit somewhere and another child sat in that chair, she became so anxious that she was unable to sit somewhere else. Hence, she could not then access whatever lesson it was. Giving her a name card to put on a chair she wanted to sit on and letting the other children know to respect that was the support she needed. It worked immediately.

2. Sensory and emotional support programmes

Autistic girls in the early years and primary school are likely to have sensory differences. They can be hyper-sensitive to sensory stimuli that others are able to filter out of their focus. Being aware of *all* the noises, smells, movements, sights, colours, light differences, patterns, temperatures, acoustics of the room, as well as internal body sensations *all* of the time is exhausting and at times, distressing. It is possible that they have lower responsiveness to some senses as well as, or instead of, hyper-sensitivity. A sensory assessment would need to be done by a sensory-trained professional such as an occupational therapist, educational psychologist or specialist teacher. Some CAMHS services offer a sensory assessment, but there are different levels of service provided in each area. If the autistic girl has an assessment, school staff and parents should be asked to fill in an observation sheet and send it to the assessor, who should come and observe the child in the school and home environment. From their report school and home can then provide a 'sensory diet', which is a set of regular sensory activities timetabled into the child's day. There may also be advice to provide a sensory area in the home and in the classroom, and sensory 'toys' or equipment. The purpose of all these is to help the child learn that she is over- or under-sensitive to different experiences and that she can 'regulate' (that is, feel calm or alert as needed) through these activities. It will take some planning to build these into an early years or primary class daily routine but the benefits for the child are lifelong. Learning that their senses work in the way they do and that they can do something to help themselves is going to be one of the most important lessons for their lives. Starting this in the early years and primary school will be of great benefit to them, and working alongside the support parents provide at home will have lasting benefits. Here are some suggested adjustments to meet the needs of the child:

- Have a visual timetable for the child to follow and use it consistently.

- Timetable the sensory activities for the child to do after coming into school, and before or after break and lunch times. Use symbols that show what will be done.

- Set aside a sensory area in the classroom and put symbols or pictures of the sensory activities on the wall. All children can access the activities but the autistic girl should have time alone there if that is what she needs.

Emotions are likely to be a huge part of the autistic girl's life. She may be able to detect the emotional states of everyone in the room and be overly sensitive to the teacher's every frown, tone of voice and sigh. She may be over-keen to please, just to keep everyone happy. Negative emotions can cause a lot of anxiety because she may not be able to understand why someone is feeling that way. She may internalise this and blame herself. Perfectionism can develop, because the feeling of dread is so strong when someone says something isn't right that she will do all she can to avoid it. Emotional understanding should include learning about the internal reactions she has about emotions, so that she recognises what internal feelings are connected to which emotions. Knowing her triggers and who she can trust to help her in these early and primary years will build up a trusted group of people to support her when the teenage hormones and emotional upheaval arrive. Remembering that anxiety is often the most common emotion among this group of children, support to understand and manage their anxiety should be built into their education from an early start. It is unlikely to go away for all her life, as many autistic adults will testify to. But strategies to manage anxiety, and sensory and social overload can be taught from an early age. Not punishing her for shutdowns or expressing her emotional distress will be very important too. To feel and be safe, less verbal interaction and a quiet place to recover are what she needs.

3. Social interactions and friendships

Support for building friendships can start early. All the children in the class can be helped to be more understanding of autism and other needs through stories that have characters with different disabilities and learning needs. Being open to discussing, accepting and celebrating difference should be a whole school policy. Challenging society's demands that we should all be the same should be part of a school's curriculum. Autistic children need to know they are a valued part of society and that starts at school. This is more successful the earlier it starts, as the social relationships between girls in the pre-teen years become much more complicated. Friendship lessons and activities can be part of the personal, social and health education (PSHE) curriculum and circle time but may work better in small group activities.

It is important for early relationships to be built so that the girl has friends she can rely on as they grow together. It is also important to let the autistic girl take the lead in working out what kind of friendships she wants, not what adults think would be good for her. As with boys, friendships that are based on common interests tend to be stronger; they can be with boys or girls and with children of different ages. Learning to trust others with her ideas and interests will be a big step for a young autistic girl, and support from an adult to help talk things through when there are disagreements or conflict can often be empowering for all the children in the friendship group. An autistic girl may prefer to have one friend as the social complexities of two or more people to include can be overwhelming, but if supported carefully and respectfully, having more than one friend can be more rewarding and guard against the devastation if one were to leave the school or go into a different class.

4. Early educational support and access to learning

An autistic girl can have learning difficulties ranging from mild to severe. She may have dyslexia or any other specific learning disability. She might have developmental language delay or moderate learning difficulties. These can be identified before or after the autism diagnosis. The autism diagnosis may not happen because her difficulties are believed to be only a learning disability, or the autism could be thought to be the reason the girl is not learning. Specialist support and assessments may be needed, and in an ideal world would always be available. In the early years, teachers are developing the learning skills of children in their class and may pick up the difficulties a child has with the conventional way of learning. Differentiation is the skill of each class teacher to adapt their teaching to the learning needs of the child.

A young autistic child often responds well to structure. The continuous provision of an early years classroom can be good for an autistic child because of the lower demands put on them, but can also be difficult because of the lower level of structure. Visual timetables are a good resource to provide some structure and can be developed with choices and sensory diet activities built in for the autistic child

(McCann 2017). When it comes to accessing learning activities, an autistic child may need to know more about what is expected, how long it will take and what to do when an activity is finished. These visual timetables can also help an autistic child learn to do some tasks and activities for themselves. A good example is getting changed for PE. A visual schedule of the sequence of getting changed can help a child become more independent and not have to rely wholly on verbal instructions.

As an autistic child goes through the primary school, the learning activities will need to take into account their processing speed and the strengths they have in knowledge and understanding. Girls are as individual as boys, but generally, chunking work, giving sensory breaks, paired work instead of group work, and very clear instructions can support learning. Extra support is most often needed for sensory, anxiety and social difficulties, which can manifest in any lesson situation. More practical ideas can be found in *How to... Support Children with Autistic Spectrum Condition in Primary Schools* by this author (McCann 2017).

5. Support for growing up

There are many challenges that an autistic girl will face as she grows up, and these begin in the later primary years as she moves towards puberty. Having social anxiety and difficulty with being able to 'read' people's intentions leaves her vulnerable to bullying and exploitation. Puberty happens as it does to other girls, but emotional and social maturity can take much longer. While their peers are developing interest in boys, music and celebrities, autistic girls may still prefer their books, My Little Ponies, maps or machines. As with all autistic children, developing their special interests into career opportunities is important, but being prepared for the world of adult relationships is just as important. Even in the early years, respect for their views and choices must be part of their support priorities. If they learn that they must become compliant and docile (as happens with many girls in our society), then they are at greater risk of being taken advantage of when older 'Early research found that individuals with intellectual disabilities [including autism] might be more at risk if they have lower IQs or less education, live alone or in a group home, *are female, and have no or few friends* (Fisher, Moskowitz and Hodapp 2013; my emphasis).

All of these factors can be a higher risk for autistic females, especially if they have not been diagnosed and supported early enough. Therefore, sex and relationship education is essential and must be relevant to their understanding; an excellent book is *Sexuality and Relationship Education for Children and Adolescents with Autism* (2013) and other books by Davida Hartman. Learning to recognise false kindness and flattery, and how to say 'no' needs to begin in the primary years, along with the biology of growing up and the changes ahead.

Conclusion

We have yet to embed training about autism in girls for early years and primary teaching staff but it is important that we do make this a priority in initial teacher training and in school professional development priorities. It may seem that the number of autistic pupils is small; currently the statistics are officially between 1:100 and 1:59 (Baio *et al.* 2018) of the population. However, these do not take into account the girls not yet diagnosed due to the later diagnosis typical for females. The prevalence of 1:4 female to male statistic is out of date and may now be closer to 1:3 (Loomes, Hull and Mandy 2017).

Early years and primary teachers are pivotal in noticing and referring those girls who previously have been missed and potentially let down by our systems. Other chapters in this book highlight the effects that this can have on a girl or woman who later finds out she is, in fact, autistic. The later mental health issues can be supported early if we identify autistic girls in the primary years. We can build the support and awareness they need and give them a greater sense of identity. That, and high expectations of what they can achieve in life, must be our priority. Start early and give them the best chance to thrive that we can. The transition to secondary school, which is explored in the next chapter, along with puberty is more traumatic for autistic girls than their peers, with more resulting exclusions or anxiety-based school refusal according to Sproston, Sedwick and Crane (2017). Unless we support autistic girls in the primary years and plan a strong and supportive transition, we are failing them and setting them up for failure. Girls are autistic for life, just like the boys.

I asked Thea's mum, 'What makes your daughter autistic?' 'Her neurology!' she replied. 'She has a very unique and different brain that is wired up in a way that makes her exquisitely sensitive to life. This is a blessing and a curse. The way she processes and interprets the world is both astounding and crushing, sometimes at the same time.'

References

American Psychiatric Association (2013) *Diagnostic and Statistical Manual of Mental Disorders: DSM-5* (5th edn). Washington, DC: American Psychiatric Publishing.

Attwood, T. (2006) *The Complete Guide to Asperger's Syndrome.* London: Jessica Kingsley Publishers.

Baio, J., Wiggins, L., Christensen, D. L., Maenner, M. J. *et al.* (2018) 'Prevalence of autism spectrum disorder among children aged 8 years. Autism and Developmental Disabilities Monitoring Network, 11 Sites, United States, 2014.' *MMWR Surveillance Summaries, 67*, 6, 1.

Department for Education (2013) *Special Educational Needs and Disability Code of Practice: 0 to 25 Years.* London: Department for Education.

Fisher, M. H, Moskowitz, A. L. and Hodapp R. L. (2013) 'Differences in social vulnerability among individuals with autism spectrum disorder, Williams syndrome, and Down syndrome.' *Research in Autism Spectrum Disorders, 7*, 8, 931–937.

Fisher Bullivant, F. (2018) *Working with Girls and Young Women with an Autism Spectrum Condition: A Practical Guide for Clinicians.* London: Jessica Kingsley Publishers.

Frazier, T., Georgiades, S., Bishop, S. L. and Hardan, A. Y. (2014) 'Behavioral and cognitive characteristics of females and males with autism in the Simons Simplex Collection.' *Journal of the American Academy of Child and Adolescent Psychiatry, 53,* 3, 329–340.e3.

Gould, J. and Ashton-Smith, J. (2011) 'Missed diagnosis or misdiagnosis? Girls and women on the autism spectrum.' *Good Autism Practice, 12,* 1, 34–41.

Grey, C. (2015) *The New Social Story Book.* Arlington, TX: Future Horizons.

Hadjikhani, N. (2014) 'Scientifically deconstructing some of the myths regarding autism.' *Swiss Archives of Neurology and Psychiatry, 16,* 8, 272–276.

Happé, F., Dworzynski, K., Ronald, A. and Bolton, P. (2012) 'How different are girls and boys above and below the diagnostic threshold for autism spectrum disorders?' *Journal of the American Academy of Child and Adolescent Psychiatry, 51,* 8, 788–797.

Harrop, C., Green, J. and Hudry, K. (2017) 'Play complexity and toy engagement in preschoolers with autism spectrum disorder: Do girls and boys differ?' *Autism, 21,* 1, 37–50.

Hartman, D. (2013) *Sexuality and Relationship Education for Children and Adolescents with Autism.* London: Jessica Kingsley Publishers.

Leekam, S. R., Libby, S., Wing, L., Gould, J. and Taylor, C. (2002) 'The Diagnostic Interview for Social and Communication Disorders: Algorithms for ICD-10 childhood autism and Wing & Gould autistic spectrum disorder.' *Journal of Child Psychology and Psychiatry, 43,* 3, 327–342.

Loomes, R., Hull, L. and Mandy, W. (2017) 'What is the male-to-female ratio in autism spectrum disorder? A systematic review and meta-analysis.' *Journal of American Academy Child and Adolescent Psychiatry, 56,* 6, 466–474.

McCann, L. (2017) *How to… Support Children with Autism Spectrum Condition in the Primary School.* Hyde: LDA Learning.

Nasen (2016) *Girls and Autism: Flying Under the Radar.* Tamworth: Nasen.

NICE (2011/2017) *Autism Spectrum Disorder in Under 19s: Recognition, Referral and Diagnosis [CG128].* London: NICE. Accessed on 4/12/18 at www.nice.org.uk/guidance/cg128#

Nixon, G. (2017) 'New thinking on wall displays in early childhood settings.' *Educa.* Accessed on 3/3/18 at www.geteduca.com/blog/displays-in-early-childhood-settings

Sproston, K., Sedgewick, F. and Crane, L. (2017) 'Autistic girls and school exclusion: Perspectives of students and their parents.' *Autism and Developmental Language Impairments, 2,* 1–14.

Sucksmith, E., Allison, C., Baron-Cohen, S., Chakrabarti, S. and Hoekstra, R. A. (2012) 'Empathy and emotion recognition in people with autism, first-degree relatives, and controls.' *Neuropsychologia, 51,* 1, 98–105

Recommended further reading

Autism Education Trust (n.d.) *Sensory Audit for Schools and Classrooms*. Accessed on 3/3/18 from www.aettraininghubs.org.uk/wp-content/uploads/2012/05/37.1-Sensory-audit-tool-for-environments.pdf

McCann, L. (2018) *Stories that Explain: Social Stories for Children with Autism in Primary Schools*. Hyde: LDA Learning.

Nasen (2014) *SEN Support and the Graduated Approach*. Tamworth: Nasen.

Nichols, S., Moravcik, G. M. and Pulver Tetenbaum, S. (2009) *Girls Growing Up on the Autism Spectrum: What Parents and Professionals Should Know About the Pre-Teen and Teenage Years*. London: Jessica Kingsley Publishers.

CHAPTER 4

Managing the Transition from Primary to Secondary School for Autistic Girls

A Case Study Approach

Judith Hebron

The move from primary to secondary school (henceforth referred to in this chapter as transition) is a momentous occasion in all children's lives: even as adults, most people can recall the sense of anticipation (and sometimes trepidation) that accompanied it. While there are many transitions throughout life, the primary to secondary one is arguably the most challenging. In England children move following as many as eight years in the same primary setting to a new and largely unfamiliar secondary school. In addition, girls are on the cusp of adolescence – or may even be going through it – adding to the numerous changes with which 11-year-olds are expected to cope. Central to this are the considerable social demands made on young people, as they mix with a new peer group, potentially only knowing a few or perhaps none of them. For young autistic girls, who may struggle with change and managing anxiety, it is understandable that this may present as an especially tumultuous time, and yet there is no previous research focusing specifically on their experiences at this point.

This chapter presents the 'journey' undertaken by two autistic girls: one from a mainstream and the other from a special school setting. It begins with an exploration of what is currently known about the primary to secondary school transition for all pupils, followed by a closer examination of how this may be more challenging for autistic children. The specific needs of girls are extracted from this literature, although at the time of writing, the transition of autistic girls has not been studied in depth. This is followed by the two case studies, exploring each girl's experiences over an 18-month period from the final term of primary school to the second year of secondary school. In doing so, it becomes possible to understand some of the challenges as well as opportunities that these girls faced, through their own eyes, as well as those of their parents and teachers. While the two experiences are different in many ways, there are also some striking similarities. The chapter concludes with suggestions for schools and parents in terms of best practice when preparing autistic girls for the transition to secondary school.

Sincere thanks go to the two girls, their parents and teachers for sharing their experiences, even the most difficult ones. Without their willingness to discuss the highs and lows of transition, this research would not have been possible. The two case studies come from a larger project exploring the transition of young people with autism conducted by the author (Hebron 2017, 2018) that was jointly funded by Early Career Research Fellowships from the Leverhulme Trust (ECF-2013-098) and Simon Endowment at the University of Manchester.

Making the transition to secondary school

The transition from primary to secondary school is a landmark in any young person's education and may be considered a rite of passage. Research into this transition is well established and has provided us with some good understanding of its inherent difficulties and benefits. It is known to be a challenging time for all students (e.g. Zeedyk *et al.* 2003), particularly as they move from the top of the primary school hierarchy to the bottom of the secondary one (Rice and Frederickson 2011). In addition, in England the average size of primary schools is around a quarter of that of secondary schools (Department for Education 2018), meaning that the young person will have to navigate a much larger environment, with considerably more students and increased associated concerns, such as noise and boisterous behaviour from older students. Linked to this are the demands of having specialist teachers for the many different curriculum subjects, as well as the social demands of making new friends and adjusting to the dynamics of a new peer group (Coffey 2013). Nevertheless, while all of these changes can be regarded as challenges, research has consistently found that detrimental effects (such as a dip in academic achievement and increased levels of worry) tend to be relatively short-term for most students (e.g. Bloyce and Frederickson 2012). The anticipation of transition is often worse than the actual experience, with potential benefits cited by children such as increased social opportunities, greater subject choice and a broader range of extra-curricular activities (Waters, Lester and Cross 2014).

However, research has highlighted that transition can remain a negative experience for up to a quarter of all children (Waters *et al.* 2014). This is an emergent research field where more research is urgently needed. It is thought that many of these children come from vulnerable groups, including those with special educational needs and disabilities (SEND). However, SEND comprises heterogeneous groups of young people, leading to a need for more targeted studies to understand which groups are more vulnerable at this time and why.

Transition for students with autism spectrum conditions (ASC)

Difficulties with change and social understanding are core components of a diagnosis of autism (American Psychiatric Association 2013), and so it seems likely that a group whose challenges are similar to those encountered at transition may be especially vulnerable. Studies to date have revealed that many of these difficulties are similar to those of the broader school community and include adapting to a new school environment with a greater number of teachers and making new friends (e.g. Peters and Brooks 2016). Nevertheless, there are concerns that these challenges are experienced more intensely by young autistic students (Dann 2011), contributing to a higher probability of negative outcomes.

A recent review of studies on the transition of autistic pupils by Nuske *et al.* (2018) reveals some worrying trends. There remain relatively few studies specifically exploring the transition experiences of young autistic people, and while this study examined research on both the transition to primary school and the primary–secondary one, there were considerably more studies in the latter case (17 as opposed to 10), with the majority of difficulties identified as taking place when moving to secondary school. At the student level, anxiety emerged as a significant challenge in a majority of studies (e.g. Tobin *et al.* 2012), although Hannah and Topping (2012) reported a more mixed picture, highlighting that anxiety levels are likely to vary considerably between individuals. Social relationships also emerged as problematic in many studies (e.g. Deacy, Jennings and O'Halloran 2015), and there were additional concerns regarding bullying (e.g. Peters and Brooks 2016).

While the focus is often on students, there are concerns that parents find the primary–secondary transition stressful and problematic too. This may involve the choice of school, difficulties communicating with staff, and a sense of powerlessness about the whole process. Teachers also report concerns at transition in terms of adequate training, communication between primary and secondary schools, and also having sufficient resources to provide an individualised transition package for the children (for a comprehensive review of these studies, Nuske *et al.*'s (2018) review is recommended to the reader). What emerges consistently across research on the transition of autistic students is that some transition strategies are particularly effective.

These include giving the student time to become familiar with the new school setting, bespoke transition arrangements, and clear communication between home and school. Nevertheless, the author's own research and experience suggest that the quality of transition varies widely from school to school and is dependent on many factors at different levels. In this context, it is currently impossible to draw conclusions over whether transition tends to be a more positive or negative experience for this group of young people.

Transition for autistic girls

As usual, girls represent a minority in these studies, and findings tend to focus on autistic young people as a group. To date, no study has focused solely on autistic girls across the transition to secondary school although some (e.g. Cridland *et al.* 2014; Peters and Brooks 2016) consider this as part of their findings. Arguably, a key consideration is that an autistic girl is to a large extent living in a boy's world (e.g. Cridland *et al.* 2014), as autism is still regarded as a 'male' condition, with girls frequently absent from studies. This can lead to a lack of understanding among school staff who may struggle to identify autistic girls' needs and perceive them as requiring less support than their male counterparts (Mandy *et al.* 2012). Girls are more likely to internalise their anxiety and frustrations, meaning that these serious issues can easily be missed, resulting in extreme distress. Linked to this is the issue of 'camouflaging' (Dean, Harwood and Kasari 2017), which means that girls may appear to be coping at school when the opposite is actually the case. Often the resulting pressure and frustration are released when they return home upset and exhausted (e.g. Hebron, Humphrey and Oldfield 2015). For those girls attending special school, there may also be a sense of isolation, as 70 per cent of students attending special schools are male (Department vfor Education 2018), and the percentage in ASC-specific classrooms is likely to be higher again.

It is acknowledged that friendship can be qualitatively different among girls compared to boys, and this becomes increasingly salient during adolescence when groupings become ever more complex (Bauminger *et al.* 2008). Of course, this often coincides with transition, compounding existing concerns. Although levels of social communication tend to be higher in autistic girls compared to autistic boys (Nichols, Moravcik and Tetenbaum 2009), a significant difference frequently remains between girls with and without autism, meaning that friendships may be more difficult to form and maintain. Given the protective nature of friendship in guarding against bullying (Kendrick, Jutengren and Stattin 2012), this further complicates the picture. Studies consistently indicate that autistic students are more vulnerable to bullying than their peers and that this tends to increase in prevalence from primary into secondary school (e.g. Hebron and Humphrey 2014). While girls may exhibit a range of types of bullying, they are more likely to engage in relational bullying (e.g. social exclusion, unkind gossip, and spreading of rumours) (Salmivalli and Kaukiainen 2004), something which is often subtle and therefore difficult for an autistic girl to understand. In addition, it can be considerably more difficult for parents and teachers to identify, especially given the widespread use of social media during adolescence (Shakir *et al.* 2018). Autistic girls may, therefore, be especially vulnerable to this once they transition to secondary school.

In broader terms, girls tend to enter adolescence earlier than boys (Lee 1980) and may already be experiencing puberty during transition. Understanding and coping with the physical changes, including the onset of menstruation and acne, can be stressful for all girls, and this is likely to be intensified in autistic girls who may already be struggling to cope with the significant changes of transition.

Therefore, it is vital that teachers understand that while many of the challenges of transition may be common to autistic girls and boys, there are some areas specific to autistic girls that may be causing hidden distress. Sadly, there is a much higher proportion of autistic young people who are school refusers than among the broader school population (Munkhaugen *et al.* 2017). While it is currently unknown how this affects autistic girls, it is likely to occur when their needs are not being met, resulting in higher levels of stress and anxiety. This may currently be the case for many young autistic women struggling with the increased demands of transition to secondary school.

The transition experiences of two autistic girls

At this point, we turn to the experiences of two autistic girls[1] as they navigate the transition from primary to secondary school. First, we explore the experiences of Rose, a student in mainstream education, followed by those of Lucy, who attends a special school. While there are some major differences in their experiences, largely due to receiving different types of educational provision, there are also some startling similarities, and these will be explored at the end of this section.

Rose

> Imagine you're on stage and you're in a stage production that lasts eight hours every day! And you're playing a part and that would wreck you. It must be exhausting! (Mother)

Rose's parents had long realised that she was 'different' from many of her peers, and despite excelling academically she experienced many episodes of behavioural outbursts during her early school years. Primary school had consequently not been a happy experience for her; she had moved schools several times and been bullied severely, resulting in a short

---

1 All names in this chapter are pseudonyms to preserve the anonymity of the participating girls, their families and their teachers.

period of home-schooling. This all changed when she came to her current primary school, where the special educational needs coordinator (SENCO) recognised her difficulties in interpreting and coping with the social demands of school. In conjunction with Rose's parents and GP, assessment was sought, and a diagnosis of Asperger's syndrome subsequently given. This enabled Rose, her family and her school to understand her challenges and build in strategies for her to cope and flourish in education. As her needs were being supported by the SENCO at her school, an application for an Education, Health and Care Plan (EHCP) was not made.

As transition approached, Rose and her family explored the secondary school options available in the area. This highlighted some sensory issues around noise that would have made these alternative choices difficult. Rose's mother reported that following visits to local secondary schools, 'The teachers were too shouty'; 'She was utterly overwhelmed by the number of children and the noise they made.' Therefore, Rose opted to transition to the secondary section of her existing 3–19 girls' academy school which seemed calmer to her and more predictable. This secondary school was on a nearby but separate site, with the move into Year 7 still perceived as a major transition for all pupils and requiring careful arrangements.

Transition arrangements – what worked

On the whole, despite some anxieties around change and new and unknown social demands, Rose's transition to secondary school was successful. Rose and her mother discussed transition when they walked to school each morning, ensuring that change and new routines were familiar well in advance of the new school year. Staff were proactive in generating opportunities for Rose to familiarise herself with the new school and especially the layout (e.g. knowing where the toilets were, which was a concern for Rose). This included an induction day and subsequent 'taster' sessions that were provided to pupils by secondary staff. As well as providing a basis for getting to know the new school, this served to 'normalise' the process, as something that all pupils did. However, this initial transition process was not without problems, as evidenced when the plans for induction day were not as anticipated:

> There'd been numerous promises made; she would be with her friends from primary and she would have a designated teacher and she'd be told where there was a designated safe place she could go, and all of it went out the window because some very well-meaning sixth form girls who were organising the little girls as they came in put her in a group with nobody she knew, and she didn't know where the safe place was and she...she coped, very proud of her, she coped, but she came home and fell apart. (Mother)

This highlights the importance of maintaining agreed arrangements and not imposing sudden changes on a situation that is already socially challenging for an autistic student. Fortunately, the year head subsequently worked closely with Rose to ensure there was consistency, and a bespoke induction day was provided for her that was successful in alleviating some anxieties.

In addition to this, opportunities were provided to help manage new social demands once transition had taken place. For example, Rose had friends in her Year 6 class who were also peer mentors, and the SENCO ensured that these girls were kept together in their new form class in Year 7. As the SENCO explained, 'These people know her ups and downs, they know her ins and outs, and they will tell her when she's overstepped the mark or whatever. And she can cope with it from them.'

At a key time in development at the beginning of adolescence, when female social groups become more complex and often fluid, this provided a sense of continuity and removed some of the additional social demands of being with an unfamiliar group of peers.

Following her move to secondary school, Rose reflected that she had 'a few bumps as you would expect, but everything's gone really well'. This underlines that a well-managed transition – that still includes some challenges (such as getting lost, forgetting equipment, and not completing homework) – can be highly effective.

Challenges at transition and beyond

Nevertheless, although much of the transition process was successful in enabling Rose to adapt to the demands of secondary education, worrying themes around adults' understanding of autism, social relationships and coping strategies emerged during Year 7 and into Year 8, and these impacted on her overall experience of school. While some of them may apply more broadly to all young people with autism, several are of particular significance to girls and young women.

Staff training in autism has increased significantly in recent years, and although there remains considerable work to be done, there is some evidence that schools are becoming better equipped to support autistic students (e.g. Cullen *et al.* 2013). However, a key concern to emerge from Rose's experiences is that understanding of autism in girls still lags behind that of boys. This became apparent at several points, with some key staff in secondary school having an incomplete understanding of autism, and more specifically its heterogeneity among girls.

For example, according to her SENCO, 'What [some staff] can't understand is what works with one child, why doesn't it work with another necessarily?' Fortunately, Rose's mother acknowledged that this improved over time as teachers got to know her daughter:

> I think for some of them what had happened at the start is they'd been good, they'd gone onto an autism website, they'd read her profile, right brilliant, but all those profiles tend to be about boys and she wasn't ticking those boxes, so we've had a couple of incidents where a member of staff has lost their temper, they've been shouting and then they've come back the next day and they've gone, 'I'm sorry Rose, I got...you know, I got that wrong.'

In addition, good links between home and school enabled Rose's mother and the SENCO to share which strategies could be effective in defusing confrontational situations, and also which approaches would be more likely to trigger them.

In particular, some issues arose due to Rose interpreting situations quite logically but also very literally (e.g. when a teacher asked for homework to be completed but not specifically for it to be handed in), meaning that staff required training to understand how more concrete instructions may need to be used with autistic pupils. Of course, Rose also needed to learn how to manage difficult situations, and in particular those where she felt that there had been an injustice. Nevertheless, this highlights how situations can be calmed or exacerbated depending on the knowledge and understanding of a member of staff.

There was also evidence of poor understanding of autism in girls from some parents in Rose's year, causing obvious upset and frustration for her own parents: 'We've had a couple of comments from some parents. One parent said, "Oh, but she looks so normal, I wouldn't think there was something wrong with her." And things like that..."but she dresses like the other girls".'

Rose's mother was concerned that this lack of under-standing could lead to social exclusion:

> I'm wary that, you know, somebody has a party or an event, and that mother knows that Rose has autism and says, 'Oh, well it'll just be hassle, let's not ask her.' Or you know, 'It'd be a bit loud for her.' Or something like that.

Clearly, this is a broader issue; with improved awareness of difference and diversity embedded in many schools, the challenge may lie in reaching out to older generations. Whether the onus to do this lies with schools or not remains a point of debate.

Difficulties in social interactions is a core challenge in autism, and this was in evidence for Rose at times, although she did have some good reciprocal friendships. Indeed, it was of note that these friends supported each other and enjoyed common interests, although Rose embraced her individuality and observed with humour the drive towards conformity and social group norms:

> Everyone has their own little clusters, it's like they're penguins grouping together into one corner; it's very funny to me, so like people are in this corner and then people are in front of here, which are the girls that are a bit naughty. Then there's the popular girls at the front, then there's my friends at the back here.

As mentioned in the introduction to this chapter, girls' social groups become more complex in the secondary years (Cridland *et al.* 2014), and this has arguably been exacerbated by the growth of social media in recent years, including the ability to see and follow people's social interactions 24/7. This was a concern for Rose and her mother, with some incidents of social exclusion emerging following the transition to secondary school; for example, 'I went on Instagram, checked on my friend's profile pages to see what they'd been up to and they'd had a big sleepover and they invited girls they didn't even like, but they didn't invite me.'

There was also an incident of relational bullying following transition to secondary school (her mother said, 'A little girl had written a list, "anybody who doesn't like Rose write on the list…"'. This girl was a pupil Rose had not known at primary school but it was still very upsetting. The school dealt with it promptly when some of Rose's friends reported it, but it highlights the need for staff to be vigilant to forms of bullying that can be subtler but no less damaging. Such forms of bullying are generally more common among girls than boys (Salmivalli and Kaukiainen 2004).

Despite some socially driven issues, Rose often seemed to cope well with her move to secondary school and the accompanying challenges. She had clearly developed some effective coping strategies, and these enabled her to have a more harmonious relationship with her peer group and fewer confrontations with staff. These strategies, supported by the SENCO and Rose's parents, included 'traffic light cards' which enabled her to leave a classroom without having to explain why to staff. In addition, many teachers accepted that she sometimes needed 'time out', so long as they were aware that she had gone to a safe place in school.

Nevertheless, it should also be remembered that autistic girls often camouflage their emotions very effectively (Dean *et al.* 2017), resulting in staff believing that all is well, when in fact the girls might be experiencing severe stress, anxiety and fatigue. This was certainly the case for Rose, who returned home exhausted each day and needed time alone before dinner to decompress and recover from the demands of the school day: 'She basically creates her own sensory deprivation area in which she recharges after school' (mother). This may be seen to a certain extent in her difficulties completing homework and a desire to separate school and home. This is likely to reflect the increased and often exhausting social demands experienced by autistic girls in school settings. As such, it is important that staff recognise these challenges, and while not necessarily removing the need to complete homework, provide – as was the case in Rose's school – opportunities for homework to be completed at some other time in the school day, such as lunchtime.

So, despite a broadly positive experience of transition for Rose, it is clear that there were challenges from different sources, and that many of these remain ongoing concerns as she moves through the secondary education years.

Lucy

> I'm proud to be here because I could've ended up downhill, but I'm uphill now. (Lucy)

Lucy is a friendly and articulate girl with lots of interests, especially computer games and Moshi Monsters. She was diagnosed with autism at the age of seven and also had a diagnosis of cerebral palsy (as well as some additional physical issues), meaning that she received a dual Statement of Educational Needs (now an EHCP) that identified both conditions as core areas of need. Lucy has an older brother with severe autism, and so her mother was aware from an early age of her autistic traits. Lucy attended a special school from Year 1 and progressed well during her time there. At primary school, she often rushed her work and could be very anxious, meaning that her academic profile was not thought to reflect her actual ability. Nevertheless, primary school had been a mostly positive experience for her, despite some earlier instances of school refusal that had been overcome, and this had not been an issue in Year 6. Lucy found friendships with her peers difficult but was very happy with adult company and tended to consider school staff her friends, including her class teacher, who had taught her for two years.

Initial transition to secondary school

When considering the transition to secondary school, there were already concerns during Year 6 that there had not been enough preparation and communication with the new school, and this was expressed by both Lucy's mother and her Year 6 teacher. As Lucy's mother explained, managing change was far from straightforward, as:

> If you give her too much notice, then she'll start stressing about it, and she'll process it too much where she can't handle it. [...] But if you don't, if you don't tell her, then she'll just back off, she'll just refuse it anyway and hit crisis.

In addition, there were some concerns that it was difficult to arrange transition visits with the secondary school due to logistical arrangements. Nevertheless, the Year 6 teacher and speech and language therapist had a range of transition activities delivered in the primary school aimed at preparing pupils for the forthcoming major changes.

Unfortunately, the transition to secondary school did not go as planned, with only two fairly brief visits, some of the anticipated visits not taking place at all, unanticipated changes in key staff, and other important concerns including delays in the arrival of new uniform and confirmation of transport arrangements. This led to Lucy becoming very anxious, to the point where her mother and teacher had to persuade her that the first day at her new school was one of the missing transition days. This all meant that Lucy was unprepared for the major upheaval of starting a new school, and although the first few days appeared to go reasonably well, her experience soon deteriorated:

> It was horrendous, she ended up just breaking down, you know on the floor in a heap, sobbing her heart out that she couldn't understand the lessons, she couldn't do the work, I don't know where I'm going [...], and it was just everything was way too much for her. (Lucy's mother)

A long-term concern of Lucy's mother was that the choice of secondary school had been based on Lucy's academic rather than social skills, meaning that she was assigned to a school for children with moderate learning difficulties. Furthermore, Lucy was very upset that she was placed in an 'ASD class' with other autistic children, rather than a mixed class, as had been the case at her primary school. While the 'ASD class' provided a higher ratio of staff to children and was specifically geared towards the needs of autistic youngsters, Lucy was adamant that it was not the right place for her and also that she could not cope with the work. A point to note here is that there are fewer girls than boys in special schools (Department for Education 2018), and the gender disparity is likely to be even more pronounced in autism-specific classrooms. While Lucy did not mention this specifically, it remains a point of concern more generally that autistic girls in special school settings may lack opportunities to interact with other girls and also that their often subtler presentation of autism may result in their needs being more difficult to identify and therefore address.

As mentioned earlier in this chapter, the issue of camouflaging among autistic girls is becoming increasingly recognised (e.g. Dean *et al.* 2017), and this appears to have been the case for Lucy. While at school, she appeared to cope, with her teacher commenting that 'When she's in school she very rarely appears to have issues.' However, Lucy was releasing all her anxiety and frustration once she returned home:

> She'll just sort of come in, bounce the door off the wall, you know, and just rant and rave and you just sort of stay out of her way, stay very calm and then she'll eventually, she will get it out of her system, but you don't actually know what the problem is until further down the line when she'll just burst into tears and then it's like 'OK, what's the problem?' (Lucy's mother)

The difference in behaviour between school and home was extreme and something which is starting to be recognised in girls (e.g. Hebron *et al.* 2015). Indeed, it was only when Lucy's teachers came to her house and witnessed her behaviour that they realised the full extent of the anxieties that she masked so effectively in school.

The constant upset led to increasing periods of school refusal, despite adjustments to her timetable. Lucy's mother eventually withdrew her from school completely, was forced to give up her job in order to look after her, and began the process of finding another school that could meet her complex needs and where a fresh start could be made. While this process was lengthy and often frustrating, Lucy's mother was able to secure a place at another special school in the area, and so a second transition to secondary school began.

A fresh start

The second transition was very different, especially in light of having failed the first time around. This one was critical if Lucy was to be able to continue her education with confidence. The new school worked with the previous one and Lucy's mother in order to understand how to proceed, and this started with multiple visits, initially short ones but steadily getting longer until Lucy could complete whole school days. While Lucy did find these visits stressful and upsetting in the early stages, the approach the school took was of absolute consistency and with an understanding that Lucy would be listened to once she was calm: 'The headmistress was just fantastic. She just looked at her and she went, "Have you stopped shouting now? I'm not listening. Speak to me and I will listen." And it was just so... she didn't rise to any of it' (Lucy's mother). Furthermore, the school gave Lucy a transition booklet that included information about her new school. This included visual explanations and photographs of staff. Together, these strategies gradually calmed Lucy's worries about school to the point that she started to look forward to going.

While Lucy's mother was concerned about the long summer holiday in terms of undoing the apparently successful transition arrangements, the new term started well, and Lucy made a highly successful transition into Year 8. Of course, there were some days where events challenged Lucy, and these are likely to be ongoing, but the change in her overall well-being was significant: according to her mother, 'She comes home and she's actually quite relaxed, she's chatty, she's happy, she's just, I've got my girl back again, I've not had that for a long time.'

In terms of what made a successful second transition, it appears that the consistent approach from the school provided a clear starting point, as well as a refusal to try to reason with Lucy while she was in crisis, even if that took time. In this context, Lucy was soon able to start to address her frustrations and anxieties and was working effectively with staff to learn how to manage problematic situations.

In addition, this school catered for children with more severe needs, and as such was organised using a primary-based model where the students stay in the same classroom with the same staff most of the day, allowing for greater predictability. Communication seems to have been very effective from the outset, with a home–school diary used on a day-to-day basis, as had been the case in primary school. Positive home–school communication remains an essential component for many young people with autism, ensuring consistency across settings, and permitting important knowledge to be shared quickly (e.g. Bond and Hebron 2016). This positive process was commented on by Lucy's teacher: 'We communicate really well. So we write to each other like, we write every day and tell her how Lucy's been and she'll [mother] write back almost every day.'

In addition, problems with inconsistencies in school transport improved, although this did remain an ongoing concern for Lucy's mother, as some of the companies used were privately contracted, with reduced understanding of children's needs (e.g. the need for the same seat and a familiar face in terms of the escort). Indeed, it is important to bear in mind that the school day is much longer for the many children in special education who rely on transport to and from school.

The effects of a positive transition and having a child who is settled in school should not be underestimated. Lucy appeared happier and more relaxed, but equally importantly was looking forward to her future with determination, stating, 'I want to prove to everybody in my family that I can do this,' and 'I'm going to be proud to wear this [uniform] until I leave to go to college.' A strong sense of belonging had already emerged by the end of her first term at the school, which is significant given that she missed a large part of her first year of secondary school. This positive impact extended beyond Lucy to her younger brother, who was more relaxed at home, and to her mother, who was able to return to work.

Lucy's transition was undoubtedly difficult, involving a great deal of upset for her and her family. Nevertheless, it is reassuring to know that positive outcomes are possible despite many challenges, some of which may be directly related to being female and autistic.

Common themes across transition

While it is impractical to try to generalise from two case studies of autistic girls transitioning to secondary school, there are nevertheless some powerful emergent themes. Therefore, it is possible to highlight a number of shared areas of experience that were relevant to both Rose and Lucy during and after their transition and which are reflected in recent research on autism in girls specifically.

First, it is important to note that many of the challenges of transition are common to boys and girls, with challenges such as coping with change, literality, and peer relationships all key considerations. However, these areas may be impacted by differences in the female presentation of autism. Both Rose and Lucy experienced high levels of anxiety and had in the past externalised their frustrations. However, with the move to secondary school and the onset of adolescence, it is vital to acknowledge that both girls were able to mask their difficulties in school and give the impression that all was fine. These anxieties and frustrations were more likely to be expressed in the safety of their homes, where their behaviour was very different from school.

Awareness of autism in girls is also a key theme to emerge, although in very different ways. While there appeared to be a lack of knowledge and understanding of autism in girls among parents and staff in the mainstream school, Lucy's relative isolation as an autistic girl in a special school setting should not be ignored, especially as she may present more subtly than boys due to masking her difficulties. Fortunately, in Lucy's case, the school staff appeared to understand this masking of anxieties.

A key point, though, is the need for staff to be able to see beyond the label of autism, avoiding stereotypes, and appreciating the young person for who she is, recognising her needs, interests and aspirations. As Lucy's mother stated, 'They [the staff] actually listen to her and they actually talk to her like she's a person.' This is something that we expect for all young people, and autistic girls are no different.

Promoting a positive transition to secondary school for girls with ASC

While not exhaustive, below are recommendations for parents and schools to take into consideration when planning and implementing transition to secondary school for autistic girls. These are drawn from the broader transition study but adapted to have a specific focus on autistic girls.

Elements that are *essential to a positive transition* for girls with autism:

- effective and bespoke transition planning between primary and secondary school that involves parents and students (the number of visits required will vary)

- open channels of communication on both sides between home and school (this may involve phone calls, email, text messages or home–school diaries as appropriate)

- support which continues beyond the settling-in period that is individualised and flexible

- getting to know the student as an individual, finding out her interests, and seeing beyond the label of autism

- ensuring all staff have an understanding of autism and of its potentially different presentation in girls (e.g. masking of difficulties, internalisation of anxieties)

- provision of adequate training in order to meet the needs of young autistic women with confidence.

Areas where *additional monitoring is needed* to accommodate potential difficulties:

- friendships and relationships with the peer group

- being bullied, teased and/or socially excluded (including via social media)

- being aware of anxiety levels and fatigue

- the impact of sensory sensitivities

- well-being and academic motivation beyond early Year 7

- broader community understanding of autism.

Conclusion

The transition from primary to secondary school is a challenging time for all young people but may be especially so for young autistic students. To the author's knowledge, the research presented in this chapter is the first to focus specifically on the transition experiences of two autistic girls. While the experiences of the two girls are different in many ways (and we must bear in mind that this is a highly individualised experience for every young person), there are also some important common themes that support and extend knowledge and understanding in this area. Many of the challenges are similar to those experienced by autistic boys, and so the 'best practice' advice to parents and schools remains centred on bespoke transition planning, involvement of the children and their parents, familiarisation with the new school and teachers, good communication between home and school (before, during and following transition), and seeing the individual beyond the label of autism. These are not technical interventions but good practice that can be adopted by any school prioritising transition as a significant time in young people's lives.

Nevertheless, Rose and Lucy's experiences also highlight some differences in the transition process that are more specific to girls. These include parents and teachers understanding the differences and subtleties of the female presentation of autism (i.e. being a girl in a boys' world); masking and/or internalising anxieties; managing the complex social networks adopted by girls; and the heightened risk of more female-specific forms of bullying. Transition can be successful, but only if the right adaptations are made for autistic girls in a supportive atmosphere that respects their individuality and their strengths as well as challenges. Of course, this is not the only transition that these young women will face in their lives, but it is potentially the first major one, and the experiences gained at this point are likely to influence future choices and decisions.

References

American Psychiatric Association (2013) *Diagnostic and Statistical Manual of Mental Disorders: DSM-5* (5th edn). Washington, DC: American Psychiatric Publishing.

Bauminger, N., Solomon, M., Aviezer, A., Heung, K., Brown, J. and Rogers, S. (2008) 'Friendship in high-functioning children with autism spectrum disorder: Mixed and non-mixed dyads.' *Journal of Autism and Developmental Disorders, 38*, 7, 1211–1229.

Bloyce, J. and Frederickson, N. (2012) 'Intervening to improve the transfer to secondary school.' *Educational Psychology in Practice, 28*, 1, 1–18.

Bond, C. and Hebron, J. (2016) 'Developing mainstream resource provision for pupils with autism spectrum disorder: Staff perceptions and satisfaction.' *European Journal of Special Needs Education, 31*, 2, 250–263.

Coffey, A. (2013) 'Relationships: The key to successful transition from primary to secondary school?' *Improving Schools, 16*, 3, 261–271.

Cridland, E., Jones, S., Caputi, P. and Magee, C. (2014) 'Being a girl in a boys' world: Investigating the experiences of girls with autism spectrum disorders during adolescence.' *Journal of Autism and Developmental Disorders, 44*, 6, 1261–1274.

Cullen, M., Cullen, S., Lindsay, G. and Arweck, E. (2013) *Evaluation of Autism Education Trust Training Hubs Programme, 2011–13: Final Report*. Warwick: University of Warwick.

Dann, R. (2011). 'Secondary transition experiences for pupils with autistic spectrum conditions (ASCs).' *Educational Psychology in Practice, 27*, 3, 293–312.

Deacy, E., Jennings, F. and O'Halloran, A. (2015) 'Transition of students with autistic spectrum disorders from primary to post-primary school: A framework for success.' *Support for Learning, 30*, 4, 292–304.

Dean, M., Harwood, R. and Kasari, C. (2017) 'The art of camouflage: Gender differences in the social behaviors of girls and boys with autism spectrum disorder.' *Autism, 21*, 6, 678–689.

Department for Education (2018) *Schools, Pupils and Their Characteristics: January 2018*. London: Department for Education.

Hannah, E. and Topping, K. (2012) 'Anxiety levels in students with autism spectrum disorder: Making the transition from primary to secondary school.' *Education and Training in Autism and Developmental Disabilities, 47*, 2, 198–209.

Hebron, J. (2017) 'The Transition from Primary to Secondary School for Students with Autism Spectrum Disorders.' In C. Little (ed.) *Supporting Social Inclusion for Students with Autism Spectrum Disorders*. London: Routledge.

Hebron, J. (2018) 'School connectedness and the primary to secondary school transition for young people with autism spectrum conditions.' *British Journal of Educational Psychology, 88*, 3, 396–409.

Hebron, J. and Humphrey, N. (2014) 'Exposure to bullying among students with autism spectrum conditions: A multi-informant analysis of risk and protective factors.' *Autism, 18*, 6, 618–630.

Hebron, J., Humphrey, N. and Oldfield, J. (2015) 'Vulnerability to bullying of children with autism spectrum conditions in mainstream education: A multi-informant qualitative exploration.' *Journal of Research in Special Educational Needs, 15*, 3, 185–193.

Kendrick, K., Jutengren, G. and Stattin, H. (2012) 'The protective role of supportive friends against bullying perpetration and victimization.' *Journal of Adolescence, 35*, 4, 1069–1080.

Lee, P. A. (1980) 'Normal ages of pubertal events among American males and females.' *Journal of Adolescent Health Care, 1*, 1, 26–29.

Mandy, W., Chilvers, R., Chowdhury, U., Salter, G., Seigal, A. and Skuse, D. (2012) 'Sex differences in autism spectrum disorder: Evidence from a large sample of children and adolescents.' *Journal of Autism and Developmental Disorders, 42*, 7, 1304–1313.

Munkhaugen, E. K., Gjevik, E., Pripp, A. H., Sponheim, E. and Diseth, T. H. (2017) 'School refusal behaviour: Are children and adolescents with autism spectrum disorder at a higher risk?' *Research in Autism Spectrum Disorders, 41*, 31–38.

Nichols, S., Moravcik, G. and Tetenbaum, S. (2009) *Girls Growing Up on the Autism Spectrum: What Parents and Professionals Should Know About the Pre-Teen and Teenage Years*. London: Jessica Kingsley Publishers.

Nuske, H., McGhee Hassrick, E., Bronstein, B., Hauptman, L. *et al.* (2018) 'Broken bridges – new school transitions for students with autism spectrum disorder: A systematic review on difficulties and strategies for success.' *Autism.* https://doi.org/10.1177/1362361318754529

Peters, R. and Brooks, R. (2016) 'Parental perspectives on the transition to secondary school for students with Asperger syndrome and high-functioning autism: A pilot survey study.' *British Journal of Special Education, 43*, 1, 75–91.

Rice, F. and Frederickson, N. (2011) 'Assessing pupil concerns about transition to secondary school.' *British Journal of Educational Psychology, 81*, 2, 244–263.

Salmivalli, C. and Kaukiainen, A. (2004) '"Female aggression" revisited: Variable- and person-centered approaches to studying gender differences in different types of aggression.' *Aggressive Behavior, 30*, 158–163.

Shakir, T., Bhandari, N., Andrews, A., Zmitrovich, A. *et al.* (2018) 'Social media and its impact on adolescents.' *Pediatrics, 141*, 1 (Meeting Abstract).

Tobin, H., Staunton, S., Mandy, W., Skuse, D. *et al.* (2012) 'A qualitative examination of parental experiences of the transition to mainstream secondary school for children with an autism spectrum disorder.' *Educational and Child Psychology, 29*, 1, 72–83.

Waters, S. K., Lester, L. and Cross, D. (2014) 'Transition to secondary school: Expectation versus experience.' *Australian Journal of Education, 58*, 2, 153–166.

Zeedyk, M., Gallacher, J., Henderson, M., Hope, G., Husband, B. and Lindsay, K. (2003) 'Negotiating the transition from primary to secondary school: Perceptions of pupils, parents and teachers.' *School Psychology International, 24*, 1, 67–79.

CHAPTER 5

Meeting the Needs of Autistic Girls at Secondary School

Gareth Morewood, Carla Tomlinson and Caroline Bond

It is only relatively recently that conferences started to take place specifically focusing on autistic women and girls. Since then, a growing understanding with regard to diagnosis and presentation of girls and women with autism has started to gain pace. With increasing research and awareness of the different profiles and presentations of males and females with autism there has been an increase in the numbers of girls being diagnosed. However, as outlined in the Introduction to this book, the current diagnostic criteria (American Psychiatric Association 2013) fail to give examples of the types of difficulties experienced by girls and women as distinct from those of boys and men. This can make it difficult for the needs of girls to be recognised in schools and consequently expectations may not be adjusted to accommodate their strengths and difficulties.

For autistic girls, their challenges may present as difficulties understanding unwritten rules and expectations, challenges with understanding and managing anxiety, and difficulties navigating the increasingly complex social world of secondary school. Girls' skills at masking their difficulties and demonstrating age-appropriate interests may make it more difficult for their needs to be identified in relation to current diagnostic criteria (Mandy *et al.* 2012). School staff and parents/carers with less knowledge of how autistic girls present may be surprised that someone who appears able, can participate in reciprocal conversations, and can use appropriate affect and gestures may have a diagnosis of autism (Gould and Ashton-Smith 2011). Therefore, a diagnosis, and perhaps most importantly, the specific challenges faced by an autistic girl, can be routinely missed (Honeybourne 2015; Moyse and Porter 2015). Once girls' needs are identified, there is also a lack of guidance on what should be put in place to meet their needs. Recently, general guidance has begun to emerge (Nasen 2016) which highlights how girls' needs might be missed due to late diagnosis or misdiagnosis and masking of their difficulties due to better superficial social skills than boys. This document also highlights the need for generic autism strategies such as a whole-school approach and visuals as well as adapted social skills groups and work around emotional well-being, gender identity and keeping safe. However, there remains a lack of research showing how schools can develop these effective approaches for autistic girls.

In this chapter we set out to describe how one mainstream high school has developed a model of working for all autistic pupils and how this has been tailored and adapted to meet the needs of autistic girls. Interviews with key staff are used to illustrate how the approach works in practice.

The Priestnall model

Priestnall School is a large 11–16 comprehensive community school with just under 1300 pupils. The number of students in receipt of Education Health and Care Plans or school level support as a result of their special needs and disabilities is broadly in line with national averages. Many of these learners have complex physical and medical needs, and there is also a significant population of autistic students. Priestnall has a well-established school-led provision for speech and language therapy and educational psychology (Morewood, Drews and King 2016) which allows for systemic work with feeder primary schools, families and the wider community. In developing this model of provision there is an increased understanding of individuals and families and how to support them. This has regularly been recognised by inspections, in the views of families and through the outcomes of the young people themselves. Each year almost all learners successfully transition into post-16 education, employment or training: a real hallmark of successfully preparing pupils for adulthood, whatever their age or starting point.

The development of awareness, understanding, training and direct support at Priestnall School started with trying to understand why 'education', in particular regular mainstream schooling, presents such a challenge for many children and young people with autism. Morewood, Humphrey and Symes (2011) highlighted a number of issues relating to the young people themselves, their teachers, the environment and, perhaps most importantly, their peer group.

Educating the peer group has been a key component of the developed approach, ranging from the young people themselves reading an agreed 'script' to peers about what autism means for them, to general awareness lessons delivered by a specialist teacher as part of an inclusive curriculum, and whole-school assemblies with additional follow-up activities for students. Positive conversations about autism are an essential element in addressing misinformation and prejudices.

In the following sections two frameworks are presented and described by the first author in order to illustrate whole-school and individual planning aspects of provision at Priestnall for all autistic pupils. Data from a recent small-scale study undertaken by the second author and looking at the perceptions of two staff working closely with autistic girls at Priestnall is then used to provide further specific examples of provision for autistic students. Interviews were conducted with a therapeutic support worker and a speech and language therapist based on site at the school, who were selected due to their close working relationships with the girls. Both members of staff supported the girls on a regular basis, which enabled them to provide an effective overview of provision for girls on the spectrum at the school.

The saturation model

The *saturation model* (Figure 5.1) was developed during a four-year Economic and Social Research Council (ESRC) research project and is discussed in the peer-reviewed paper by Morewood *et al.* (2011). This model provides an overarching structure of provision for all autistic pupils at Priestnall and ensures that the needs of autistic pupils are considered at all levels within the school.

Figure 5.1 The saturation model (Morewood *et al.* 2011)

Priestnall School, in partnership with colleagues at the University of Manchester, developed this model as the foundation for bespoke training and direct work across other schools and communities both in the UK and abroad, whilst considering the key elements of:

- the agent of change

- developing the school environment

- providing a flexible provision for learning

- ensuring direct specialist support and interventions

- establishing policy that is embedded in practice

- providing high-quality training and development for staff and parents/carers

- supporting peer education and self-awareness

- creating a positive ethos/culture.

The development of these key themes, stemming from the original (2011) research, both at Priestnall School and across partner schools and communities, has provided a holistic approach to supporting young people with autism and their families in line with an inclusive vision as articulated by the Salamanca Statement (UNESCO 1994). We have continued to develop the model further since the original research and the fulcrum on which the effectiveness of provision rests continues to be the *agent of change*. This is a central figure who can shift beliefs and coordinate the whole-school response necessary for effective inclusion. At Priestnall School the first author, who is Director of Curriculum Support and Special Educational Needs Coordinator (SENCO), continues in that lead role, working with all stakeholders: the local authority (LA), parents/carers, young people, school staff and headteachers, along with specialists, in ensuring that understanding and provision is embedded into *whole-school policy*, practice and thinking. The 'agent of change' must also empower others within the school and community; this corporate responsibility model (Morewood 2018) has been the natural evolution of the approach as more staff, peers and families gain increasing knowledge and wider skills through ongoing training, professional discussions and joint working. This also fits with a recent blog by Milton (2017), who argues that 'instead of working against a person's "autism", practitioners can work with autistic people and their families with mutual respect', which is central to the work at Priestnall.

The continually evolving model continues to draw upon whole-school and community approaches to emotional regulation and supports increased understanding and the *development of environmental factors* (Morewood *et al.* 2011):

- physical environment

- social environment

- communication environment

- emotional environment.

The *flexibility* of the approach has enabled us to identify and address specific aspects of the environment which may have a greater impact for autistic girls. It would appear from our ongoing work with girls that the more subtle, environmental factors are vital when considering mainstream schools, girls and autism. The consideration of sensory needs also appears to be a significant area for education to consider (Honeybourne 2015); many autistic females have complex hidden needs which significantly impair their ability to engage with mainstream education and learning. In undertaking a sensory audit of provision and considering the emotional levels of students throughout the day, we can modify and adapt environmental factors to better support learning and engagement. This can sometimes be as straightforward as altering the classroom for a particular lesson or providing some time for self-regulation during the last half hour each day to support transition home. The importance of managing environmental factors to support autistic girls was also highlighted as a significant consideration by the interview participants; for example, the provision of alternative spaces for learning when classroom demands were too great was noted by one participant: 'It might be them doing the same work that was done in the classroom but in a smaller environment.'

Another factor for promoting flexibility which emerged from the interviews was the importance of sharing information between staff. This included the provision of student passports (Morewood 2014, 2015) documenting the particular needs of the girls and the ways in which staff could best support them. The interviewees suggested that it was enough for the girls simply to be aware that members of staff working with them were aware of their difficulties and that it would not present a challenge should they need to leave the classroom in times of high anxiety. This appeared to be effective in reducing anxiety when the demands of the mainstream classroom became too much.

Another specific example of understanding the specific needs of autistic pupils is with regard to *specialist support* through speech and language therapy and the extent to which this happens in isolation simply becomes a 'provision', or is embedded. We have found it to be most effective when the therapist works with other staff and the young person in ensuring key aspects of that 'direct support', identified in the saturation model, are within 'real' contexts and address the different challenges that the girls encounter. In gaining a greater understanding of autistic girls, we need to be prepared to deliver specialist services differently; as with definitions and diagnostic criteria, provision also needs to be re-imagined and developed as our understanding increases; personalisation is key to provision.

Our *training of education professionals* (in addition to the direct work with young people and their families) supports an approach to develop a fuller understanding of the child's experience of anxiety and how it impacts upon them, and is a core element of the revised delivery model identified previously. The ultimate goal is to use a range of tools based on good practice, research and increasing understanding of individuals, which will both reduce the experience of anxiety and enable better self-management of anxiety in the future. This is the core element of the evolving model and one that is particularly useful as a 'whole-school approach' with regard to all pupils, most importantly autistic girls. The interviewees felt that only through regular and consistent training would staff become more aware of the needs of autistic pupils and how they could provide more effective support. Participants suggested that training needed to be regular, rather than just a one-off continuing professional development exercise to ensure that any updates in the field were communicated to staff. This was viewed as most effective when clearly part of whole-school development plans and understood by the governing body. It was acknowledged, however, that such training was not yet specific to girls but rather a more general raising of awareness in relation to autism. When considering the lack of specific knowledge available, this is understandable. This highlights the importance of providing specific training for school staff on how the needs of autistic girls may differ to those of boys, and resulting implications for more tailored provision.

Another important element, the student's *peer group*, cannot be underestimated. Peers may not understand why others behave and interact in the way that they do; they may resent the extra attention or affordances given to them (for example, teaching assistant support, bespoke timetable, individual sessions, etc.); be offended if their social advances are ignored or rejected; and/or exclude, tease or bully them as a result. This pattern of rejection can lead to the autistic pupil becoming isolated from peers and consequently providing fewer opportunities for peers to develop an understanding of autism and supportive strategies for autistic students with whom they regularly come into contact or share lessons. At Priestnall autism awareness-raising assemblies and specifically designed lessons delivered by an experienced teacher from our partner special school keep positive and open discussions high on the agenda, as outlined previously. This was reflected in interviews with staff who commented on the issue of raising peer awareness; this was perceived to be especially important given the increased potential for a later diagnosis for female pupils in comparison to their male peers. The assumption was that more often than not friendship groups of female pupils would be unaware of such a diagnosis, unlike male pupils who 'sort of come with that diagnosis already'. This often led to difficulties for the girls in social interactions with friends where 'there is a lot of falling out because people think they don't care or they're not a good friend'. In this sense, the importance of sharing information regarding diagnosis was viewed as invaluable.

The development of an inclusive curriculum includes challenging negative and discriminatory stereotypes through life education lessons; for example, building on the *culture* of open discussions regarding hidden disabilities, and therefore directly increasing the understanding and knowledge base of peers and staff within the school. Schools should guard against underestimating the impact of an inclusive curriculum and address misconceptions as and when they arise: 'If children's perceptions of people who are different from themselves are based on stereotypical thinking it is likely that they will retain this misinformation for the rest of their lives unless positive steps are taken to counter this learning' (Brown 1998, p.23).

Although the interview participants identified many factors that are common to autistic boys and girls, they also emphasised that recognition of gender differences can help to inform awareness and planning at a subgroup level. This recognition of gender differences was a recurrent theme. Participants reported differences in the presentation of traits between male and female autistic pupils alongside the unique strengths of the girls (Marshall 2014) and the very specific needs they might have as a consequence of their difficulties. These challenges included navigating the subtle communication styles apparent in female friendships and coping with misconceptions from staff regarding autism spectrum conditions (ASC) and females. Participants also expressed the view that only through understanding such differences would autistic female pupils achieve the support they needed (Moyse and Porter 2015). Regarding the differences in the presentation of traits, the importance of highlighting this to staff working with autistic girls was emphasised:

> They actually just withdraw, they become very introverted. When people hear a female student is on the spectrum they just go, 'Really, well I never!'

> You hear that all the time: 'I just never would have known that'…girls are very good at masking, boys aren't.

The interviewees reported staff observations of differences between autistic male and female pupils that included the greater desire for females to explore their condition and their desire to be more involved in the decisions made regarding their provision. Participants clearly recognised how provision was continually evolving as a consequence of increasing experience of working with girls on the spectrum; for example, 'Staff are now responding differently to the needs of girls' as it's 'filtering through and it's something we're recognising'. There was a sense that raising awareness regarding the specific presentation of traits in girls had been hugely beneficial to the girls in the respect that they were able to be themselves and no longer had to mask their symptoms.

These specific examples illustrate how the saturation model provides an overarching framework for whole-school good practice for autistic boys and girls, which can then be personalised further through tailored individual plans.

Developing tailored plans

Although many needs of autistic pupils will be addressed through the implementation of the broader strategies outlined in the saturation model, individual pupils may also require more bespoke plans. In a report for the National Autistic Society, Harker and King (2004) identify seven key features of provision:

- person-centred planning

- developing independence and understanding of behaviour

- an autism-friendly environment

- managing risk

- developing social networks

- clear policies and processes

- understanding communication and emotional needs.

At Priestnall, these factors are considered in relation to all autistic pupils but have sometimes been adapted in specific ways for girls. In relation to *person-centred planning* it is important that such discussions are truly personalised: simply 'applying' a published structure doesn't work – understanding the individual and building trust is key in being able to develop a person-centred planning structure (MacDonald 2015). There is a strong possibility that the time-consuming nature of ensuring bespoke arrangements with regard to person-centred planning means that schools try to force individual girls into prescribed systems; this is often driven by other pressures (time, finance, expertise, etc.) as opposed to deliberate actions and purposeful decision making.

A recent meta-analysis revealed that autistic people experience a much lower quality of life compared to the rest of the population (van Heijst and Geurts 2015), potentially amplified by the delay in diagnosis for girls, and also that at a societal level, autism represents a significant economic burden associated with greatly increased health, education and social care use (Lavelle *et al.* 2014). This clearly highlights the real need for increased thinking and understanding at school and family level as we prepare the young people with whom we work to develop independence and make the transition to adulthood.

In relation to individualised planning, personalised interventions for girls mentioned by interview participants often reflected those generally mentioned in research literature (e.g. Bond and Hebron 2016), such as flexibility over timetabling if pupils were struggling to access the curriculum or the provision of a '*safe space*' during both structured and unstructured times where pupils could go and work alone if desired. This was viewed as one of the most effective means of reducing the anxiety experienced by female pupils on the autistic spectrum.

As mentioned previously, Priestnall's NEET (not in education, employment or training) figure is zero, or very close to it year on year. This is no coincidence. Proper *preparation for adulthood* requires important foundations from much earlier than the last few years of school. Working with specialists (therapists, teachers, etc.) in helping individual girls gain a good understanding of themselves in relation to the environment and others is essential. As Temple Grandin aptly puts it, 'The problem is, what's in *my* autistic brain is not necessarily what's in *someone else's* autistic brain' (Grandin and Panek 2013, p.34). There is the potential that autistic girls are less likely to maintain employment (Nasen 2016) and engage in meaningful relationships unless they can develop a better understanding of themselves as part of their education (Kanfiszer, Davies and Collins 2017). The success of Priestnall's work has stemmed from the understanding that internal understanding of 'themselves' is a key element of provision.

An important element reported in the interviews was collaborative working. Such collaboration involved building relationships with the girls themselves as well as working effectively with parents/carers, support staff and multi-agency working (e.g. Child and Adolescent Mental Health Services). One vital aspect of this communication was to facilitate the development of a shared understanding of the needs of the girls and work collaboratively to plan and implement actions and thus reduce their anxieties. Working with parents/carers was regarded with special importance and seemingly served to provide a mutual support network within which school and parents could feel supported through the sharing of information regarding individual girls. Communication with parents/carers was reported to be both regular and comprehensive and served to provide a bridge between home and school. For example, if a pupil had 'had a meltdown' because she had lost her timetable, staff at school were immediately aware of this through email communication and were able to provide appropriate support, as identified in the student passport, as soon as the pupil arrived.

A further consideration made by both interview participants was the importance of collaborative working with the girls themselves as a means of facilitating the best possible provision for them and ultimately enabling their transition to adulthood. It was suggested that often the girls 'initially…don't trust because they don't know… They're like who are you and how can you help?' The essential value of building relationships was key to engaging the girls; an important area of this was to engage in helping the family, as well as the individual girl, to understand what autism means. Many families appreciated additional support/meetings to discuss home life and how to support at weekends/holidays as well. This joint approach through positive discussions allowed for significantly increased trust between all those involved and subsequently improved outcomes for all.

In relation to behaviour, many schools consider managing behaviour and accommodating the special interests expressed by autistic young people as the most demanding elements of an inclusive provision (Robertson, Chamberlain and Kasari 2003). Our work in developing an increased understanding with regard to *emotional regulation* has been a key factor in moving away from social and behaviourally based approaches. We have now developed a more eclectic methodology considering emotional regulation as a lifelong developmental process underpinned by attention and social engagement, which are essential for optimal social, emotional and communication development and the development of relationships for all children and adults. Considering emotional regulation from the perspective of changes that occur over short periods of time, even from moment to moment, has also been a significant part of our developing provision. Difficulties arise for teachers and practitioners if they cannot recognise when children are displaying challenges with emotional regulation, or with a task (Jahromi, Meek and Ober-Reynolds 2012). As these so-called 'challenging behaviours' work as attempts to communicate/control, it is often beneficial to provide strategies that help both teachers and pupils understand their emotions and react to them in an appropriate manner, which is done through planned and ongoing staff training and direct work.

Staff interviews linked the emotional demands of autistic girls managing school with anxiety. Perhaps most important was the recognition that often the girls were experiencing anxiety as a consequence of their attempts to mask symptoms and cope with the daily demands of school but that they would not necessarily need the overt support that boys received. The suggestion was in many cases that it was enough to actively 'monitor them from a distance to make sure they are coping okay' and often it was sufficient for the girls to know that 'there are things in place that they can access if they need to…mostly they do that independently'. As such, they were less likely to need one-to-one support in class, unlike male pupils on the autistic spectrum.

Structuring an *autism-friendly environment* is also essential. Change, transitions and unexpected breaks in routine can add to anxiety and create a further barrier to learning and participation.

The cohort of female autistic students at Priestnall often experience significant challenges with regard to learning in a social setting, particularly in relation to the complex language environments with limited visual support. Understanding and communicating with other members of the school community and reading social situations that arise can also be problematic. Direct support and intervention to scaffold pupils' understanding of language and ability to cope with change is crucial (for example, speech and language therapy; Morewood and Drews 2015). Coping with change was also identified as being of equal concern for autistic girls as for boys by the interview participants.

Risk management is often seen as a medicalised term that seeks to identify, evaluate and reduce risks associated with individuals. Too often, school-based risk management approaches are about imposing systems on individuals. Our approach is much more collaborative: building from the bespoke person-centred planning discussions, we will work with individual girls and jointly identify areas, lessons, systems and structures that have differing levels of risk for the individuals. Then, as part of a solution-based approach, plans are agreed to minimise the risks identified. Collaboratively co-producing approaches to minimise risks is very different to imposing risk management systems on individuals; careful thought is required in the approaches developed from existing autism knowledge when applied to girls.

Developing *social networks* is vital with regard to supporting the place of girls within the community and society; at school this can be through interventions with peers around shared interests or facilitating clubs/groups at social times (Bond *et al.* 2016). Social media can be an important way of reducing social isolation and developing friendships through sharing common interests with others, although there are also risks to be managed (National Autistic Society (NAS) n.d.). Assisting with the explicit teaching (individually and through the mainstream curriculum, as identified previously) of the use of social media is vital. Teaching girls not to accept literally what others say online, keeping themselves safe from bullying and recognising when 'friendships' may not be genuine can all be significant factors in reducing their vulnerability so that they can benefit from the positive aspects of online communities (NAS n.d.).

Interview participants highlighted that social support appeared to be particularly important for autistic girls. A key intervention mentioned was a social skills support group aimed specifically at improving the girls' knowledge and understanding of the 'hidden curriculum'. It is well documented in the existing literature (e.g. Moyse and Porter 2015) that this is a particular area of difficulty for autistic girls, especially during adolescence when friendships become increasingly complex. Such difficulties identified included making and maintaining friendships, showing empathy and knowing the right thing to do in social interactions (Jamison and Schuttler 2017). These were perceived by the participants to be specific to the needs of autistic girls, with the implication that not getting it right is more problematic than for boys. The group was reported to involve a variety of useful strategies such as role-play or video clips of effective communication to help develop friendship and conversational skills as well as dealing with conflict (Centre for Autism n.d.).

One reported consequence of such structured sessions was the development of more informal peer 'buddy systems'. This had extended to former pupils returning to run twilight sessions to offer support through the sharing of their own personal stories. The perception of staff was that the younger girls found it useful to 'understand the world from the perspective of somebody who has a similar outlook'. Clear gender differences in provision were identified here, and it was reported that no former male pupils with autism had returned to provide such support. Although group peer support sessions had been offered to male pupils, it was emphasised that this tended not to be as effective, as the male pupils, were reluctant to engage. This was perceived to be a consequence of the greater awareness around males and autism and perhaps the lesser need to 'understand' themselves compared to females.

Understanding *communication and emotional needs* is also salient. The need to differentiate language and/or the curriculum to accommodate autistic learners requires teachers to move beyond 'the usual', which in the current climate of educational reform and austerity adds a further barrier to the wider inclusion of autistic young people.

As mentioned earlier, an essential element of our approach to support pupils to manage stress and anxiety is our developing work with emotional regulation. It is also important to recognise the requirement for a focus on positive mental health, and in doing so support an increased understanding that autistic children may not have the same awareness of the importance of emotions, particularly for girls. In this context, the following areas identified by Rieffe *et al.* (2011) need careful consideration:

- Children with autism may not be aware of the relationship between physical symptoms and emotional arousal.

- Children with autism may have a more fragmented understanding of their emotional state and their levels of emotional arousal.

- Poor coping strategies can increase the likelihood of depression and anxiety.

In relation to mental health, interview participants highlighted the importance of access to therapy for autistic students, which was offered as a consequence of the availability of an on-site therapeutic worker (appropriately qualified and registered with the British Association for Counselling and Psychotherapy). These one-to-one sessions provided ongoing support for pupils if necessary and were largely reported to be of particular interest to the girls as a consequence of their vulnerability to anxiety and other challenges to mental health such as depression and self-harm. These sessions provided an opportunity for the girls to open up regarding their particular difficulties and feel a greater level of understanding of their specific needs.

In addition to reflecting on needs and provision, the interview participants identified a range of positive outcomes related to the support put in place for autistic girls at Priestnall. These focused on immediate benefits such as improved relationships with peers to longer-term consequences such as diminished risk of school refusal and successful transitioning to post-16 education or training. Although the value of working systemically to support girls in school and embed good practice as a preventative approach to supporting girls with autism was emphasised, it was also recognised that opportunities for training specific to autistic girls remain limited and an area for development.

Conclusion

This chapter illustrates a range of effective systemic and individual approaches adopted by a mainstream school for all autistic pupils and which have been adapted and developed to support girls. The chapter illustrates how the strategies recommended by Nasen (2016) can work in practice, and it is hoped that this example might inform practice in other mainstream schools. Although interviewees identified some potential challenges and the need for continued improvement of provision for autistic girls, many of the strategies highlighted were a reflection of general provision available through the saturation model which is already in place for all autistic pupils at Priestnall.

At a systemic level the findings suggest that training in relation to the presentation of traits in female autistic pupils and appropriate support packages are paramount to improving outcomes. Awareness-raising amongst peers, given the late diagnosis of many female pupils, and specific training for staff in the presentation of autistic traits in females, particularly highlighting the tendency towards internalising symptoms. Such an enhanced understanding of the specific difficulties autistic girls face has the potential to improve their mental health through the provision of appropriate strategies; for example, support with social relationships and managing anxiety. There is a role for other professionals to work collaboratively with schools to ensure that autistic girls are no longer 'flying under the radar' through the systematic training of staff at a whole-school level. Moreover, raising awareness of the specific needs of autistic girls amongst peers is another area where professionals have the potential to contribute, given the nature of the difficulties experienced by girls.

The interviews also revealed the importance of considering the needs of the individual when planning and implementing personalised intervention programmes (Milton 2017) regardless of the gender of the child. The examples from Priestnall illustrate that many generic autism strategies only require minor modification to support autistic girls effectively. Building relationships with the girls themselves and working collaboratively with others, including staff and parents/carers, is central to developing effective provision for autistic girls. It is only by incorporating their voice through a consideration of their particular needs and strengths that the engagement of autistic girls in the support process will be facilitated. This focused understanding has the potential to allow the girls to remove their so-called 'mask', freeing them up to reveal their true selves.

This chapter has also demonstrated the importance of some strategies which are more specific to the needs of girls, such as the buddy system where 'personal stories' can be shared, and social support groups to help girls navigate the hidden curriculum (Jamison and Schuttler 2017; Moyse and Porter 2015). These are novel examples of specific provision in one secondary school which have the power to make a difference for autistic girls. The next step is to find out from the girls themselves how they perceive their experiences of secondary school and how effectively they are supported. This will further the development of a strong evidence base from which to develop provision and training for wider impact.

References

American Psychiatric Association (2013) *Diagnostic and Statistical Manual of Mental Disorders: DSM-5* (5th edn). Washington, DC: American Psychiatric Publishing.

Bond, C. and Hebron, J. (2016) 'Developing mainstream resource provision for pupils with autism spectrum disorder: Staff perceptions and satisfaction.' *European Journal of Special Needs Education, 31,* 250–263.

Bond, C., Symes, W., Hebron, J., Humphrey, N. and Morewood, G. (2016) *Educating Persons with Autistic Spectrum Disorder – A Systematic Literature and Country Review.* NCSE Research Reports No. 20. Trim: National Council for Special Education.

Brown, B. (1998) *Unlearning Discrimination in the Early Years.* London: Trentham Books.

Centre for Autism (n.d.) Interview with Dr Jacqui Ashton-Smith in *Research Bulletin 4: Autism Spectrum Disorder and Girls.* Middletown: Centre for Autism. Accessed on 4/12/18 at www.middletownautism.com/files/uploads/d01f596756cf9da5c62a770710aaf9ed.pdf

Gould, J. and Ashton-Smith, J. (2011) 'Missed diagnosis or misdiagnosis? Girls and women on the autism spectrum.' *Good Autism Practice Journal, 12,* 34–41.

Grandin, T. and Panek, R. (2013) *The Autistic Brain: Thinking Across the Spectrum.* New York: Houghton Mifflin Harcourt.

Harker, M. and King, N. (2004) *Tomorrow's Big Problem: Housing Options for People with Autism: A Guide for Service Commissioners, Providers and Families.* London: National Autistic Society.

Honeybourne, V. (2015) 'Girls on the autism spectrum in the classroom: Hidden difficulties and how to help.' *Good Autism Practice Journal, 16,* 11–20.

Jahromi, L. B., Meek, S. E. and Ober-Reynolds, S. (2012) 'Emotion regulation in the context of frustration in children with high functioning autism and their typical peers.' *Child Psychology and Psychiatry, 53,* 12, 1250–1258.

Jamison, T. R. and Schuttler, J. O. (2017) Overview and preliminary evidence for a social skills and self-care curriculum for adolescent females with autism: The girls night out model.' *Journal of Autism and Developmental Disorders, 47,* 1, 110–125.

Kanfiszer, L., Davies, F. and Collins, S. (2017) '"I was just so different": The experiences of women diagnosed with an autism spectrum disorder in adulthood in relation to gender and social relationships.' *Autism, 21,* 6, 661–669.

Lavelle, T. A., Weinstein, M. C., Newhouse, J. P., Munir, K., Kuhlthau, K. A. and Prosser, L. A. (2014) 'Economic burden of childhood autism spectrum disorders.' *Pediatrics, 133,* 3, e520–e529.

MacDonald, M. (2015) 'SEND Pathfinder Information Pack: Version 5.' Accessed on 5/2/18 at www.sendpathfinder.co.uk/preparing-for-adulthood-information-pack

Mandy, W., Chilvers, R., Chowdhury, U., Salter, G., Seigal, A. and Skuse, D. (2012) 'Sex differences in autism spectrum disorder: Evidence from a large sample of children and adolescents.' *Journal of Autism and Developmental Disorders, 42,* 7, 1304–1313.

Marshall, T. A. (2014) *I Am Aspiengirl: The Unique Characteristics, Traits and Gifts of Females on the Autism Spectrum*. Australia: Tania. A. Marshall.

Milton, D. (2017) 'The Future I'd Like to See.' National Autism Project. Accessed on 30/7/18 at http://nationalautismproject.org.uk/the-future-id-like-to-see-dr-damian-milton

Morewood, G. D. (2014) 'Our effective alternative to IEPs (student passports).' *SEN Hub Magazine,* Optimus Publishing, 10–11. Accessed on 13/2/19 at www.gdmorewood.com/wp-content/uploads/2015/05/Student-Passport-article-Morewood-2014.pdf

Morewood, G. D. (2015) 'Passports to Partnerships' [Video file]. Gareth D Morewood: Research, Training and Consultancy. Accessed on 30/7/18 at www.gdmorewood.com/books-videos/student-passports-film

Morewood, G. D. (2018) 'Gareth D. Morewood, Director of Curriculum Support, Priestnall School.' In D. Bartram (ed.) *Great Expectations: Leading an Effective SEND Strategy in School*. Woodbridge: John Catt Publications.

Morewood, G. D. and Drews, D. (2015) 'Developing a unique speech and language therapy model.' *Assessment and Development Matters*, *7*, 2, 26–28.

Morewood, G. D., Drews, D. and King, R. (2016) 'Developing school-led SEND provision: A developing model of school-to-school support.' *Assessment and Development Matters*, *8*, 2, 7–10.

Morewood, G. D., Humphrey, N. and Symes, W. (2011) 'Mainstreaming autism: Making it work.' *Good Autism Practice*, *12*, 2, 62–68.

Moyse, R. and Porter, J. (2015) 'The experience of the hidden curriculum for autistic girls at mainstream primary schools.' *European Journal of Special Needs Education*, *30*, 187–201.

Nasen (2016) *Girls and Autism: Flying under the Radar*. Tamworth: Nasen.

National Autistic Society (n.d.) 'Staying Safe Online.' Accessed on 21/7/18 at www.autism.org.uk/staying-safe-online#

Rieffe, C., Oosteveld, P., Terwogt, M. M, Mootz, S., van Leeuwen, E. and Stockmann, L. (2011) 'Emotional regulation and internalizing symptoms in children with autism spectrum disorder.' *Autism*, *15*, 6, 655–670.

Robertson, K., Chamberlain, B. and Kasari, C. (2003) 'General education teachers' relationships with included students with autism.' *Journal of Autism and Developmental Disorders*, *33*, 2, 123–130.

UNESCO (United Nations Education Scientific and Cultural Organisation) (1994) *The Salamanca Statement for and Framework for Action on Special Needs Education*. Paris: UNESCO.

van Heijst, B. F. and Geurts, H. M. (2015) 'Quality of life in autism across the lifespan: A meta-analysis.' *Autism, 19*, 2, 158–167.

CHAPTER 6

The Specialist Secondary Experience

An Alternative View of Secondary Education for Autistic Girls

Sarah Wild

In this chapter I aim to provide a general perspective on supporting autistic girls which is drawn from my experience of working with a community of autistic teenage girls at Limpsfield Grange School. I hope that the areas of staying safe and staying well are pertinent to all adolescent autistic girls, and that the following words are of some use to a wide audience of readers.

Limpsfield Grange School is a residential special school for girls with communication and interaction difficulties aged 11–16. The vast majority of girls who attend Limpsfield Grange are autistic and have high and unrelenting levels of anxiety which limits their capacity to live their lives.

Students at Limpsfield Grange School require access to the breadth of the full mainstream curriculum, but due to the anxiety arising from their sensory, social and communication difficulties they are unable to manage a mainstream school environment even with high levels of support. Limpsfield Grange provides a curriculum which enables learners to gain a wide range of GCSEs or equivalent qualifications by the end of Year 11, and many of our students leave with between six and eight GCCEs. Limpsfield Grange is a Surrey County Council provision, although our students are from all over the UK. Students who attend Limpsfield Grange have an Education, Health and Care Plan (EHCP), and referrals are made through the Surrey County Council SEND (special educational needs and disabilities) team.

Students at Limpsfield Grange access a structured environment and high levels of targeted intervention and differentiation throughout the school day. Our students work broadly at age-related levels of attainment and access a mainstream curriculum. Students are grouped according to age and key stage, and class sizes are between eight and ten students, with one teacher and one teaching assistant per group. Students are expected to travel around the school site to access learning in a range of specialist teaching areas without adult support for these transition times. Traditionally unstructured social times of the school day (before school, break and lunch times) have been structured and highly staffed. During times such as break or lunch time the girls are engaged in small group activities led by adults; this is because the unstructured nature of social times is very difficult for our students, which can lead to heightened anxiety for the girls and associated challenging behaviour.

Limpsfield Grange is a 24-hour school. We have a number of residential places, and girls access shared rooms in our Victorian manor house. Our residential provision enables us to work with girls across our 24-hour curriculum to develop key independence and communication skills, in addition to our strong focus on wellbeing. Residential students take part in a wide range of activities which develop their social skills and dramatically improve their self-esteem and confidence.

I have seen many changes in the landscape of female autism during the time I have been headteacher of Limpsfield Grange – the only state-run school for autistic girls in the country. When I first became headteacher in 2012, I spoke to a member of the local education team and told them that we had a large number of autistic girls at school. I'll never forget the anger and disappointment which I felt at their response:

'Girls don't have autism – you must be mistaken.'

Luckily we now live in marginally more enlightened times. Understanding of female autism is developing, as is the amount of research focusing on female autism. A growing number of women and girls are being identified as autistic. The wider community have started to accept that autistic women and girls (and some autistic men and boys) present differently to our preconceived notion of autism. Our view of the autistic spectrum is becoming broader.

Empowering autistic females to face their specific challenges was recognised in April 2018 by the United Nations, for World Autism Awareness Day:

> Girls with disabilities are less likely to complete primary school and more likely to be marginalized or denied access to *education*. Women with disabilities have a lower rate of *employment* than men with disabilities and women without disabilities. Globally, women are more likely to experience physical, sexual, psychological and economic *violence* than men, and women and girls with disabilities experience gender-based violence at disproportionately higher rates and in unique forms owing to discrimination and stigma based on both gender and disability. As a result of inaccessibility and stereotyping, women and girls with disabilities are persistently confronted with barriers to *sexual and reproductive health services* and to information on comprehensive sex education, particularly women and girls with intellectual disabilities including autism. (United Nations 2006; my emphasis)

The challenges outlined by the United Nations can be seen in the everyday experiences of autistic women and girls in the United Kingdom. Autistic girls are still less likely to be diagnosed than autistic boys. In an article for *Spectrum News* in May 2018, Dr William Mandy of University College London identified that boys display stable, similar autistic characteristics throughout adolescence, while autistic girls are more likely to see characteristics ramp up during the teen and pre-teen years. This pattern of behaviour could explain why boys are diagnosed with autism earlier than girls and how guidelines for diagnosing autism in children could be biased against girls. Autistic girls are more likely to start secondary school without a diagnosis, and many struggle to manage the transition or the demands of the secondary context. Autistic girls are less likely to access services that have been designed with them in mind, because until recently commissioners didn't believe they existed. It's hard to quantify the impact of so many autistic girls flying under the radar, because the research relating to autistic females is limited. It is possible that many autistic girls struggle through secondary school until it becomes so overwhelming that they stop attending, and that a great number of them suffer from such high and restricting levels of anxiety that they stop living their lives as they would wish.

At Limpsfield Grange we work with the girls so that they understand themselves; our girls have high and persistent levels of anxiety that impacts constantly on their capacity to live their lives. We believe that autistic people having a good quality of life is the most important key to being a successful adult. We listen to the voices of the whole school community – our students, parents and wider family members, staff and governors – to create a holistic approach meeting students' and families' needs to enable the girls to become happy autistic adults who are satisfied with their lives. We have designed a curriculum which focuses on the areas of wellbeing, achievement, communication and independence to empower our students to participate in society. We wish for our girls to become happy healthy citizens.

We believe that our community has a part to play in raising awareness of female autism. The girls, along with author Vicky Martin, have written two novels about an autistic girl, *M Is for Autism* (2015) and *M in the Middle* (2017). Both novels allow the reader to view the world through the anxiety-ridden eyes of an autistic girl called M. We've made quite a few films, including a documentary with ITV called *Girls with Autism*, to show people what it is really like to be an autistic teenage girl, and how teenage autistic girls are so different to each other. All of our films and resources are on our website for people to use freely.[1]

So what can schools and professionals do to ensure that autistic girls have a successful and healthy secondary school experience? At Limpsfield Grange we believe that staying well, staying safe and creating a clear pathway for a successful adult life are the key ingredients which enable teenage autistic girls to be satisfied with their quality of life.

Staying well

At Limpsfield Grange, ensuring that students are well and safe is at the heart of everything we do. The two areas are related – if you are not emotionally, mentally or physically healthy, you are less likely to be safe. For autistic girls, promoting good health is primarily about emotional and mental wellbeing, and about managing anxiety.

Recently an ex-student returned to Limpsfield Grange for a visit. She had started a degree course in a subject that she loved and had secured some excellent part-time work in her chosen area. However, she was clearly not well. Seemingly random uncontrollable panic attacks had prevented her driving, and her sky-high anxiety had stopped her sleeping for weeks on end. Her life was slowly shutting down, and she was very worried that soon she would not be able to manage her studies. The situation was very distressing for all involved, with very limited solutions on offer to her.

---

1 https://limpsfieldgrange.co.uk

The girls at Limpsfield Grange are not alone in suffering from extremely high levels of anxiety, and this seems to be a feature of female autism at any age. Our students experience unimaginable levels of anxiety all day, every day, and their anxiety is likely to be a constant feature in their lives. For some girls, this pressure makes them explode, and this is seen as a typical autistic response to anxiety. However, the vast majority of girls at Limpsfield Grange internalise their anxiety and implode.

Anxiety can be attributed to a range of factors, including:

- trying to imitate social behaviour all day, without really understanding what it means

- constantly vetting and editing personal responses to social situations without understanding what the acceptable social response is

- being overwhelmed by the level and nature of sensory information that is received

- changes; the possibility of change; unpredictability

- difficulties with understanding time and what is going to happen next.

In our novel *M Is for Autism* the girls describe anxiety as 'an uncontrollable wild, savage beast that prowls beside me' (Martin and the Students of Limpsfield Grange 2015). Anxiety can be all-consuming and can lead to patterns of intrusive thoughts, feelings of helplessness or being overwhelmed. It is hard to learn when your head is full of anxiety; you just don't have enough head space left to take in new things. Anxiety can be very restricting and disabling; it can leave you stranded in your bedroom for extended periods; it can leave you feeling powerless or force you to ritualise some behaviours to keep it at bay. Anxiety is exhausting and unwieldy and can have a significant impact on an autistic girl's mental health and on her family. Often families describe the impact of anxiety as constantly walking on eggshells in their home. Anxiety significantly reduces the quality of life for autistic girls and their families, and can limit family experiences like going on holiday or going out to a restaurant. In some extreme cases parents have to stop working to look after their autistic daughters because their anxiety levels are so high everyday life is severely restricted.

Different life stages can induce anxiety, and puberty is a source of anxiety that we commonly experience at Limpsfield Grange. Autistic girls can struggle to understand and internalise that puberty lasts for a few years, or that you have more than one period in your lifetime, or that the changes that happen in puberty are irreversible. The fact that puberty is something they can't control is often very difficult for the girls to manage. Some autistic girls might try to stop or contain puberty through excessive exercise or reducing their calorie intake; some might stop eating entirely, with the aim of delaying physical development and periods. With the addition of secondary school, increased demands and pressures and an increasing complexity in social dynamics, the perfect storm of body changes, hormones and anxiety can make life very difficult.

Signs that anxiety is building can include:

- Meltdowns becoming more frequent, or prolonged, violent or intense.

- An increased avoidance of social situations or social spaces in school.

- Poor attendance at school. This can be because being ill allows the young person to experience a lower demand situation, and have a higher level of control over social interactions. It is important to look at patterns of attendance – are there particular days where attendance is noticeably lower? What lesson happens on those days when a young person tends to be absent? Are they experiencing particular problems in areas of the curriculum, with particular peers or staff, or experiencing difficulties with physical areas of the school?

- An increased demand for routines to be kept the same, and the need to exert a higher than usual level of control over situations or environments.

- Panic attacks.

- A spike in irrational fears relating to people, places or objects.

- Increased difficulties with sleep. Sometimes this is linked to an increase in ritualised behaviours around bedtime routines.

- Perfectionism and related frustration and anger when things are not perfect.

- An increase in stimming behaviours such as flapping, spinning, pacing or rocking.

- Self-harming behaviours beginning or increasing. Self-harming is a serious issue and is sadly prevalent within the female teenage autistic population. Self-harming can take many forms, including cutting, head banging, hand biting, ingesting dangerous items, pulling out hair, restricted eating. Individuals that self-harm do so for a myriad of reasons – to feel in control; to punish themselves; to experience a feeling of release; to vent pent-up anger or frustration; to communicate unhappiness or deep sadness; to gain the attention of a specific adult; to belong to part of a wider self-harming group. Some individuals will conceal their self-harm; others will be very open about it. If you know an autistic girl is self-harming, contact your local Child and Adolescent Mental Health Services (CAMHS) team or SelfharmUK[2] for advice and support.

---

2 www.selfharm.co.uk

- Restricted patterns of eating. Eating is often problematic for autistic girls, with many experiencing difficulties with textures and sensations associated with different food types. However, it is not uncommon for autistic girls to severely restrict their food intake when they are very anxious. It is important that this area is monitored closely, as there is growing evidence that autistic females may experience higher rates of eating disorders than the neurotypical population (Westwood and Tchanturia 2017). For more information about eating disorders and support, contact your local GP services or BEAT.[3]

- In more extreme cases, autistic girls can express significant desires to seriously hurt themselves or to die, and immediate support should be sought from CAMHS or medical professionals in this case.

Strategies for working with high levels of anxiety can include:

- Identifying situations that lead to anxiety.

- Talking through any planned changes in advance. It is also helpful if changes for the day can be physically recorded for the student to refer to over the day – in a school diary, for example.

- Talking about how their body feels when they are anxious, as it is possible that they will not have connected the physical sensation (for example, feeling nauseous) with feeling anxious.

- Teaching calming strategies. This can be anything from concentrating on your breathing to using some calming hand lotion, going for a walk or listening to music or a relaxation app; whatever makes the individual feel better.

- If something has gone wrong, talking about how it could be different next time, and making a plan for it to be different.

---

3 www.beateatingdisorders.org.uk

- Asking, 'What is the worst thing that can happen?' and then discussing their fears, putting them into perspective and context.

- Using cards with 'big deal' on one side and 'not a big deal' on the other. Ask the young person to categorise what the issue would be, and then talk through reasons why it might be less of a big deal than they think.

- The anxiety bucket. Get a selection of different-sized balls. Write the causes of anxiety on each ball and add to the bucket (plant pots work well). Talk about how the bucket fills up if you keep adding anxieties to it. Discuss what makes the young person feel calm. For each calm activity or calm item identified, cut a hole in the bucket, corresponding to the size of the balls. Talk about the fact that you need to build in things that will keep you calm throughout the day or your anxiety bucket will overflow, leading to feelings of being overwhelmed.

- Celebrating difference. Everyone has things that they find difficult and things that they find easier. Build the young person's confidence and self-esteem, so that they believe in themselves, and develop their resilience.

- Acknowledge that feeling anxious is okay and a normal part of life, and that managing it is an important life skill.

- Talk about the fact that some things can't change so we have to work out a way to manage difficult situations.

- Highlight the fact that some worries are for adults only to worry about.

It's important to discuss with autistic girls the fact that anxiety is likely to be an ever-present aspect of their lives, and that they will need a flexible range of strategies and tools to manage their anxiety throughout their lives.

Staying safe

'Secretly I just want to be normal.'
Martin and the Students of Limpsfield Grange (2017)

The girls at Limpsfield Grange want to be like everyone else: to be 'normal'. They want people to like them, they want friends, they want to have a relationship, and they want to be popular. For our community of students this can also mean that they are vulnerable and at risk of exploitation. Many girls have very low self-esteem, based on years of trying to fit in and feeling like they are failing, or being told that they are different even when they've tried their best to conform.

In our experience at Limpsfield Grange the most important thing to the girls is friendship – having a best friend, someone who understands them and cares about them. The girls that we work with are very mindful of what other people think about them. It's not that autistic boys don't want friends, but in our experience boys seem less active in trying to secure friendships, whereas girls start reaching out at an early age, trying to connect with their peers. But the girls often don't understand how to start a friendship, how to build it, repair it and sustain it.

When friendships and social interaction aren't successful, autistic girls start watching how their peers behave in social situations and try to replicate their social behaviours. Autistic girls can suppress their natural instincts to effectively construct their social selves. However, because this version of them is not quite authentic, friendships and social interaction still don't work out, and the girls can become even more aware that they are different and feel very isolated and alone. At the same time, the effort of double-thinking their every move, while simultaneously watching and analysing other people's reactions to them, leaves autistic girls mentally and emotionally drained. By the time they go home, having tried to please everyone and hold it together all day, they are exhausted. That's when meltdowns or shutdowns occur because the girls have used up absolutely everything just getting through the day. This is often called 'masking' or 'social camouflaging'.

Explicitly teaching and facilitating friendships and relationships, if this is something that a student is motivated by, is part of what we do at Limpsfield Grange. It starts with building self-awareness – What am I like? What do I like about myself? – and develops into awareness of other people – What do I like about other people? What do I get from being with other people? What would I like to get from a friendship? We also work with all of our classes and explain everyone's individual needs so that the girls develop a good understanding of their peers' strengths and areas for development. This quickly grows into really strong peer support and impressive levels of empathy between the girls. For some of our students, friendship is about having one person who 'gets' them, who they don't have to explain themselves to. For other girls, friendship is about a shared specialist interest, like Ponycon (a My Little Pony convention), anime or *Dr Who*. Friendships can be quite intense and we work with the girls on sharing friends, allowing friends space to be themselves, and repairing friendships when they go wrong.

Relationships are the key to working with autistic girls. To enable autistic girls and young women to be safe, there have to be judgement-free relationships built on trust, honesty and openness, and firm, clear, consistent boundaries. This is particularly key when working on romantic relationships and sex education.

Part of the received social wisdom about autistic people is that they don't want to have romantic relationships with other people, that they are not sexual beings and that they'd prefer to be on their own. Although this might be true of some autistic people, as it is of some neurotypical people, it is clearly not applicable to all. Our experience at Limpsfield Grange shows us that almost all of our girls want to have a romantic relationship with someone. However, establishing a romantic relationship can be tricky because many autistic girls don't really understand where other people's communication comes from or what it means. Interpreting people's behaviour when you don't understand what it means is at best confusing and at worst risky. A robust, honest and real-life approach to relationships and sex education is essential to keeping young autistic women safe. Very often autistic girls are people pleasers and will also not want to seem naïve, so it is important that relationship and sex education is based on the student's understanding. It is vitally important that professionals acknowledge and address gaps and misconceptions in a young person's prior knowledge about sex and relationships. Often autistic girls have endured endless sex education classes without realising that everything discussed is applicable to them. Other individuals may have listened to everything and thought it was a list of things they had to action before their 16th birthday.

A relationships and sex education programme that is personalised and delivered regularly in small chunks is critical, as is the ability for autistic girls to ask questions either face to face or remotely. Explicitly teaching privacy awareness and rules around personal space and touching other people is important, as this is something that is often implied in communication and may be something autistic girls misunderstand. It is also important that relationships and sex education sessions use unambiguous, real-life terminology to reduce confusion. One girl at Limpsfield Grange quite cheerfully talked about how much she'd like to go dogging until staff explained that it wasn't an activity that involved any actual dogs…

It is vital that autistic girls understand that if they are involved in an intimate act they can stop it at any time, and that 'no' means 'no'. Often autistic girls think that the other person knows what is in their mind, and don't physically tell them to stop, leading them to view their sexual encounter as non-consensual. A helpful resource is the Thames Valley Police *Tea and Consent* film (2015).

Autistic girls and women can be incredibly vulnerable. Many are black-and-white thinkers who take a lot of what people tell them at face value. Often autistic girls are reaching out and trying to connect with people, without understanding any of the associated risks. They will believe that people are who they say they are, and they can be easy to manipulate because they want people to like them. Other people can also become a specialist interest, and it is important to explicitly teach rules about appropriate levels of contact, and what constitutes antisocial behaviour or stalking.

The girls have often learnt how to 'mask' their difficulties through mimicking social behaviours without understanding what the behaviours mean or where they can lead. At times this can mean that they behave in a provocative or risky way without understanding the consequences of their behaviour. They can behave in these ways because they have seen other people behave like this. Their autism sometimes limits their capacity to transfer learning from one situation to another. The girls can find themselves in high-risk situations repeatedly without seemingly ever being able to learn how to avoid risk. This can cause some professionals to make judgements about them, and believe wrongly that high risk-behaviour is something that they like or is something that they choose. A frightening number of autistic women have been sexually assaulted more than once, or have ended up in destructive relationships with people that control them. Many autistic women have shared their experiences of being manipulated by others socially or sexually, and the physical emotion and psychological pain that has caused (Holliday Willey 2012).

At Limpsfield Grange we have seen an increase in the number of students who identify as gay/lesbian or non-binary, or who experience gender dysphoria. This is an area that can cause extreme anxiety in both autistic teenagers and in their families. The two areas should not be confused or conflated. Sexual identity or orientation is defined as an enduring pattern of romantic or sexual attraction (or a combination of these) to persons of the opposite sex or gender, the same sex or gender, or to either sexes or more than one gender. Gender identity is defined as one's personal experience of one's own gender. Gender identity can correlate with assigned sex at birth, or can differ from it completely. Gender dysphoria is a condition where a person experiences discomfort or distress because there's a mismatch between their biological sex and gender identity. It's sometimes known as gender identity disorder (GID), gender incongruence or being transgender.

Dr Wenn Lawson (2015) states that 20 per cent of the autistic community live with gender dysphoria. Dr Lawson stresses the importance of respect and support when discussing sexuality and gender identity with young autistic people. At Limpsfield Grange we listen to and support each autistic young person without prejudice, and support them to live the life that they choose. It is important to support parents and families, who sometimes find this area challenging. For more information about autism sexuality and gender dysphoria see National Autistic Society (2018) and the work of Dr Wenn Lawson (see also Lawson and Lawson 2017).

The pressure to be normal is immense during the teenage years, for all teenagers. It is so important that our brilliant autistic girls don't become crushed by the weight of trying to fit in. Remind them of the words of Maya Angelou: 'If you are always trying to be normal, you will never know how amazing you can be.'

Creating a pathway for a successful adult life

As E. E. Cummings (2015) said, 'It takes courage to grow up and become who you really are.' Change is kryptonite for many autistic people, and growing up is all about change. So how can we support autistic girls and their families to navigate the choppy waters of adolescence and early adulthood? How do we prepare them to make the successful next step on the journey of their lives? At Limpsfield Grange we believe that developing communication skills, growing independence and having a clear idea of who you are, and what you want your life to be like, are key ingredients to creating a pathway to a successful adult life.

By the time they leave us, the girls at Limpsfield Grange are articulate and able to reflect on their emotions and experiences, and this is the result of lots of time spent talking about everything! We start in Year 7 working on identifying and labelling emotions. We coach the girls in identifying and talking about their triggers: for anxiety, for anger or frustration, for sadness. The girls develop their self-awareness and their communication skills simultaneously, and it is this rapid change that parents comment on when their daughters join us. It's really important that the girls can identify how they feel and what they want, so that they can begin self-advocating. We don't believe in suffering in silence at Limpsfield Grange. The girls will always find some things really tough, and they have to develop the capacity to identify the support that they need and ask for it, politely but assertively. If the girls can ask for the support and guidance that they need, then it is the responsibility of the neurotypical world to provide it, so that they can be the best brilliant version of themselves.

Communication isn't just transmitting information, it's about receiving and decoding messages from other people. Autistic girls are constantly trying to work out what other people mean. Not understanding what other people mean is confusing and can lead to high levels of anxiety, isolation and exhaustion. To help with this, at Limpsfield Grange we use a technique called 'wondering out loud'. We wonder if a person is behaving in a certain way or is saying something because of how they feel or something they have experienced. We talk through the process a person went through to arrive at a conclusion, making the invisible thought processes visible, and make it clear how that could impact on or influence their behaviour. It's a really effective approach which can be used in real life or when watching TV or a film. This approach helps to contextualise the behaviour of others, hopefully reducing anxiety.

If you have met one autistic person, then you have met one autistic person. Autistic people are as different from each other as neurotypical people are, and this is always abundantly clear when considering independence. When working with autistic girls to develop their independence, it is key to understand their motivation. What do they want to be able to do and why? Establishing joint agreement about the areas of independence to be worked on is vital, as is explaining the sequence of small steps required to become independent. If living in New York is the goal, make clear all of the small steps of independence that need to be achieved to get there.

Being independent is also essential to being safe and reducing vulnerability. At Limpsfield Grange we are passionate about ensuring our learners are engaged and active participants in their lives. Passivity and over-reliance on adults or other peers is potentially dangerous. Being wholly reliant on other people means you can be easily exploited. We want the girls at Limpsfield Grange to be happy, healthy, empowered and included citizens, who can make choices, determine their own future and help to shape the world they live in. Developing independence enables them to be active in society, and pursue their ambitions. We want the girls to be satisfied with the quality of their lives.

Promoting independence can be difficult, as quite often the activity you are engaging the girls in isn't on their agenda. They may think it is perfectly fine that they can't brush their teeth or wash their hair independently; it's just not important to them. So the first thing we do is create engagement. We use specialist interests as a motivator, and reward the girls for trying things that they clearly have no interest in. Once a skill has been practised a few times in one setting, then we try to transfer the activity to another setting, to help the girls generalise the skill. We take lots of photos and film of the girls practising skills and then share this so they have a memento that they have completed the activity successfully before.

An #ActuallyAutistic adult observed on social media that autistic people have specialist interests which are negative and not to be encouraged, while neurotypical people have hobbies which are positive and are to be encouraged. Sometimes parents and professionals spend a lot of time and energy trying to divert attention away from specialist interests, when it would be better to harness them. This is particularly true in the case of career paths. Many of the girls at Limpsfield Grange have animals as their specialist interest, and this has led to some amazing long-term paid work opportunities and routes for further study. Our students have trained to be veterinary nurses, study equine management, or have worked in a paid capacity with animals. Similarly we have a growing number of students interested in anime who have gone on to study gaming design at university. If you are studying or working in an area that you love, you'll be a great student or employee – dedicated, passionate and focused.

Following autistic adult women sharing their life experiences either in person or via social media or books is a great way to help autistic girls start to see the future. Sarah Hendrickx's *Women and Girls with Autism Spectrum Disorder: Understanding Life Experiences from Early Childhood to Old Age* (2015) and Rudy Simone's *Aspergirls: Empowering Females with Asperger Syndrome* (2010) are good places to start, as are Robyn Steward's resources[4] or Alis Rowe's The Curly Hair Project.[5] *It is important that autistic girls are encouraged to imagine their own future. They don't have to do things the way they have always been done, they can invent new ways to do things. Advances in technology mean that it is now perfectly plausible to run a global business from your bedroom. Young autistic women can demonstrate how thinking autistically is a great advantage for business because you create solutions that neurotypical people can't imagine.*

It is not acceptable that in 2019 being an autistic female means you are marginalised or discriminated against. We all need to listen to and support autistic girls to ensure that they are satisfied with the quality of their lives, and that they lead the lives that they choose. Together we can create the right conditions to enable them to be happy healthy included and empowered citizens. Because, as M would say, 'I'm not weird. I'm awesome.'

---

4 www.robynsteward.com
5 https://thegirlwiththecurlyhair.co.uk

References

Cummings, E. E. (2015) *Enormous Smallness: A Story of E. E. Cummings.* Brooklyn, NY: Enchanted Lion Books.

Hendrickx, S. (2015) *Women and Girls with Autism Spectrum Disorder: Understanding Life Experiences from Early Childhood to Old Age.* London: Jessica Kingsley Publishers.

Holliday Willey, L. (2012) *Safety Skills for Asperger Women.* London: Jessica Kingsley Publishers.

Lawson, W. (2015) *Gender Dysphoria and Autism.* London: Network Autism.

Lawson, W. and Lawson, B. (2017) *Transitioning Together: One Couple's Journey of Gender and Identity Discovery.* London: Jessica Kingsley Publishers.

Mandy, W. (2018) 'In DSM-5, guidance on girls with autism is short but savvy.' *Spectrum News.* Accessed on 7/8/18 at www.spectrumnews.org/opinion/columnists/dsm-5-guidance-girls-autism-short-savvy

Martin, V. and the Students of Limpsfield Grange (2015) *M Is for Autism.* London: Jessica Kingsley Publishers.

Martin, V. and the Students of Limpsfield Grange (2017) *M in the Middle.* London: Jessica Kingsley Publishers.

National Autistic Society (2018) 'Sex Education and Puberty.' Accessed on 13/12/18 at www.autism.org.uk/about/communication/sex-education.aspx

Simone, R. (2010) *Aspergirls: Empowering Females with Asperger's Syndrome.* London: Jessica Kingsley Publishers.

Thames Valley Police (2015, 16 November) *Tea and Consent* [Video file]. Accessed on 13/12/18 at www.youtube.com/watch?v=pZwvrxVavnQ

United Nations (2006) 'Convention on the Rights of Persons with Disabilities.' *Treaty Series, 2515*, 3.

Westwood, H. and Tchanturia, K. (2017) 'Autism spectrum disorder in anorexia nervosa: An updated literature review.' *Current Psychiatry Reports, 19*, 7, 41.

Recommended further reading

ASC Girls Forum (2017) *Girls and Autism: Flying Under the Radar.* Accessed on 5/12/18 at www.nasen.org.uk/resources/resources.girls-and-autism-flying-under-the-radar.html

PART 3

Wider Professional Support and Intervention

CHAPTER 7

Psychiatric and Neurodevelopmental Aspects of Girls with Autism

Christopher Gillberg

Girls with autism were almost non-existent in psychiatric literature until the early 1990s when our research group published a paper about six girls with social deficits and learning problems (Kopp and Gillberg 1992). Asperger did not provide any details about any possible female cases he might have come across, and Kanner, even though three of his first eleven published cases were girls, did not go into much discussion about whether or not there might be gender differences in clinical presentation. However, Asperger speculated that 'in the autistic individual the male pattern is exaggerated to the extreme... It could be that autistic traits in the female only become evident after puberty. We just don't know' (Hans Asperger in Frith 1991, p. 85).

Gradually, it seemed that the scientific community and clinical experts just took it for granted that autism is 'typically' a male condition and that the few females they included in their studies or saw in their clinics were, at least as regards their 'behavioural phenotype', blueprint copies of the males. Over the past 25 years, interest in the possible 'specifics' of 'female autism' has grown, and in the very recent past, research into the area has more or less exploded. In this chapter I will try to summarise what is currently known about autism in girls (and also cover some studies of adult women) with a clear focus on psychiatric and medical aspects.

Are there as many girls as there are boys with autism?

Until recently it has been taken almost as a hard fact that the male:female ratio in autism is about 4–5:1 or even up to 7–10:1 and that it is even higher among those with higher levels of IQ and much lower among those with severe intellectual disability (e.g. Rydzewska *et al.* 2018; Westman-Andersson, Miniscalco and Gillberg 2013). However, clinical studies have almost always yielded much higher ratios than epidemiological, population-based studies, indicating that referral bias (including underlying assumptions that autism 'almost only' exists in boys, hence boys would be referred to clinics much more often) could play an important role. Girls with autism tend to be a bit like average boys but much less socially intuitive than average girls (Halladay *et al.* 2015). Some authorities in the field now argue that there should be different diagnostic algorithms for girls compared with boys. Others argue that if autism is defined the way it is, then you have to meet the agreed criteria in order to receive the diagnosis. Nevertheless, in other fields of medicine, criteria for a diagnosis are often different for males and females (e.g. the cut-off for a diagnosis of anaemia is usually different for males and females). There is good evidence that boys and men in the general population have more 'autism-type' features than girls and women (e.g. Posserud, Lundervold and Gillberg 2006). This would suggest that criteria for defining autism in girls and women should be based on comparison with females in the general population, not with the whole population of males and females.

Age at diagnosis

Girls, on average, receive their diagnosis of autism several years later than boys. Those few girls who get a diagnosis very early in life tend to be 'just like the boys' in clinical presentation. The more cognitively impaired they are, the more likely that the diagnosis will be made early. The male:female ratio in autism with severe intellectual disability is often under 2:1. The higher the IQ and the more 'unlike male autism', the later the diagnosis in girls and women who 'have autism' tends to be. This may be the case even when girls formally meet all the criteria for autism according to the *DSM-5* (American Psychiatric Association 2013). Some women nowadays receive a diagnosis of autism without a documented early life history of autism, and it is doubtful whether these cases represent 'real autism'. One has to remember that virtually all patients attending a psychiatric clinic have some degree of social interaction and behavioural problems that 'resemble' autism, particularly in the eyes of the inexperienced examiner.

The female autism phenotype: Is there such a thing? And is it 'biological'?

There are other chapters in this book that deal with the possibility of a female autism phenotype that is different from that of the male, so I will not go into detail here. However, some of the things that seem to be fairly well documented as 'differences' in studies will be listed briefly.

There is widespread agreement that more females than males with autism want to 'fit in' and behave as social chameleons, 'Zelig-types', and through imitation of other people develop a catalogue of social script scenes that they believe will fit different social contexts. This can be 'successful' in the sense that other people might not notice their difficulties in social interaction immediately but has the disadvantage of draining the person with autism of energy. Sometimes the girl or woman misjudges the social context and starts to behave and say things that would have fitted in the context that she believes is at hand but is actually not. She may even become aware of the mistake she made after a couple of minutes of 'conversation' and then want to 'reboot' and get onto 'the right script'. In trying to do so, she loses the ability to comprehend the overall situation altogether, and the situation becomes absurd with responses to the other people's questions and comments that are totally out of place.

There is some agreement that girls with autism (more often than boys with autism) either talk-talk-talk or keep more or less totally quiet to the extent that people start wondering if they are extremely shy or have selective mutism.

More girls than boys start out with restricted food and feeding behaviours at a very young age; many even meet criteria for avoidant restrictive food intake disorder (ARFID – see below). This obvious problem often overshadows the underlying social interaction/intuition problems, and the focus on the disturbed eating behaviour may lead to a delay of several years before the diagnosis of autism is made.

Relative to boys with autism, girls can appear to be extremely skilled in their motor behaviours from a young age and start walking as early at nine months, dance and do pirouettes high on tip-toe. On the other hand, many girls tend to be totally unaware of how they look and may forget that there is a rear view (e.g. hair may be well combed and straightened at the front but all tousled and in a mess at the back). They may worry very little if at all about dress, even though in a small number of cases, there may be extreme fixations on only 'the best clothes'!

Many girls with autism say 'no' to just about everything.

The role of the so-called comorbidities and the concept of ESSENCE

Autism, in cases that come to clinics early in life, is almost always associated with other problems that cannot be accounted for by the diagnosis of autism per se. The associated problems/diagnoses/disorders are often lumped together under the somewhat mistaken notion of 'comorbidity'. In boys with autism, autism is often the first diagnosis to be made, and the 'comorbid' disorders are recognised (and possibly diagnosed) later – sometimes several years later. In girls with autism, the 'comorbidities' are often the first problems to receive a diagnosis or a label, and the autism diagnosis, if made at all, comes years or even decades later.

The concept of ESSENCE (Gillberg 2010) – referring to early symptomatic syndromes eliciting neurodevelopmental clinical examinations – takes into account the almost universal overlap of neurodevelopmental disorders (e.g. attention deficit hyperactivity disorder (ADHD), developmental communication disorder (DCD), speech and language disorder, intellectual disability and tic disorders) with autism and with each other. If a person receives a diagnosis of any of these disorders early in life, he/she is almost certainly going to meet criteria for one of the other disorders in the ESSENCE group within a few years (see Table 7.1). If a person meets criteria for two of the disorders, he/she has a high risk of meeting criteria for three. It is not unusual for a person with autism to fulfil autism criteria at age three, and then also meet criteria for ADHD at age five, for DCD at age six, tic disorder at age eight, depression and anxiety at age ten. This is true both in boys and in girls with autism, but it is much more likely that only a few of these diagnoses (e.g. depression and anxiety) will ever be established in childhood in girls.

Table 7.1 Early symptomatic syndromes eliciting neurodevelopmental clinical examinations (ESSENCE)

Syndrome	Prevalence (%)	Reference
Autism	1.0	Nygren *et al.* 2012
ADHD (with or without ODD oppositional defiant disorder)	3.7	Kadesjö and Gillberg 2001
Tourette's syndrome	1.1	Kadesjö and Gillberg 2000
ID/intellectual disability	1.5	Gillberg and Söderström 2003
Speech/language disorder	4.0	Miniscalco *et al.* 2006
DCD/developmental coordination disorder	4.9	Kadesjö and Gillberg 1999
RAD/reactive attachment disorder	0.5–1.5	Minnis *et al.* 2013
Selective mutism	0.2–2.0	Kopp and Gillberg 1997
Affective disorder including bipolar	Unknown	Biederman *et al.* 2003
Behavioural phenotype syndromes	2.0	Gillberg 2018

cont.

Epilepsy syndromes with ESSENCE	0.5	Reilly *et al.* 2014
Estimated total prevalence of ESSENCE with 'comorbidity' taken into account	**10**	**Gillberg 2018**

Attention deficit hyperactivity order

About half of all boys and girls with a diagnosis of autism will also meet criteria for ADHD within a few years. Quite a number of children (not least girls) with a primary diagnosis of ADHD will eventually come under suspicion of autism (or Asperger syndrome) too. Quite a number of young girls with autism are hyperactive during their first years of life. This may subside in cases receiving a correct diagnosis of autism early on, perhaps because of the often individually tailored new educational approaches taken once it becomes clear that the girl actually has a very different style of communication and attention to tasks. However, in cases where the autism diagnosis is missed for years, the hyperactivity tends to continue, and at least half of such cases will eventually be shown to have comorbid ADHD. ADHD is the most treatable of all the ESSENCE disorders and it is therefore essential to consider this diagnosis in all cases with suspected or diagnosed autism.

Developmental coordination disorder

In the past there was a notion that boys with autism were agile and motorically well developed. There is now overwhelming evidence that both boys and girls with autism have high levels of motor coordination problems and that about half of them meet criteria for DCD. Many girls with autism are extremely awkward motorically to the extent that they appear shy and withdrawn because they cannot cope with the motor demands of various tasks they are given. This can lead to anxiety and depression and diagnoses of anxiety disorder and major depression rather than the more basic syndromes of autism and DCD.

Tic syndromes

Tics are extremely common in autism, perhaps particularly in those with good cognitive skills (Ehlers and Gillberg 1993). Many girls with autism have tics, sometimes even extremes of tics, but the motor or vocal behaviours often remain undiagnosed or are considered to represent stereotypies (which they are not). It is quite surprising the way very obvious jerky tics, 'hard blinking' or explosive vocal tics are so often overlooked. It is important to separate tics from stereotypies, given that tics are treatable with other approaches (pharmacological and behavioural). Having said that, it is also important to point out that tics should only be treated with medication if they are severely impairing in and of themselves.

Pathological/extreme demand avoidance

Pathological/extreme demand avoidance (PDA/EDA) appears to be a problem type that is increasing in prevalence in several groups of children. Up until recently, it was considered to represent a separate category within the autism group, or at least closely related to problems that were described as 'autistic'. Many clinicians felt (and a few studies supported this) that PDA was probably more common in females with autism as compared with males. PDA is not an official *DSM* (American Psychiatric Association 2013) or *ICD* (World Health Organization 2018) diagnosis, but clearly a concept that clinicians increasingly use. In one study specifically attempting to separate a female from a male autism phenotype, the following features stood out as particularly typical of girls with autism: 'avoids demands', 'very determined', 'careless with physical appearance and dress' and 'interacts mostly with younger children' (Kopp and Gillberg 2011). Some girls with autism and PDA also suddenly 'decide' that they will not respond to questions and develop behaviours that fit with the clinical diagnosis of selective mutism.

Anxiety

Anxiety, particularly in connection with distress from change of environment or sensory overstimulation, is a common phenomenon in autism at all ages. Some clinicians would diagnose this separately as an anxiety disorder, and many girls who only later get a diagnosis of autism have been primarily diagnosed as suffering from generalised anxiety disorder (GAD), separation anxiety disorder or even panic disorder. Social anxiety can be a major problem in such cases, but many females with autism have developed (sometimes masterfully) a 'social style' after having watched soap operas or observed friends that they then copy.

Depression

Depressive symptoms very often develop in both boys and girls with autism, particularly in those with relatively better overall cognitive functioning. This is sometimes caused by their growing insight that they are 'different' and that they have a hard time fitting in with other children. It is probably not more typical of girls, but in clinical practice, many girls with autism are first diagnosed with major depression in their teenage years, before anyone starts thinking about the possible underlying combination of autism, DCD, and perhaps ADHD (which is a very common triad in psychiatry, but often missed altogether under the 'cloud of depression or anxiety') (Solomon *et al.* 2012).

Eating disorder, specifically anorexia nervosa and ARFID

More than half of all young children with autism have eating/feeding problems that often amount to a very impairing problem clinically. Some of these children now get the diagnosis of avoidant restrictive food intake disorder (ARFID), others are characterised as picky eaters and some are labelled as having early-onset anorexia (Lucarelli *et al.* 2017). Whereas boys with the combination of autism and picky eating are usually appropriately given an early diagnosis of autism (and the eating problem is often seen as a symptom of maintenance of sameness), girls tend to get the focus shifted onto the eating problem alone. Girls with early-onset eating disorders or gastrointestinal problems that come to the attention of medical services should always be screened for autism and other ESSENCE (Råstam *et al.* 2013).

About one in five to one in three of all cases of teenage-onset anorexia nervosa actually have a very high level of autistic sympto-matology and most of these meet or have met criteria for autism (which is still very often not recognised) (Råstam, Gillberg and Wentz 2003). Given that teenage-onset anorexia nervosa affects about 1 per cent of the whole female population (and only one per thousand of the male population), there should be about 0.2–0.3 per cent of the whole teenage girl population who have autism plus anorexia nervosa. It does seem likely that this – usually undiagnosed – proportion of the female population with autism contributes greatly to the unrecognised ('hidden' or 'covert') cases of female autism, and that, were they to be included in future epidemiological studies, the male:female autism ratio would be dramatically reduced (see above).

Self-injurious behaviours

Self-injurious behaviours (SIB) are very common in autism, perhaps particularly in those with intellectual disability. These are very often obvious and dramatic in nature with self-hitting and head banging being the most characteristic. However, teenagers who self-mutilate in private (cutting, pinching, hair pulling) are often diagnosed as having some kind of personality disorder (especially borderline personality disorder). A few studies have found that young girls with such SIB often have autism or another type of ESSENCE problem, such as ADHD, and studies looking at the rate of such SIB in populations with autism or ADHD have found much increased levels, particularly in females (Balàzs *et al.* 2018; Maddox, Trubanova and White 2017).

Personality disorder

The diagnosis of personality disorder is widespread in adult psychiatry. Follow-up studies of children with autism or Asperger syndrome have found that individuals with these childhood diagnoses often receive a diagnosis or meet criteria for personality disorders of various kinds (perhaps particularly schizoid, schizotypal, narcissistic and obsessive-compulsive disorder) (Hellgren, Gillberg and Enerskog 1987; Gillberg *et al.* 2016).

Catatonia

Catatonic features and catatonia occur from adolescence in 15–20 per cent of all people with autism, possibly less commonly in females. However, when it occurs, it can be extremely severe with frozen postures lasting for minutes to hours, inability to move without being physically touched or pushed, 'sleeping' with head inches above the pillow, abrupt muteness and a variety of SIB that are performed in a highly repetitive manner.

Bipolar disorder

Bipolar disorder co-occurs with autism in a subgroup of familially linked cases. Whenever there is a family history of bipolar disorder, mood swings in females with autism should be considered in the light of a possible diagnosis of bipolar disorder (Skokauskas and Frodl 2015). Some female cases, in which there is gradual realisation that the core features of the problem have actually always fitted with the diagnosis of autism, also have extremes of emotional lability from the first years of life, and it is particularly in such cases that it is important to consider the possibility of bipolar disorder from an early age, given the evidence that the earlier the successful treatment of this problem, the better the very long-term psychosocial outcome.

Psychosis and forensic psychiatric problems

A small minority of women with autism develop psychosis. Some of these have recurring psychotic episodes often ushered in by periods of 'perceived stress' (stress that is sometimes something that other people would consider anything but stressful). Occasionally, long periods of time (even years) with hallucinations and other schizophrenia symptoms occur in women who have had mild or moderate autism from early childhood. It is always important in such cases to be aware of the possible underlying disorder associated with 22q11 deletion syndrome (Niklasson *et al.* 2001).

On rare occasions a woman with autism is apprehended and sentenced for criminal offences, including violent crime, although evidence does not suggest that offending is higher among individuals with autism (compared to those without) (Helverschou *et al.* 2015). Confessing to the crime is probably more common in this very small subgroup of women with autism (who have often been diagnosed as having a personality disorder rather than autism before the criminal act). There is a need for much more in-depth studies of the pathways to crime and for the situation of 'criminal women with autism' more generally as a highly vulnerable group.

Paediatric acute onset neuropsychiatric syndrome

Some girls and boys with mild autistic features and other neuro-developmental problems, who usually do not meet full criteria for any of the categorical diagnoses, suddenly (over a day or a week) develop extremely severe symptoms of just about anything featured under the ESSENCE umbrella plus also very often enuresis and separation anxiety disorder. Such acute onset of symptoms should always lead to a suspicion that the category of paediatric acute onset neuropsychiatric syndrome (PANS) might apply (Johnson *et al.* 2019).

Behavioural phenotype syndromes

There is always a need to consider a variety of underlying genetic and other behavioural phenotype syndromes (including foetal alcohol and foetal valproate syndrome) in cases of autism, regardless of gender. Conversely there is always a need to consider the possibility of autism and/or other ESSENCE in such syndromes.

Many girls with the fragile X syndrome and premutation fragile X syndrome have marked autistic features and it is important to always bear this association in mind when working up autism/ESSENCE in females.

Girls with 22q11 deletion (22q11del) syndrome appear to have marked autistic symptoms and to have such severe social deficits that a diagnosis of autism is considered. However, very few of these individuals actually meet criteria for autism once the 'slow processing' (slow to warm up, slow to react, inertia) is factored in. However, in all girls raising any screening suspicion of possibly having autism, 22q11del must be considered a possible background factor (see below).

Foetal alcohol syndrome (FAS) is considered by many to be one of the behavioural phenotype syndromes group of conditions, even though the strongest link to the clinical manifestations of this syndrome is likely not genetic, but the toxic effect of alcohol on the developing foetus brain. There are clearly also genetic factors involved, given that there is a strong genetic link between ADHD in the mother and ADHD in the child and links between ADHD in the young girl and later alcohol abuse in the young woman (young parent). Clinical experience and limited research suggest that both girls and boys with FAS have a very high risk of showing the features of both autism and ADHD from about three years of age onwards (Aronson, Hagberg and Gillberg 1997).

The need for medical/psychiatric work-up and interventions

All medical doctors, not just paediatricians and psychiatrists, need to know more about females with autism. All patients with any kind of long-standing problems (and also the few with extremely severe and acute onset of problems) need to be considered from the point of view of autism and other ESSENCE (Kopp, Kelly and Gillberg 2010).

The diagnosis of autism and other ESSENCE

There are many well-validated screening tools for autism, including the A-TAC (Autism – Tics, ADHD and Other Comorbidities Inventory; Hansson *et al.* 2005), ASSQ (Autism Spectrum Screening Questionnaire; Ehlers, Gillberg and Wing 1999) and SRS (Social Responsiveness Scale; Constantino *et al.* 2003), and any of these can be used in in- or outpatient clinics to locate individuals with a high risk of having autism. There is one particular scale – the ASSQ-REV – that was developed specifically for recognising females at high risk for autism (Kopp and Gillberg 2011). Females scoring above cut-off on any of these, and who at interview (self or parent) exhibit several symptoms, should be referred to appropriate services for diagnosis. These tend to vary both as regards availability and quality and, in the future, given the relatively high frequency of autism/ESSENCE problems in the general population, it would perhaps be preferable to have local outpatient psychiatric teams develop sufficient experience and expertise in making the diagnoses themselves.

There is no need to always use specific instruments (e.g. Autism Diagnostic Interview – Revised (ADI-R), Autism Diagnostic Observation Schedule (ADOS), or Diagnostic Interview for Social and Communication Disorders (DISCO)) to make the diagnosis of autism. A good in-depth early history taken by a clinically experienced psychiatrist/neurologist/paediatrician from a parent, observation of and interaction with the girl/teenager/woman, thorough checking of the *DSM* or *ICD* criteria for autism, ADHD, DCD, tic disorders etc., plus an age-relevant test of cognitive functioning (such as one of the Wechsler scales) will usually be sufficient to arrive at an appropriate diagnosis (including of some of the comorbidities) without the use of the autism-specific instruments that are currently in vogue. In reviewing the data available for making a diagnosis, it is important to take a female–female perspective, i.e. comparing the individual assessed for autism with other females of the same age rather than with males with autism.

Once a diagnosis has been established, there is a need to screen for all possible comorbidities (including depression, anxiety, speech and language disorder, eating disorder, tic disorders, etc.), perhaps using scales such as the A-TAC or the FTF (Five to Fifteen), and to be specific about the level of cognitive functioning (ID, borderline, average, and above average) and expressive language level and comprehension. Very often, the so-called comorbidities are actually more treatable than the autism (e.g. ADHD, DCD, tics). Even though information about the autism and insight into the specifics of how autism affects the individual's style and degree of functioning may be all important, the need to consider a trial of stimulant medication for possible ADHD and targeted task motor training for DCD must be highlighted.

Medical work-up and interventions

The next step is to always consider what degree of medical work-up is needed. There can never be a question of whether or not some degree of medical work-up is indicated. A medical doctor skilled in the medical work-up of neurological, neurodevelopmental and neuropsychiatric disorders *must* assess all females with a diagnosis of autism. This chapter is too brief for a full description of what needs to be done in terms of work-up, but it varies according to age of the individual at the time of diagnosis, comorbidity, intellectual and language level and on findings obtained at the physical examination. For a full consideration of what should be done, the reader is referred to Coleman and Gillberg (2012) in which there is an algorithm of how the medical examination should be pursued in autism.

Vitamin D deficiency/insufficiency

When it comes to medical treatment aspects, it is important to highlight the very common problem of hypovitaminosis D in females (even more than in males) with autism. Many girls and women with autism, particularly in the Western world (plus Japan), say that they cannot tolerate the sun or are fixated on 'never getting malignant melanoma', and if they do not take vitamin D supplementation orally, they will become vitamin D deficient. It is important to always check vitamin D levels in the blood in females with autism and give proper advice as to the need to be in the sun/level of supplementation needed to acquire sufficiently high blood levels of the vitamin. Sunscreen should probably be avoided in most cases (because of possible harmful hormone-disturbing substances in most sun protection lotions); instead, using reasonable clothing and avoiding spending too much time in the sun is the safest way of not getting burnt. However, it is important for most people to spend as much 'non-burn' time in the sun as possible.

Polycystic ovary syndrome

Polycystic ovary syndrome (PCOS) should be considered in all cases of female autism. There is good evidence that PCOS is overrepresented in autism and vice versa. In some families, the maternal grandmother, the mother and the child all have PCOS and autism. In all women presenting for autism assessment, the possibility of PCOS should therefore be considered. Also, gynaecologists should be aware of the association of PCOS with autism (Cherskov *et al.* 2018). The association of PCOS with autism is possibly due to the intrauterine exposure of female foetuses to high levels of testosterone in utero (which is known to be strongly associated with both PCOS and autism).

Extreme diets

Diets need to be discussed in a thoughtful way. Many females with autism have unusual or dangerous diet habits that can lead on to all sorts of deficiency syndromes, including vitamin D, iron, zinc and omega-3 deficiency. The widespread belief that gluten intolerance (and to some extent lactose intolerance) has something to do with autism has little or no scientific underpinning. Omega-3 supplementation has moderately positive effects on attention deficits in children with ESSENCE and appears to improve several aspects of reading in school-age children regardless of underlying neurodevelopmental problems (Johnson *et al.* 2019).

Stimulant and other treatments for ADHD
About one third of all teenage girls and adult women with autism meet criteria for ADHD, and some of them will benefit greatly from treatment with a stimulant and other interventions known to be helpful in ADHD.

Targeted motor training for DCD
The motor clumsiness that is also very common in intellectually able girls and women with autism/Asperger syndrome can be positively affected by focused motor task training programmes, and for some, these can be important parts of the overall intervention (Bonney, Ferguson and Smits-Engelsman 2017; Smits-Engeslman *et al.* 2018). For others, the motor clumsiness, at least in adult age, is not experienced as a major problem and therefore not a target for intervention.

Histories of sexual abuse and/or suicide attempts
There are at least two things that doctors – including psychiatrists – often feel uncomfortable asking young (and older) patients, perhaps particularly girls and women, about: sexual abuse and suicide. One of the reasons for their shying away from interviewing about these things is probably that they do not really know what to do if the answer to 'Have you ever been sexually abused?' or 'Have you ever seriously considered/are you considering taking your own life?' is 'Yes'. Is it the medical doctor's responsibility to do something about it? Maybe provide the opportunity for the patient to 'talk about it' or

even consider admitting the patient to inpatient psychiatric care? The self-reported incidence of sexual abuse among young autistic women is 'shockingly high' (Bargiela, Steward and Mandy 2016). The risk of attempted and completed suicide is much higher in autism than in non-autism (Hirvikoski *et al.* 2016). The evidence is there that these factors/risks are associated with autism, perhaps particularly in girls (or could it be that boys and men with autism do not report such things even though they have been abused or considered suicide?), but the reality is that we do not really – yet – know what to do about it.

In the case of suicidal thoughts and attempts, it is essential to screen for depression and other major psychiatric disorder, and to treat such problems appropriately – medically and psychologically. When it comes to experiences of sexual abuse, the effects of such childhood exposure range from epigenetic changes to lifetime psychological trauma to 'so what?' reflections, and any approach to intervention has to be individualised. There is no universal remedy for the effects of childhood sexual abuse suffered by so many individuals with autism.

A female life with autism

This chapter has explored our emergent understanding of the prevalence of autism among girls and women, as well as considering some of the differences and subtleties of female presentation. Clearly, there are many potential comorbidities, and the concept of ESSENCE can help in building a clearer understanding of the complexities inherent in an autism diagnosis. This approach, along with our developing understanding of the female autistic phenotype, will facilitate earlier identification of girls with autism, providing opportunities for the development of more supportive medical and educational systems. I will end by describing a fairly typical case of 'female autism' from infancy through to adult age.

Anna

Anna was born six weeks prematurely and had respiratory distress. An older brother attended a special school because of mild learning problems and overall very aloof behaviour but was only diagnosed with autism and ADHD in the 1990s when he was already 40 years of age. In her first year, the parents were unconcerned about Anna; she was an 'easy baby', even though Granny wondered why she never smiled. At around one year of age she started refusing solid foods and would only eat when seated in the same chair at the same place at the table. She avoided demands and would withdraw to a corner and sit there with her head down, sometimes for an hour or more. She said little before age two and then started talking in a loud shrill voice with very well-developed vocabulary but with an unusual lisp. She seemed to be interested in other children but would never actively join a group or approach individual children. When she started school, teachers would often ask her parents, 'Has anything bad happened today?' because Anna had seemed especially low, sad or angry but would not share with anybody what it was that bothered her. She got good grades but almost always refused to speak out loud in the classroom. Alone with teachers she would whisper responses to questions. She was pale, 'highly strung', eyes wide open and seemingly very anxious, particularly in connection with change of routine or plans. She had no close friends but would sometimes sit near a group of other girls without speaking to them.

At age 16, two years after she had her first menstruation, she lost a lot of weight in a very short time, and six months later was hospitalised for two months with a diagnosis of anorexia nervosa and depression. Her body mass index (BMI)[1] on admission to the hospital at age 16 was 13.5 (BMI calculated in

---

1 According to NHS, the ideal BMI range is 18.5–24.9.

the year 2000, when she was seen at age 30 in an outpatient clinic for autism). She gained some weight but would only agree to eat the food prescribed by one particular doctor to whom she would speak; with all other people she refused to say a word. She was discharged from the hospital when her BMI had reached 16 and she has retained this level of extreme thinness ever since. She has been amenorrhoeic from age 16 through to age 45 when she was last seen.

After the hospital period she 'decided' that she would make friends with other people, and she started talking freely and often, excelled in many subjects in high school and at university (where she studied philosophy) and gave public talks seemingly without any anxiety or stage fright. She worked as an assistant to a professor of languages for seven years, but when he died, funding for her post disappeared and she has been unable to find a new regular job since the age of 32. At age 30, three years after her brother was diagnosed with autism, she consulted an autism specialist who gave her the diagnosis of Asperger syndrome (and chronic anorexia nervosa) on the basis of meeting all six Gillberg and Gillberg (1989) criteria for Asperger syndrome (and *DSM-III-R* criteria for anorexia nervosa; American Psychiatric Association 1987). She lives alone, 'semi-retired', gives public lectures on autism, and says that now that she knows herself better (because of the diagnosis related to autism) her life is 'quite OK'. She asserts that the best thing that ever happened to her was getting the diagnosis of Asperger syndrome. 'All the bits and pieces fell into place – suddenly everything made sense.' Her full-scale Wechsler Adult Intelligence Scale score was 126, well above average, with extremely low scores on processing speed (corresponding to IQ 85).[2]

---

2 Scores ranging from 90 to 109 are considered to be in the average range; 120–129 fall in the superior range and 85–89 is in the low average range.

There is no doubt, on the basis of a DISCO-10 interview (Wing *et al.* 2002) with her mother performed when the mother was 70 years of age, that Anna must have met criteria for autism even before the age of two years. In many ways she was a classic case of infantile autism (with high IQ), but she did not have any very conspicuous stereotypies, although her mother stated that she herself had always wondered why Anna held her hands together on the back of her body even from the age of two or three, and said that she would flap and flick her hands and fingers there (unlike her brother, who would flap his hands fully visibly while rocking his body back and forth from about the age of 14 months).

Anorexia, depression and anxiety (plus once obsessive-compulsive disorder?) were the diagnoses she had been given by psychiatrists and general practitioners when she had consulted them for her problems or when she had been hospitalised. Even after her brother had been diagnosed with autism and she consulted two different psychiatrists for low mood and hopelessness, the issue of autism either never came up or was dismissed as 'ridiculous' ('just because your brother has autism does not mean *you* do').

References

American Psychiatric Association (1987) *Diagnostic and Statistical Manual of Mental Disorders: DSM-III-R* (3rd edn, revised). Washington, DC: American Psychiatric Press.

American Psychiatric Association (2013) *Diagnostic and Statistical Manual of Mental Disorders: DSM-5* (5th edn). Washington, DC: American Psychiatric Publishing.

Aronson, M., Hagberg, B. and Gillberg, C. (1997) 'Attention deficits and autistic spectrum problems in children exposed to alcohol during gestation: A follow-up study.' *Developmental Medicine and Child Neurology, 39,* 583–587.

Balàzs, J., Gyori, D., Horvath, L. O., Meszaros, G. and Szentivanyi, D. (2018) 'Attention-deficit hyperactivity disorder and nonsuicidal self-injury in a clinical sample of adolescents: The role of comorbidities and gender.' *BMC Psychiatry, 18,* 34.

Bargiela, S., Steward, R. and Mandy, W. (2016) 'The experiences of late-diagnosed women with autism spectrum conditions: An investigation of the female autism phenotype.' *Journal of Autism and Developmental Disorders, 46*, 3281–3294.

Biederman, J., Mick, E., Wozniak, J., Monuteaux, M. C., Galdo, M. and Faraone, S. V. (2003) 'Can a subtype of conduct disorder linked to bipolar disorder be identified? Integration of findings from the Massachusetts General Hospital Pediatric Psychopharmacology Research Program.' *Biological Psychiatry, 53*, 952–960.

Bonney, E., Ferguson, G. and Smits-Engelsman, B. (2017) 'The efficacy of two activity-based interventions in adolescents with developmental coordination disorder.' *Research in Developmental Disabilities, 71*, 223–236.

Cherskov, A., Pohl, A., Allison, C., Zhang, H., Payne, R. A. and Baron-Cohen, S. (2018) 'Polycystic ovary syndrome and autism: A test of the prenatal sex steroid theory.' *Translational Psychiatry, 8*, 136.

Coleman, M. and Gillberg, C. (2012) *The Autisms*. Oxford: Oxford University Press.

Constantino, J. N., Davis, S. A., Todd, R. D., Schindler, M. K. *et al.* (2003) 'Validation of a brief quantitative measure of autistic traits: Comparison of the social responsiveness scale with the autism diagnostic interview-revised.' *Journal of Autism and Developmental Disorders, 33*, 4, 427–433.

Ehlers, S. and Gillberg, C. (1993) 'The epidemiology of Asperger syndrome: A total population study.' *Journal of Child Psychology and Psychiatry, 34*, 1327–1350.

Ehlers, S., Gillberg, C. and Wing, L. (1999) 'A screening questionnaire for Asperger syndrome and other high-functioning autism spectrum disorders in school age children.' *Journal of Autism and Developmental Disorders, 29*, 129–141.

Frith, U. (ed.) (1991) *Autism and Asperger Syndrome*. London: Jessica Kingsley Publishers.

Gillberg, C. (2010) 'The ESSENCE in child psychiatry: Early Symptomatic Syndromes Eliciting Neurodevelopmental Clinical Examinations.' *Research in Developmental Disabilities, 31*, 1543–1551.

Gillberg, C. (2018). *ESSENCE 2018 Book of Abstracts*. Gothenburg, Sweden: Danagård Litho.

Gillberg, C. and Söderström, H. (2003) 'Learning disability.' *The Lancet, 362*, 811–821.

Gillberg, I. C. and Gillberg, C. (1989) 'Children with preschool minor neurodevelopmental disorders. IV: Behaviour and school achievement at age 13.' *Developmental Medicine and Child Neurology, 31*, 3–13.

Gillberg, I. C., Helles, A., Billstedt, E. and Gillberg, C. (2016) 'Boys with Asperger syndrome grow up: Psychiatric and neurodevelopmental disorders 20 years after initial diagnosis.' *Journal of Autism and Developmental Disorders, 46*, 74–82.

Halladay, A. K., Bishop, S., Constantino, J. N., Daniels, A. M. *et al.* (2015) 'Sex and gender differences in autism spectrum disorder: Summarizing evidence gaps and identifying emerging areas of priority.' *Molecular Autism, 6*, 36.

Hansson, S. L., Svanstrom Rojvall, A., Rastam, M., Gillberg, C., Gillberg, C. and Anckarsater, H. (2005) 'Psychiatric telephone interview with parents for screening of childhood autism – tics, attention-deficit hyperactivity disorder and other comorbidities (A-TAC): Preliminary reliability and validity.' *British Journal of Psychiatry, 187*, 262–267.

Hellgren, L., Gillberg, C. and Enerskog, I. (1987) 'Antecedents of adolescent psychoses: A population-based study of school health problems in children who develop psychosis in adolescence.' *Journal of the American Academy of Child and Adolescent Psychiatry, 26*, 351–355.

Helverschou, S. B., Rasmussen, K., Steindal, K., Sondanaa, E., Nilsson, B. and Nottestad, J. A. (2015) 'Offending profiles of individuals with autism spectrum disorder: A study of all individuals with autism spectrum disorder examined by the forensic psychiatric service in Norway between 2000 and 2010.' *Autism, 19*, 850–858.

Hirvikoski, T., Mittendorfer-Rutz, E., Boman, M., Larsson, H., Lichtenstein, P. and Bölte, S. (2016) 'Premature mortality in autism spectrum disorder. *British Journal of Psychiatry, 208*, 3, 232–238.

Johnson, M., Fernell, E., Preda, I., Wallin, L., Fasth, A., Gillberg, C. and Gillberg, C. (2019). Paediatric acute-onset neuropsychiatric syndrome in children and adolescents: an observational cohort study. *The Lancet Child & Adolescent Health, 3*, 3, 175–180.

Kadesjö, B. and Gillberg, C. (1999) 'Developmental coordination disorder in Swedish 7-year-old children.' *Journal of the American Academy of Child and Adolescent Psychiatry, 38*, 820–828.

Kadesjö, B. and Gillberg, C. (2000) 'Tourette's disorder: Epidemiology and comorbidity in primary school children.' *Journal of the American Academy of Child and Adolescent Psychiatry, 39*, 548–555.

Kadesjö, B. and Gillberg, C. (2001) 'The comorbidity of ADHD in the general population of Swedish school-age children.' *Journal of Child Psychology and Psychiatry, 42*, 487–492.

Kopp, S. and Gillberg, C. (1992) 'Girls with social deficits and learning problems: Autism, atypical Asperger syndrome or a variant of these conditions.' *European Child and Adolescent Psychiatry, 1*, 89–99.

Kopp, S. and Gillberg, C. (1997) 'Selective mutism: A population-based study: A research note.' *Journal of Child Psychology and Psychiatry, 38*, 257–262.

Kopp, S. and Gillberg, C. (2011) 'The Autism Spectrum Screening Questionnaire (ASSQ)-Revised Extended Version (ASSQ-REV): An instrument for better capturing the autism phenotype in girls? A preliminary study involving 191 clinical cases and community controls.' *Research in Developmental Disabilities, 32*, 2875–2888.

Kopp, S., Kelly, K. B. and Gillberg, C. (2010) 'Girls with social and/or attention deficits: A descriptive study of 100 clinic attenders.' *Journal of Attention Disorders, 14*, 167–181.

Lucarelli, J., Pappas, D., Welchons, L. and Augustyn, M. (2017) 'Autism spectrum disorder and avoidant/restrictive food intake disorder.' *Journal of Developmental and Behavioral Pediatrics, 38,* 79–80.

Maddox, B. B., Trubanova, A. and White, S. W. (2017) 'Untended wounds: Non-suicidal self-injury in adults with autism spectrum disorder.' *Autism, 21,* 412–422.

Miniscalco, C., Nygren, G., Hagberg, B., Kadesjö, B. and Gillberg, C. (2006) 'Neuropsychiatric and neurodevelopmental outcome of children at age 6 and 7 years who screened positive for language problems at 30 months.' *Developmental Medical Child Neurology, 48,* 361–366.

Minnis, H., Macmillan, S., Pritchett, R., Young, D. *et al.* (2013) 'Prevalence of reactive attachment disorder in a deprived population.' *British Journal of Psychiatry, 202,* 342–346.

Niklasson, L., Rasmussen, P., Oskarsdottir, S. and Gillberg, C. (2001) 'Neuropsychiatric disorders in the 22q11 deletion syndrome.' *Genetics in Medicine, 3,* 1, 79–84.

Nygren, G., Cederlund, M., Sandberg, E., Gillstedt, F. *et al.* (2012) 'The prevalence of autism spectrum disorders in toddlers: A population study of 2-year-old Swedish children.' *Journal of Autism and Developmental Disorders, 42,* 1491–1497.

Posserud, M. B., Lundervold, A. J. and Gillberg, C. (2006) 'Autistic features in a total population of 7–9-year-old children assessed by the ASSQ (Autism Spectrum Screening Questionnaire).' *Journal of Child Psychology and Psychiatry, 47,* 167–175.

Råstam, M., Gillberg, C. and Wentz, E. (2003) 'Outcome of teenage-onset anorexia nervosa in a Swedish community-based sample.' *European Child and Adolescent Psychiatry, 12,* Suppl 1, I78–190.

Råstam, M., Taljemark, J., Tajnia, A., Lundstrom, S. *et al.* (2013) 'Eating problems and overlap with ADHD and autism spectrum disorders in a nationwide twin study of 9- and 12-year-old children.' *Scientific World Journal, 2013,* 315429.

Reilly, C., Atkinson, P., Das, K. B., Chin, R. F. *et al.* (2014) 'Neurobehavioral comorbidities in children with active epilepsy: A population-based study.' *Pediatrics, 133,* e1586–1593.

Rydzewska, E., Hughes-Mccormack, L. A., Gillberg, C., Henderson, A. *et al.* (2018) 'Prevalence of long-term health conditions in adults with autism: Observational study of a whole country population.' *BMJ Open, 8,* e023945.

Skokauskas, N. and Frodl, T. (2015) 'Overlap between autism spectrum disorder and bipolar affective disorder.' *Psychopathology, 48,* 209–216.

Smits-Engelsman, B., Vincon, S., Blank, R., Quadrado, V. H., Polatajko, H. and Wilson, P. H. (2018) 'Evaluating the evidence for motor-based interventions in developmental coordination disorder: A systematic review and meta-analysis.' *Research in Developmental Disabilities, 74,* 72–102.

Solomon, M., Miller, M., Taylor, S. L., Hinshaw, S. P. and Carter, C. S. (2012) 'Autism symptoms and internalizing psychopathology in girls and boys with autism spectrum disorders.' *Journal of Autism and Developmental Disorders, 42,* 48–59.

Westman Andersson, G., Miniscalco, C. and Gillberg, C. (2013) 'Autism in preschoolers: Does individual clinician's first visit diagnosis agree with final comprehensive diagnosis? *Scientific World Journal, 2013,* 1–7.

Wing, L., Leekam, S. R., Libby, S. J., Gould, J. and Larcombe, M. (2002) 'The Diagnostic Interview for Social and Communication Disorders: Background, inter-rater reliability and clinical use.' *Journal of Child Psychology and Psychiatry, 43,* 3, 307–325.

World Health Organization (2018) *International Classification of Diseases for Mortality and Morbidity Statistics, Eleventh Revision* (ICD-11). Geneva: WHO.

CHAPTER 8

A Clinical Psychology Perspective on the Experiences and Mental Health Challenges of Girls With Autism

Judy Eaton

This chapter aims to address the mental health challenges faced by girls with autism from a clinical psychology perspective.

I am a clinical psychologist with many years' experience of working in Child and Adolescent Mental Health Services (CAMHS) in the United Kingdom. I have worked in both community National Health Service (NHS) teams and in adolescent inpatient services. It was during my time working in an inpatient unit that I became particularly interested in the mental health issues faced by girls with autism. Despite an estimated prevalence rate of 0.2 per cent (Brugha 2009) for autism in females derived from a whole population study and historical data that suggested that autism is a predominantly male condition, I was disturbed by the number of adolescent girls in inpatient units who had autism (diagnosed either prior to their admission or when they were inpatients). The issues and challenges of diagnosing girls with autism are described elsewhere in this book, and also in Eaton (2017). However, it did raise the question for me of how, and whether, these young women could be better supported. Since moving on from inpatient services, I have continued to assess and work with a large number of girls and adult women with autism, most of whom have experienced mental health challenges but have been supported to find a way of living that suits them and allows them to work, bring up a family and play an active role in society.

It is important to acknowledge that mental health difficulties can develop in females with autism. However, I strongly believe that this is largely due to lack of understanding of the 'female' presentation of autism. I use this term carefully as it is becoming clear that to adopt a gendered version of autism is not necessarily accurate or correct – there are many girls who present with a more obvious, 'male' version of autism and many boys who present in more of a 'female' manner. There is also a significant number of young people who describe themselves as 'gender fluid' or prefer not to identify as either male or female. The most important point from this is to be aware that autism can present in a variety of different ways. Lack of understanding or awareness, or refusal to make 'reasonable adjustments' in education, employment and community participation are often the underlying reason behind the mental health issues faced by women with autism.

What has become very clear to me over the course of a long career in clinical psychology is that most people with autism do not want to be considered as 'weird', or defective in some way. They do not want to be 'changed' or forced to become a version of themselves they cannot maintain. They simply want to be understood and accepted for the awesome, amazing, creative people they are.

In this chapter I contextualise possible mental health difficulties experienced by girls with autism by first considering the challenges of social relationships for them before discussing some of the mental health and educational challenges they may experience.

Social relationships

This part of the chapter will cover the friendship challenges faced by many girls and young women with autism. As has been stated in other chapters, one of the reasons that girls tend to be diagnosed with autism later than boys is their (often superficially) better social skills. When considering the nature of children's friendships in the playground it is helpful to think in terms of 'groups'. First, there are the 'popular girls' – those who are the leaders and the girls who everyone wants to be friends with. Second are the group of girls who are on the outside looking in, always trying to find a way to join in. Finally, there are the girls on the outside looking out – those who appear to be in their own world and quite happy in their own company.

In my own clinical experience, there are quite distinct personality types in girls with autism – some are 'quirky' and different from a very early age and tend to gravitate towards other quirky and different children or are quite happy to play on their own in the playground. Others are quite charismatic and dominant personalities; they will often want to be in charge and organise how games are played. Some, however, will watch, observe and copy what the other girls say and do, how they speak and interact with each other. All of these personalities can be easily accommodated in the pre-school and infant school and, to some extent, in the early part of junior school. The difficulties for girls with autism often start to become more apparent around Years 4 or 5 (when they are 8–10 years old).

For those who like to be in control, what can initially be seen as a confident approach towards other children gradually becomes perceived as 'bossy'. The lack of social imagination seen in children with autism often means that they simply cannot compromise or imagine a different way of playing or outcome to their game. This can lead to anger and anxiety and ultimately to rejection by the other children.

Girls who copy and imitate their peers often find that this strategy becomes far less effective as they approach adolescence (Bauminger et al. 2008; Carrington, Templeton and Papinczak 2003). Girls' friendships become so much more complex as they grow up. The concept of talking behind someone's back or making nasty comments about people when they leave the room is often confusing and anxiety, provoking for girls with autism. They may try to imitate this behaviour and get the timing and content completely wrong. They simply have not 'read' the subtle social rules around this type of behaviour. In addition, for many when they try to imitate others in other ways, they again somehow get it subtly 'wrong'. Their make-up and clothes choice might be 'over the top' or somewhat unusual. This can make them very prone to bullying and teasing by their peers.

In addition, during the early school years, many friendships are often facilitated by parents. Play-dates are organised and party invites sent out strategically to include certain children. As girls approach adolescence, they are much more likely to be quite vocal about who they do (and do not) want at their parties and social gatherings!

Interventions that specifically focus upon improving social skills can equip girls with autism with more appropriate ways of interacting with their peers. However, it is important to be aware of the different personality types. As stated, some girls are very happy with their own company or may relate better to boys or older adults, and who is to say that this is not perfectly appropriate for that young person if this is what they choose? In addition, having worked extensively with both younger girls and adult women with autism, it is important to appreciate the price that many pay for their desire to socialise. Socialising and interaction generally can be extremely tiring for girls with autism. Constantly needing to 'put on a mask' and behave in a way that enables them to fit in with others often leads to them becoming exhausted and 'burned out'. It is important to appreciate the need for (and allow) time alone to recharge their 'social battery'.

Girls with autism can also be sexually vulnerable. Sometimes the combination of a desire to 'fit in' with peers or be popular along with poor or reduced ability to 'read' intentions can lead to girls with autism being encouraged or coerced into sexual activity they are not emotionally ready for. This is particularly true in terms of what is colloquially known as 'sexting' (the sending of explicit pictures via social media). This also has implications if, by any chance, a girl over the age of 16 was to send a picture to a boy (or girl) who was under the age of 16.

It is vital that parents ensure that they have sound security on home computers, and programmes produced by the CEOP (Child Exploitation and Online Protection) programme can be very helpful. It is also important to be aware that typically developing children are also vulnerable. However, they tend to be better at picking up unspoken rules and sharing information amongst themselves. Girls with autism may need to be explicitly taught about online safety and sexual vulnerability. They are much less likely to simply 'pick it up' via everyday interaction with their peers.

Social media and social pressures can make it more difficult for young people with autism to express their individuality and develop solid self-esteem. Bullying of those who are 'different' is an unpleasant fact in today's society. In my clinical practice, parents often express sadness about their child's lack of social awareness or lack of friends. However, it is important to listen to what the individual child wants and support their choices with regard to what type of social interaction suits them best.

Anxiety and depression

The incidence of anxiety and anxiety-related difficulties in individuals with autism is reported to be high. A conservative estimate is that 40 per cent of those with a diagnosis will experience significant levels of anxiety (Van Steensel, Bogels and Perrin 2011). In my clinical experience, the correct figure is much higher. A variety of theories for this are explored more fully in Eaton (2017) and possible causes include having been bullied, social anxiety, sensory issues and difficulties with emotion regulation.

The ways in which anxiety manifests itself in girls with autism vary. Some will become increasingly unable to manage everyday life. They may experience sudden and dramatic mood swings. This is particularly true of those girls who try to 'mask' or camouflage their difficulties at school. These girls fly under the radar – often keeping themselves to themselves and rarely speaking out whilst in public, only to explode and become extremely upset and dysregulated as soon as they reach the safety and security of their own homes. There is often no apparent trigger and the young person's reaction can seem completely out of proportion to the situation. Others are not so good at 'masking'. They may struggle to stay calm and 'hold it together' at school and may become angry, shout at the teacher or storm out of the classroom. Many parents report a 'Jekyll and Hyde' personality change with swearing and shouting and even aggressive outbursts which are out of character. Some report that the young person appears out of control, with a 'glazed' look.

These are the more obvious and apparent outward signs of anxiety in young people with autism. This type of emotional outburst can be difficult and upsetting to witness and often the young person feels terrible after the event. However, in some ways this type of behaviour is easier to spot and support, because it is so visible.

Often girls with autism are very poor at vocalising how they are feeling. They are generally not good at recognising the signs within their body that they are becoming upset or anxious. Frequently, an outburst will appear to come out of the blue. Very often the intervention strategies that are suggested for helping with anxiety are based upon the principles of cognitive behavioural therapy (CBT). Successfully accessing this type of therapy relies upon the young person being able to link thoughts, feelings and bodily sensations – something that is frequently difficult for girls with autism.

What is often needed is more specific support and teaching around how certain situations make someone feel inside and assisting the young person to develop a better emotional vocabulary. Individuals with autism have poor social imagination and less effective (but not non-existent) theory of mind (the ability to infer the thoughts, feelings and emotions of others). This sometimes makes it hard for them to appreciate that other people do not automatically know what is upsetting them or making them anxious.

What can be more worrying and difficult to support are those girls who internalise their anxiety. These might be the girls who say very little about how they are feeling until they reach crisis point. Subtle signs are often there. Chewing or biting of nails or clothing or unusual repetitive movements or blinking are often seen. These girls may also develop disordered eating patterns (which will be discussed in more detail later in this chapter). They may also begin to withdraw. This type of behaviour is often missed by teachers and educators as the girl is simply perceived as being 'good' or compliant.

This may start as a reluctance to speak (selective mutism), or a reduced desire to go out of the house. However, this can very soon become chronic. Withdrawal into a fantasy world – whether this is an internal fantasy world or as part of a computer game – is also common. Some girls are very creative and draw or write elaborate stories. Again, this type of behaviour is often perceived as worrying and somehow 'wrong' by parents. They worry that their daughter is not happy or is somehow missing out on 'normal' social interaction opportunities. Some of this type of behaviour is perfectly normal 'regulating' behaviour for girls with autism. They need time alone, away from the crowd.

However, it can become more worrying if the young person refuses to come out of their room or begins to 'dissociate' and is essentially unreachable for periods of time. Some young people become so anxious that they begin to experience brief psychotic episodes where they may hear voices and appear quite unwell.

Allowing time to regulate and 'recover' during periods of heightened anxiety is both helpful and necessary for good mental health. However, there does have to be a balance. If a young person begins to display this type of behaviour or develops more significant features of depression (poorer than usual sleeping pattern, loss of appetite, sudden deterioration in self-care ability and a reduction in engaging in activities that were previously enjoyable), professional help should be sought.

It is always preferable, though, to try to help the young person manage these difficult feelings earlier rather than when things have reached crisis point. Mental health issues for young people today are at an all-time high and many health services are struggling to cope with the demand for support. Girls with autism may be more prone to experiencing anxiety than their non-autistic (or neurotypical) peers but high levels of anxiety are not inevitable. Sometimes fairly simple things like helping the young person to understand their own feelings and express themselves alongside acknowledging and accepting aspects of their life that may cause anxiety (such as sensory overload, social 'burnout' or academic struggles) can be enough to reassure and support them.

Self-harm

A great deal has been written about self-harming or self-injurious behaviour in individuals with autism. This has, however, tended to focus upon those people who are non-verbal and have a learning disability. What has been less well researched, and is reported anecdotally during clinical work, is the extent to which this type of behaviour is also prevalent within those with autism who are intellectually more able. It is often thought that self-injurious behaviour in people with poor verbal ability is a sign of frustration at their inability to effectively communicate needs or distress. What is often overlooked is the extent to which even more verbally and intellectually able individuals with autism will often struggle to verbalise their feelings. Often when in great distress, the ability to think and speak rationally will be impaired. In these cases, self-harming behaviour such as head banging or hitting themselves can be interpreted as a sign of frustration and anxiety. In addition, contrary to popular belief, 'stimming' or unusual and repetitive movements are common. For some people repetitive behaviours can be calming or are used as a strategy to reduce anxiety.

There may also be a sensory reason for some behaviours that, on the face of it, could appear to be self-harming or self-injurious.

Yasuda *et al.* (2016) examined pain sensitivity in people with autism and reported that the majority of case studies examined noted hypo-sensitivity to pain. Other studies reported hyper-sensitivity to pain, with individuals often reporting mixed reactions to painful stimuli. This is often observed clinically when young people can react quite dramatically to a paper cut but often do not register times when they have actually badly injured themselves.

For others, the self-harm may be a sign of emotional distress. Bjarehed and Lundh (2008) studied self-harming behaviour in typically developing adolescents and reported that it is very common. With the growth in social media sites since this study, as self-harm is known to be 'contagious', it is likely that this continues or has even increased in prevalence.

Lundh, Walgby-Lundh and Bjarehed (2011) found that girls were more likely to self-harm as a result of emotional distress than boys. It has been speculated that inflicting pain or injury on oneself is a behaviour that emerges most commonly when individuals feel alone or helpless and is used as a way of managing intense psychological pain. It is perhaps not surprising, therefore, that many girls with autism begin to self-harm, given their poor emotional literacy and difficulty explaining how they feel. What is worrying is the extent to which some girls with autism can take this self-harm. Some appear to have exceptional pain tolerance levels and also seem to be less aware of the possible consequences of their self-harm.

Once again, interventions that help young people to express how they are feeling can be helpful. Programmes such as dialectical behavioural therapy skills training can be very helpful, as what is essentially being provided are clear strategies for tolerating and managing feelings of distress. It provides people with a 'toolbox' of things to try when they are struggling.

Witnessing self-harm or becoming aware that it is happening can be very difficult for both teaching staff and parents. However, keeping an open dialogue about it and supporting the young person to both talk about their feelings and develop strategies to find alternatives to self-harm are essential. There are often huge amounts of shame associated with self-harm for the individual concerned. A quiet, calm, practical and non-panicked approach is helpful.

Anorexia and eating difficulties

This part of the chapter deals with both eating difficulties and eating disorders for girls with autism.

Selective eating, where only a few food types either are chosen or can be tolerated is common in young children. Many typically developing toddlers go through phases of refusing certain foods and this is often seen as part of normal development. However, Sharp *et al.* (2013) reported that compared to other groups, children with autism are five times more likely to develop selective eating patterns and, more importantly, that these patterns can continue through to adulthood. Many children with autism limit themselves to certain types of food (often 'beige' food such as bread, pasta and potato-based products) or will only accept certain brands of food. This often causes great anxiety for parents and carers who worry that their child may not be getting adequate nutrition.

The reasons for selective eating in children with autism are complex. First, predictability and routine are often very important, and they simply choose foods they know they like. Uncertainty about trying new food can be anxiety-provoking and it can be easier to stick with the familiar. For others, there may be a variety of sensory reasons for choosing certain textures and tastes of food. In many children, the first sign of this will be difficulties weaning or a disproportionate adverse reaction to the smell and/or texture of certain foods. The *DSM-5* (American Psychiatric Association 2013) now includes avoidant and restrictive food intake disorder as a distinct diagnostic category, and in the work done by psychologist Dr Elizabeth Shea, certain food types in children with autism provoked an extreme disgust response (Shea 2015a, 2015b). She likens this to someone being offered a bull's eyeball to eat. For other children it can be the smell of the food (or in terms of eating at school, the smell of the school dining room) that causes difficulties. The sound of other people eating can also be intolerable. All of this can make mealtimes a challenge.

Another reason for eating difficulties in some children with autism is what appears to be a reduced awareness of the sensation of either hunger or fullness. Interoception is the ability to recognise and interpret bodily signals. This can include the bodily sensations of hunger and fullness and can lead to a child or young person simply forgetting to eat or drink. This obviously has an impact upon their mood, wellbeing and ability to concentrate and focus during a school day. Many parents and teachers will recognise the concept of a 'hangry' (hungry/angry) child. There is limited research into whether this affects girls and boys with autism equally. Clinical experience would suggest that it is fairly similar.

However, where there is a much more compelling gender difference is in the development of eating disorders in girls with autism. There are a variety of different types of eating disorder (including avoidant and restrictive food intake disorder, discussed above). Anorexia nervosa is typified by extreme restriction of food intake and often results in very low body weight. Bulimia nervosa often involves a cycle of binge eating followed by purging. Girls with bulimia often maintain a more normal body weight but experience other debilitating symptoms.

The reasons for this gender difference are complex. Girls who develop eating disorders tend to be intelligent perfectionists, often with high baseline levels of anxiety. As their eating disorder develops and their body mass index gets lower, there is an impact upon cognitive functioning, often resulting in extremely rigid and inflexible thinking patterns. In studies of girls in inpatient units who have a diagnosis of anorexia nervosa, there appears to be a disproportionate number of young women who would meet criteria for a diagnosis of autism. Without a full diagnostic assessment, it is often difficult to establish whether, in fact, the rigid and inflexible thinking was always there or whether it is a feature of the effects of starvation upon the brain.

There also appear to be issues for some girls with autism around growing up or reaching puberty. Many girls with autism have a significantly lower social and emotional age compared to their typically developing peers. They often struggle with the idea of their body changing and starting their menstrual periods. Maintaining a low body weight can be a way of delaying puberty and its associated bodily changes.

For others, teasing or bullying about their body weight or body shape can be taken very literally, and the combination of a rigid thinking style with (possibly) a reduced sensation of hunger can make girls with autism very good at restricting their food intake. For some young women with autism, restricting their eating has nothing to do with body weight or body image. Earlier in this chapter, I discussed the ways in which girls with autism manage their anxiety levels. Some display their anxiety in very obvious ways, others find that by controlling their environment (in this case by controlling what they eat) they feel less anxious.

Whatever the underlying reason behind the development of eating difficulties in girls with autism, treatment and management of these difficulties can be challenging. The usual way of treating an eating disorder involves a combination of a fairly prescriptive diet plan alongside family therapy. Some girls with autism find the structure of an eating plan helpful, but others, particularly those who strongly resist demands and have a need for control, find this type of intervention intolerable. Many girls with autism also find family and other 'talking' therapies difficult due to their challenges in verbalising their feelings, adapting the way they think or taking other peoples' feelings into account. These challenges are further compounded if the young person has sensory difficulties around certain types and textures of food as it can be difficult to unpick their issues.

In terms of intervention, although this may at first appear counterintuitive, reducing the anxiety around food and food intake appears key. Dr Elizabeth Shea (2015a) advises allowing the young person to select her own preferred and 'safe' foods and to take a very gentle and considered approach to encouraging her to eat. It is also helpful to consider ways to help her to reduce her anxiety levels. Like self-harm, eating difficulties are often the outward sign of other things going on in the young person's life which they may not be able to easily verbalise. Obviously, if the issue becomes serious, it is necessary to seek professional support. Thankfully there are now a number of eating disorder services that have expertise in managing young people with autism.

Academic difficulties and school refusal

There has been great debate over the years regarding the use of 'low-functioning' and 'high-functioning' autism, and the term 'Asperger's syndrome' – which was often associated with high intelligence – has been removed from the diagnostic manuals. In my clinical experience it can be extremely misleading to focus too much on the concept of someone being 'high-functioning'. Some of the most cognitively able people I have come across in the course of my clinical work have struggled hugely with tasks that involve planning, sequencing and organising themselves. Some have struggled to find their way from classroom to classroom once they transition to high school. Many have significant difficulties remembering the books and equipment they need for the day. One particular young person had an IQ in the 'superior' range but frequently got lost when catching the bus home from sessions. High IQ does not always translate into good functional living ability.

Much of this has to do with poor, or impaired, executive function which is a common feature of both autism and attention deficit hyperactivity disorder (ADHD). In fact, around 40 per cent of children with autism will also have features of comorbid ADHD. As described above, executive function is the process by which people are able to plan, sequence and organise activities. It also impacts upon the ability to think about the consequences of actions or to consider whether it is an appropriate time to join in a conversation or make a particular comment. Children with poor executive function also find it hard to socialise appropriately and make and maintain friendships. All of this can have a huge impact upon self-esteem and how a child is perceived in a classroom situation.

On top of this, many children with autism have a 'spiky' profile of cognitive ability. This means that they may be exceptionally good at some tasks and exceptionally poor at others. Oliveras-Rentas *et al.* (2012) reported that in children with autism, a typical pattern emerged in cognitive ability testing – children frequently had good functional vocabulary, but poor social comprehension in addition to slow visual processing speed and impaired working memory (the ability to hold information in one's head for a short period of time). It is easy to see how children with autism who display these particular difficulties might find a typical mainstream school classroom a challenge. These difficulties become more of an issue as the curriculum demands increase throughout primary school and into secondary school. Being asked to remember instructions or write something down quickly from the board can be difficult. Literal language understanding and poor social comprehension can lead to misunderstanding and confusion about task expectations. This can sometimes lead to parents and teachers feeling that the child is 'lazy' or 'defiant', when in fact they simply cannot comply or complete what they have been asked to do.

As stated earlier in this chapter, girls with autism respond in a variety of ways to the anxiety that this type of situation often results in – they may act out, hide under the desk or run out of the room, or they may withdraw into a world of their own or 'daydream'. Some can, and do, hold it all together until they get home. As well as being difficult for the child, this can also be very stressful for parents who are often on the receiving end of distressed behaviour, especially if they are told by teachers that the child is 'absolutely fine' in the classroom.

Very often this can result in school refusal. The exact number of girls with autism who are either home or un-schooled is unclear. Many will develop physical symptoms of stress and be unable to attend school due to ill health. There is emerging evidence that for many of these girls, this can lead to features of post-traumatic stress disorder. For example, Mafesky *et al.* (2013) observed structural changes in the brains of young people with autism that were similar to those seen in individuals with a history of chronic trauma. As a consequence, their education is disrupted, and they have reduced opportunities to socialise and be with their peers.

Much of this type of stress could be massively reduced by having a better understanding of the child's needs and making reasonable, and often very simple, adjustments to minimise stress, such as providing homework on a printed sheet, coloured timetables and support with organisational skills, or taking time to cue in the girl who has switched off and is apparently 'daydreaming'.

Of course, there is also the issue of pastoral support around break times. For many children, the mid-morning and lunch-time break is an opportunity to let off steam and socialise with friends. For girls with autism, this is often another opportunity to 'fail' or experience bullying and rejection. Social skills support or even simply a 'safe place' within school where they can recharge their social 'battery' can be invaluable, as can buddy schemes and lunch time clubs where young people with autism can find their 'tribe' and be accepted.

Conclusion

In conclusion, I hope this chapter has highlighted some of the potential difficulties girls with autism might face. However, it is not all doom and gloom. School years, and particularly adolescence, can be difficult times for all children. We live in a social-media driven, competitive society where both adults and children judge each other by the number of 'likes' they have on Instagram posts. Social media also has an upside though, particularly for anyone who identifies as 'different' or neurodiverse. There are whole communities out there where people can find other people like them, who think the same way or like the same kinds of things. On the whole, society is far more aware now of both neurodiversity and gender diversity, and knowledge around the multi-faceted presentation of autism is growing.

I have met a large number of adult women who have accepted and actively embrace their autistic identity. Many work in creative fields, most are self-employed. Some did not do well at school and found it hard to concentrate on topics they found difficult or were not interested in but have gone on to excel in areas they have a passion for. The key to good mental health in girls with autism appears to be acceptance, reasonable adaptations and an end to trying to wedge square pegs into round holes!

References

American Psychiatric Association (2013) *Diagnostic and Statistical Manual of Mental Disorders: DSM-5* (5th edn). Washington, DC: American Psychiatric Publishing.

Bauminger, N., Solomon, M., Aviezer, A., Heung, K., Brown, J. and Rogers, S. J. (2008) 'Friendship in high-functioning children with autism spectrum disorder: Mixed and non-mixed dyads.' *Journal of Autism and Developmental Disorders*, *38*, 7, 1211–1229.

Bjarehed, J. and Lundh, L. G. (2008) 'Deliberate self-harm in 14-year-old adolescents: How frequent is it, and how is it associated with psychopathology, relationship variables and styles of emotional regulation?' *Cognitive Behaviour Therapy, 37*, 1, 26–37.

Brugha, T. (2009) *Autism Spectrum Disorders in Adults Living in Households Throughout England: Report from the Adult Psychiatric Morbidity Survey 2007*. The NHS Information Centre for Health and Social Care. Accessed on 8/10/18 at http://content.digital.nhs.uk/catalogue/PUB01131/aut-sp-dis-adu-liv-ho-a-p-m-sur-eng-2007-rep.pdf

Carrington, S., Templeton, E. and Papinczak, T. (2003) 'Adolescents with Asperger's syndrome and perceptions of friendships.' *Focus on Autism and Other Developmental Disabilities, 18*, 4, 211–218.

Eaton, J. (2017) *A Guide to Mental Health Issues in Girls and Young Women on the Autism Spectrum: Diagnosis, Intervention and Family Support*. London: Jessica Kingsley Publishers.

Lundh, L. G., Walgby-Lundh, M. and Bjarehed, J. (2011) 'Deliberate self-harm and psychological problems in young adolescents: Evidence of a bi-directional relationship in girls.' *Scandinavian Journal of Psychology, 52*, 5, 476–483.

Mafesky, C. A., Herrington, J., Siegel, M., Scarpa, A. *et al.* (2013). 'The role of emotion regulation in autism spectrum disorder.' *Journal of the American Academy of Child and Adolescent Psychiatry, 52*, 7, 679–688.

Oliveras-Rentas, R. E., Kenworthy, L., Robertson, R. B., Martin, A. and Wallace, G. L. (2012) 'WISC-IV profile in high functioning autism spectrum disorders: Impaired processing speed is associated with increased autism communication symptoms and decreased adaptive communication abilities.' *Journal of Autism and Developmental Disorders, 42*, 5, 655–661.

Sharp, W. G., Berry, R. C, McCracken, C., Nuhu, N. N. (2013) 'Feeding problems and nutrient intake in children with autism spectrum disorders: A meta-analysis and comprehensive review of the literature.' *Journal of Autism and Developmental Disorders, 43*, 9, 2159–2173.

Shea, E. (2015a) 'Eating disorders or disordered eating? Eating patterns in autism.' Network Autism. Accessed on 8/10/18 at http://network.autism.org.uk/good-practice/case-studies/eating-disorder-or-disordered-eating-eating-patterns-autism

Shea, E. (2015b) 'Supporting autistic people with eating issues.' Network Autism. Accessed on 8/10/18 at http://network.autism.org.uk/knowledge/insight-opinion/understanding-and-managing-eating-issues-autism-spectrum

Van Steensel, F., Bogels, S. and Perrin, S. (2011) 'Anxiety disorders in children and adolescents with autistic spectrum disorders: A meta-analysis.' *Clinical Child and Family Psychology Review, 14*, 3, 1071–1083.

Yasuda, Y., Hashimoto, R., Nakae, A., Kang, H. *et al.* (2016) 'Sensory cognitive abnormalities of pain in autism spectrum disorder: A case control study.' *Annals of General Psychiatry, 15*, 8, 1–8.

CHAPTER 9

Speech and Language Difficulties and Service Provision for Girls with Autism

Alexandra Sturrock with Etienne Goldsack

In this chapter we will consider the communicative needs of females with autism from the perspective of speech and language therapy services. First, we will familiarise ourselves with the role of SLT in autism provision. Then we will consider how speech and language difficulties present in females with autism and how these differences may have a specific impact on SLT services. We will focus on speech and language difficulties in girls with an intelligence quotient (IQ) in the typical range, because language impairment in girls with lower IQ is possibly just as well explained with reference to wider learning disabilities and autism literature. We will also focus on SLT provision through school services as this is the most likely age of involvement for our team. However, we hope that details of the cases and interventions used here can be easily applied to other ages and settings.

Both contributing authors in this chapter are practising SLTs with a specialist skill-set in autism assessment and intervention. Alexandra is a clinical specialist, diagnostician and researcher into females with autism. Etienne also works in autism provision, but her true expertise lies in her own diagnosis. She will share some of her personal reflections at the end of the chapter.

SLT provision

What are SLTs?

Speech and language therapists (SLT) specialise in the details of assessment and therapeutic intervention associated specifically with speech (how we *say* words) and language (how we *understand* words and *use* them to communicate ideas). We may work with children or adults, be it in a highly medical or educational setting, and focus on anything from speech sounds to eating and drinking difficulties. However, when thinking about autism we are primarily interested in social communication difficulties, that is, difficulties with the social use of language to communicate. SLTs often provide a bridge between our own clinical skills and educational or care models of working. As such, our fellow multi-disciplinary team (MDT) may include teachers, teaching assistants (TAs), specialist educators, family members/carers, social services, psychologists, psychiatrists, paediatricians, general practitioners and nurses. We are also members of the Allied Health Professionals (AHP) and so frequently work with physiotherapists and occupational therapists.

Where do SLTs work?

This will depend on the type of service we are providing. We are often found embedded within educational services. If you work in a school or college with high levels of special educational needs (SEN) there may be an SLT integrated into your team. How we are employed will impact on the service we provide. If our contract is with the education providers, then we will be based in the building, and client targets will be shaped by educational priorities. If we provide therapy through a healthcare system (i.e. the National Health Service in the UK), then we will be part of a wider clinical team, targets will be linked to *those* service directives and we may be located elsewhere for part of the week. There are pros and cons in both cases. SLTs will also be found within autism diagnostic teams or post-diagnostic specialist services and even in mental health provision. In these roles we will be clinic based and follow clinical pathways and protocols. However, wherever and however we work, our input should always be person centred, with a focus on improving functional communication by integrating therapy and targets into daily living and education. This will involve close working with the whole of the person's support network.

What do SLTs do?

Our basic remit is to assess and collect information about the child's language and communication, and use this to develop individualised therapeutic programmes of support. This is likely to look subtly different for every individual.

Assessment

Our first job will be to see what has already been done for the child, identify priority targets with family or educators and get a functional account of communication difficulties. If we assume here that the child has an existing diagnosis of autism, then it is likely she will have an extensive back history of clinical records. In these initial stages we are looking for evidence about the child's intellectual ability, motivation to communicate, special interests and preferences, and any barriers to communication. Wherever possible, we will always include the child's self-reflection in our assessment. There are a number of tools which can be used for this purpose, and with minor adaptations these will be accessible to most verbal children. I have found many girls with autism to be relatively good at self-reflection. Providing them with quiet space, time, written information and explicit direction will improve their identification of strengths and weaknesses in social communication.

SLTs also specialise in performing and interpreting formal language assessments. Results can either confirm existing beliefs about the child's abilities, or sometimes demonstrate underlying difficulties covered up by layers of masking or challenging behaviour. Our assessments will test *use* and/or *understanding* of language at various levels: single word vocabulary, sentence level and higher levels of narration or conversation. We will also look in detail at pragmatic and semantic language difficulties, and the reason for this will be explained in more detail later in the chapter.

Note: It is not uncommon for children with autism to have at least superficially good *expressive* language (especially when talking about their own special interests). Parents and teachers may comment on their child's great vocabulary and complex use of language, and girls in particular may be very talkative within the home environment. It then seems impossible that the same child might have relatively low *receptive* language (for example, when being asked to focus on things that other people want to talk about). However, many individuals with autism report real difficulties focusing on and processing other people's speech. One girl I recall had many receptive language scores within the first percentile (extremely poor function). She had been masking those difficulties by copying children during class-based tasks, maintaining learnt routines and following play behaviour during break. It is worth remembering that underlying language difficulties may be obscured by behaviours that seem like wilful inattention, disruptiveness, passivity or withdrawal.

Intervention/therapy

Assessment findings will usually be written up as a report and fed back to parents and educators. Recommendations within the report should include adaptations for the functional language environment; for example, describing the child's current language level and strategies for encouraging self-advocacy and academic inclusion. Ideally it should feed into MDT discussions and overarching education and health plans. It will also form the backbone of the therapist's intervention plan. Intervention will be highly individualised; however, the SLT is likely to provide some *direct therapy* (face-to-face contact with the child), *indirect programmes* established by the SLT but presented by parents and educators, and support team *training*.

Direct intervention might include focused 'within class' support, private one-to-one sessions, paired work, small groups or even whole classroom activities. Vignettes later in the chapter will give examples of activities I have undertaken with girls during some of these sessions. Indirect therapy will follow a specific programme devised by the SLT but presented by trained members of the teaching team or parents. The SLT will provide baseline and outcome measures to check the programme is working. Evidence suggests that parent- or teacher-led therapy programmes of this type can be an effective way of managing communication difficulties (Enderby *et al.* 2009), and it is thought to help generalise language skills into the wider functional environment.

Communication profiles for girls with autism

So, now we turn to the communicative strengths and weaknesses of females with autism. There are many areas where diagnosed girls and boys have similar profiles of communication and so, where relevant, we will talk about the autism group as a whole. I will highlight where there is evidence of a different pattern of strengths and weaknesses according to gender. It is important to remember that any difference between females and males reflects only the group norm. It could not predict the sex of the child, but instead reflects a typical pattern for the group. I have personally met girls who seemingly fit better with a classic male profile of communication and vice versa. However, group norms remain useful in order to understand specific support a child might need when fitting into their peer group. So, with that in mind…

Structural language

In this chapter we are focusing on the girls with autism who are accessing mainstream school and therefore could be assumed to have *normal range* intelligence. This is important because overall structural language measures (i.e. single-word vocabulary and sentence-level language) will improve in line with cognitive ability. It is not in the scope of this chapter to discuss communication difficulties at every level of IQ. Even restricting ourselves to considering the *normal* range population, we are still including everyone from IQ 70 (borderline learning difficulties) to 130 (superior). This means when we talk about structural language skills within that group we are also talking about a very wide range of verbal ability.

As a very broad rule of thumb, children with borderline cognitive difficulties may have some good skills at word and sentence level but will likely have low scores on formal tests and certainly have difficulties with processing the type of language commonly used by their peers, and they may need some picture support and demonstration to help with learning.

Children with an average IQ (around 100) will very likely have typical scores on formal language assessments at word and sentence level. They may have specific difficulties with tasks that require listening to detail or processing language for long periods, especially where interpreting or mentally storing information is required.

Even children with excellent language test scores and literacy levels can report functional difficulties when required to listen and process language for long periods of time. They may be able to use analytical cognitive skills to help follow and interpret spoken language, but this can come at a cost associated with fatigue and even stress. At this higher level it is unclear whether functional language difficulties are linked to specific language difficulties or whether it is better understood in terms of lower levels of attention or deficits in auditory processing, memory, sensory filtering or social/contextual interpretation, or whether it is a difficulty integrating multiple streams of information. In any case, functional difficulties processing spoken information have been reported to me similarly by academics, teachers and successful business people with a diagnosis.

Note: While cognitive ability can largely predict structural language levels, there is no evidence (that I am aware of) that females and males with autism will perform differently on these types of assessments.

Semantic differences

'Semantics' refers to meaning in language, which sounds straight-forward but, for example, when you think of the word 'bank' you may be thinking of a river bank or a building to deposit money in. You have to understand both meanings and be able to select the correct one for the situation. If you said, 'Meet the girl dressed in scarlet,' I would have to know that scarlet was a type of red. If you said, 'We are going to a furniture store,' I would have to know that this type of shop sold chairs and tables, and not chocolates and flowers. Word meaning is therefore more complex than it seems; it relies on good stored knowledge and flexible categorisation which can take into account multiple interpretations. Word meaning often relies on contextual information, which is a recognised area of difficulty for some individuals with autism, regardless of intellectual ability. Difficulties have been noted identifying categories for words (e.g. banana is a type of fruit) (Dunn and Bates 2005), and generating words relating to a topic (e.g. name ten occupations) (Bowler, Gaigg and Gardiner 2008). The problem may come from an underlying difference in word organisation and recall at a neural level (Dunn and Bates 2005), or reduced flexibility in switching between different word meanings (Minshew, Meyer and Goldstein 2002). This can result in some functional differences in productive speech; for example, a greater tendency to list, more repetitions and idiosyncratic usage of words (e.g. 'un-nice' instead of 'unpleasant'). Word recall problems can have a functional impact on the flow of conversation, and lead to an odd use of language and conversational breakdown.

Note: Goddard *et al.* (2014) showed that females with autism would outperform males with autism in a task generating vocabulary from a given category. A study I recently conducted with colleagues also showed that girls with autism would generate more correct category words than boys with autism (Sturrock *et al.* in preparation)

Pragmatic language difficulties

This refers to how structural language is used and can be interpreted within a specific context. As an example, if I said, 'I feel cold,' my literal meaning is that I/myself am feeling something and that is cold, to which a perfectly adequate response from a second person would be 'oh'. However, it is also possible that the statement is an *indirect request* to share a blanket or to go home and sit by the radiator, to which an adequate response is not 'oh'. The way we use language and interpret it depends on the context; who am I, who is the person that I am talking to, what is the immediate situation and what relevant knowledge do I assume we share? Most children with autism will have a functional difficulty with pragmatic skills (Eigsti *et al.* 2011), and this is not entirely mediated by general cognitive abilities. In clinic several individuals noted their annoyance when people used the phrase 'in a minute', which can be used to represent *an amount of time*, but rarely literally a minute. Figurative language like metaphors (e.g. 'my teacher is a dragon'), understatements (e.g. 'we just got a few things from the shops') and hyperbole (e.g. 'you've got millions of CDs') all require interpretation based on context to understand actual meaning. A task investigating this in children with autism found them more likely to make errors in interpretation than children with typical development (Mackay and Shaw 2004).

Note: When we compared females with autism to males with autism on pragmatic tasks, we found females to perform better, although both scored lower than typically developing (TD) peers (Sturrock *et al.* in preparation).

Sarcasm of course relies on pragmatic language skills because to say 'nice dress' when it is clearly ghastly relies on the person interpreting the contextual, not the literal information. People with higher IQ and autism often report being aware of some of these conventions, but it can still slow them down in real time. One woman described having to consider the literal option every time she heard figurative language, in order to then rule it out and move on with other language processing.

Pragmatic interpretation may also rely on non-verbal communication; for example, the statement 'it's over here' is so ambiguous it requires some type of pointing or eye gaze to be interpreted. Gesture is another area of communication which can be lost on someone with autism. One young woman I worked with succinctly explained that she spent so much time thinking about what people were saying that if she also had to worry about what they were doing with their hands or faces she would never get anything done. She coped by just wiping this from her to-do list and focusing on speech, thereby missing many valuable visual cues to communicative meaning. Non-verbal communication can include paralinguistic behaviours like physical gesture, facial expression and eye gaze (which can be *too much*, *too little* or *atypical* in some way). It can also include prosodic features of speech: rate (too fast/too slow), volume (too loud/too quiet), intonation, timing and rhythm (which can be typical or unusual). These non-verbal aspects contribute more to our overall communication than verbal language, so if someone is not able to process this information they are losing important communicative information. Paul *et al.* (2009) showed differences in prosodic and paralinguistic communicative behaviours between autistic and non-autistic groups.

Note: There is some evidence to suggest that females with autism may perform better on at least their use of communicative gestures than male peers (Holtmann, Bölte and Poustka 2007), though Hiller, Young and Weber (2014) felt they were still likely to struggle with interpreting gesture in other people.

Paul *et al.* (2009) also showed differences in pragmatic behaviours between typically developing groups and high-functioning/Asperger's groups, who were more formal, provided inappropriate levels of detail, were tangential, overly focused on their own interests, unresponsive to examiners' cues, and showed little reciprocity in turn taking. In terms of pragmatic skills these differences show a poor application of language to context. However, there is some evidence that females with autism may be slightly better at elements of reciprocity in social communication than males with autism (Hiller *et al.* 2014).

There is probably some mediating effect of cognitive ability on pragmatic skills, and this can affect clinical and research conditions. One young lady I worked with talked through her process of interpreting pragmatic answers correctly. She described herself as a fan of detective shows and enjoyed looking for clues in conversations. So, for each item on the assessment she used analytical rather than intuitive skills, which must have been enormously draining for her when compared to typically developing peers. She did have an extremely high IQ, which helped. However, despite her phenomenal performance on test material, she struggled considerably to develop peer relationships, which is surely the real test of good pragmatic ability.

Impact of communication difficulties

It is also important to consider the impact of these communication difficulties on females with autism. We do know that typically developing females use language rather more than males to discuss emotions, and that subtle use of social communication is rather more important in friendship building (Newman *et al.* 2008). A similar pattern was identified in the autistic population (Sedgewick *et al.* 2016), with communication skills seen as more integral to friendships in females than males. A very moving analysis of peer interactions between one female with autism and a lunch group of TD girls showed how she was unable to modify her communication to fit in with the group (Dean, Adams and Kasari 2013). The children attempted to modify her behaviour, first with subtle feedback, then direct feedback, then by negative commentary, but finally they withdrew their attention altogether. It is possible that females' social networks rely on a rather more complex use of social language than males', and this puts females with autism at a disadvantage within their own peer group. Certainly, parents and the individuals themselves have been found to rate communicative difficulties higher than what might be indicated from objective analysis of language (Holtmann *et al.* 2007; Lai *et al.* 2011; Sturrock *et al.* in preparation). This may reflect the relative difficulties they experience when compared to their gender norm peer group and wider societal expectations.

SLT intervention in practice

So, a girl with autism may have some language and communication features in common with her male peers, but she will also have specific strengths and weaknesses quite personal to herself. The intervention required will depend on her own cognitive and language capacity, what she has learnt from her communication environment so far, and what her peer group demands might be. As with male peers, we may offer advice on appropriate use of language and visual aids for the child, and programmes of direct or indirect work for building structural, semantic or pragmatic language skills.

Below are a number of vignettes which represent sessions I have offered females with autism, and which seem to typify some of the more common social communication targets.

A conversation group

In one school several girls reported difficulties socialising during break (a common phenomenon) and so we arranged a conversation group within a lunch session. The girls themselves had mixed abilities in conversational skills: some with more motivation than capacity; some who could be described as aloof and alone; and others who would talk, but only to staff.

The group required some structured activities and discussion topics to focus attention and to reduce demands. These were initially chosen by myself, but as the group became more established, activities were chosen collaboratively. We took part in arts and crafts and group meditation sessions to help people feel at ease. We also discussed fun topics from magazines and some articles specifically relevant to the girls and autism; for example, 'What sensory difficulties do you have?' 'What support would you like in school?' 'What would you like other people to know about your condition?'

Guides were provided about good conversational practice (see Figure 9.1). Modelling of appropriate social etiquette and behaviours by staff was also important.

✓ We will all listen to each other when we talk
✓ We will all try to talk in the session
✓ We will take it in turns to suggest group activities
✓ We will accept feedback about the things we say and do in the group
✓ We will try to think of positive things to say about other each other's ideas
✓ We will try to ask questions about each other

Figure 9.1 Conversation group guidelines

This activity was about raising confidence and practising emerging skills in a safe environment. As such, the girls were not rated on their performance, but gentle feedback was given throughout; for example, 'I like the way you asked that,' or 'Is there a better way of saying that?' It would have been easy to introduce targets around this activity and maybe rate the individuals at the end of the session for self-reflection purposes. However, I think it would then be important to have placed the activity during class time, rather than free periods when the students need some opportunity to relax. It was very simple to run and very enjoyable. It could easily be handed over to trained staff to continue or adapted to meet the needs of older or younger girls.

Developing social skills

A social skills group is an excellent accompaniment to a conversation group although, to my mind, fundamentally different and I would always want to keep them separate. While girls might learn about good conversational practice in a social skills group (for example, appropriate eye contact, distance to conversational partner, active listening, turn taking, etc.) it is not always the best place to practise those skills due to the session being clinician-led and therefore not very natural. Alternatively, imposing learnt skills during a conversation group could impede real-time interactions, making a conversation less realistic and more anxiety-provoking. However, run simultaneously, experiences from conversation practice could be a great source for discussion in a concurrent social skills group.

There is no doubt that females with autism need support with social development. They are motivated in this area and often have existing skills which need developing or honing. However, this is an area where there may be a great deal of variation in ability. Constraining the group to individuals with completely overlapping needs could mean numbers would be reduced to one. Therefore, making a social group of mixed ability is not only beneficial but possibly also inevitable. In the group I ran we made a careful analysis of needs first, then drew up some realistic targets which could be addressed at the various levels of ability we had in the class. Topics included 'making friends', 'stranger danger', 'developing self-esteem', 'better conversation skills' and 'self-advocacy'. Girls with higher-level skills were quite happy to take on a supporting role to others, and the girls with more difficulty in this area enjoyed gaining insight from their peers. However, it needed to be managed in order not to make the participants feel the tasks were either too easy or too complex for them.

In these groups each girl was involved in her own target setting and encouraged to make self and peer reflections at the end of each session. This gave them a sense of control and engagement in developing their skills.

Discussion groups: changing bodies

An additional group activity would be a discussion group focusing on specific areas of concern for the girls. A commonly identified difficulty is coming to terms with puberty. The members of my group were at various stages of development both physically and sexually, but there were some common concerns; for example, changes to physical body shape, starting periods and increased awareness of sexual issues.

It goes almost without saying that this is work of an MDT nature. Within a school setting, teachers and nurses should be involved all the way and may even be leading on this issue. But an SLT could be involved in adapting standardised materials and making sure the language is appropriately clear and literal. Visual information may need to be developed, even for very able girls. Concrete examples of what something might look like and feel like can be very powerful. Images of changing physical form may be harder to accept for this group and so more discussion time should be built into the session. Girls may need opportunities to reflect on the issues and return to them at a later date. They may require written forms of information to help them with this reflection.

In my sessions I also introduced discussion about sensory issues, and we used the Adult/Adolescent Sensory Profile (Dunn 2002) supported by additional visual information to identify specific issues for the girls, such as tight-fitting clothes (bras), changes in personal odour, and sensitivity to textures (wearing a sanitary pad). For issues that were too personal, girls were offered private sessions, but group discussion was often a good way of providing a non-threatening introduction to the topic. Some issues went well outside of the remit of a speech therapy session, but, as familiar medical professionals, it is a safe place to discuss onward referrals with parents, teachers and the girls themselves.

Recognising emotions

One potential area of difficulty can arise from a poverty recognising facial expressions. This will impact on a person's ability to understand the motivation of others in social situations. Typically, I would assess people with higher IQ and autism using mind reading activity sheets (Baron-Cohen 2004). A common pattern for this group can be to only recognise basic emotions like happy, sad, angry, surprised, worried, but have poor knowledge of more complex concepts and, in particular, mixed emotions. Females I have worked with have also described difficulty identifying the same emotion in different faces because the natural differences between people (e.g. the physical shape of the mouth or brow) are more significant than the shared characteristics of, for example, being happy. Looking at faces can also become a source of anxiety. However, this is exactly what is needed in order to develop skills in this area. During therapy sessions I have supported girls to develop a photo database of emotions. To reduce stress related to looking at too many human faces I have asked them to do web searches for the target emotion, first in favourite film or cartoon characters, animals, and children (which can be easier to look at). Only when that is complete will I ask them to find a picture of an adult woman and man also representing the same emotion. This task can reduce barriers to engagement and is often enjoyable. It is quite amazing what animal expressions people have documented on the internet (confused llama, stubborn gorilla, cheerful hamster all spring to mind).

Finally, the resulting picture data base can be used to discuss broad similarities between the facial expressions of the underlying emotions in question. It can provoke useful discussion about mixed emotions and how an individual can feel conflicted about a situation and therefore show multiple emotions in quick succession, or even simultaneously. Sessions of this type can also be used to discuss ways to clarify intent during conversation; for example, nice ways of asking the speaker, 'What did you mean by that?'

Preparing for independence: thinking and planning

This was a short block of therapy, more like a consultation than conventional therapy, really. It is most suitable for more able young women who are coping with their current situation but who need help transitioning to greater independence. I have used it with females moving into college, university and independent living where they have emerging, but certainly not established, organisation and planning skills.

The sessions involved three stages. First, we discuss a number of fictional scenarios where a young women needed to make a choice and there could be confusion about the right course of action. Then we introduced some visual thinking and planning strategies (see Figure 9.2).

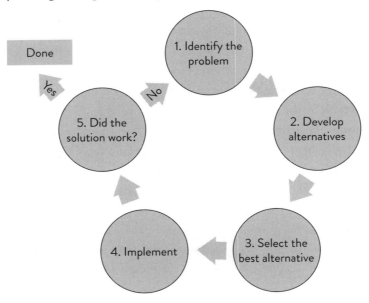

Figure 9.2 Visualisation of the steps to solve a problem

During these early trials we collaboratively choose themes that are relatively simple and not highly emotional. Using a form of mind mapping we identify a range of potential solutions to our fictitious problem (see Figure 9.3).

All options are added to the mind map, even if they are bizarre or unlikely solutions, which can make the activity a little more fun. We rate the solutions between one and five for suitability and decide on the pros and cons for each idea. In this way a best solution is reached. In the final stage of the process we apply the new strategies to real-life situations that the young woman is happy to discuss in session.

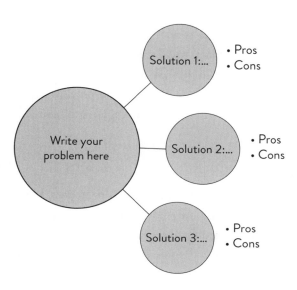

Figure 9.3 Visual strategy for choosing the best solution to your problem

These sessions can also be used to advise on the use of calendars, diaries and technology to help with organisation and planning. We can discuss what type of format work best for the individual and what sort of reminders she needs to engage with the strategy. This can then be supported and reinforced by the teaching team and family members in a functional setting.

Implications of gender differences in autism for SLT practice

Early years

This is a relatively basic concept but important in practice; females in the general population are less likely to have early language delay and will have relatively advanced early years expressive language when compared to males (Bouchard *et al.* 2009). There is recent research that suggests this pattern is mirrored in toddlers who are at risk of autism, with females demonstrating larger expressive vocabulary than males (Fipp-Rosenfield *et al.* 2018). This could mean females with autism will be less likely to be referred to SLT services in early years. Our services are an important route into diagnostic pathways for young boys (Kozlowski *et al.* 2011). However, with differences in their language profile this is a route to diagnosis potentially missed in girls.

Access to SLT

If language is not the primary need for females in early years, it may be that speech therapists are only involved once diagnosis is in place and social communication difficulties have begun to develop, often in middle to later childhood and adolescence. This does not mean that the need for communication support was not always there, but that the type of need was subtle, not in line with the greater difficulties associated with male norms and therefore not identified as significant enough for intervention. There is an argument in the wider field of language development that when females and males are judged against unisex norms we will see an over-diagnosis of language difficulties in males and under-diagnosis of the same in females, with females in a more disadvantageous position due to needing support but not receiving it (Erikkson *et al.* 2012). This argument would also hold true in females with autism. Subtle pragmatic difficulties may be going unidentified for this group, which means they are missing out on critical timely support.

Referral for intervention

In some of the more highly performing girls it may feel difficult to justify access to SLT according to existing service criteria. However, I hope it is clear that with the right type of referral these girls could certainly benefit from some dedicated SLT assessment and intervention. Appropriate and timely involvement with services may even help avoid secondary difficulties developing, such as mental health problems. Highlighting social communication difficulties and functional deficit in comparison to their peer group will be essential to a successful referral, as will highlighting the impact communication difficulties are having on well-being and friendship building. With these arguments in place before requesting a referral, it would be hard to deny the particularly well-positioned skill-set the SLTs can provide in terms of in-depth assessment and support.

Difficulties with assessment

There are a lot of considerations when assessing a female with autism for language and communication skills. It may be very challenging to identify communicative difficulties from observations alone, or even teacher/parent reports, because of the high levels of mirroring and masking that the girl is likely to do (Tierney, Burns and Kilbey 2016). The SLT will have to be highly attuned to subtle signs of difficulty and difference within the girl's social network. Language tests may also be problematic. In some cases, females with autism may achieve unrepresentatively high scores in formal language assessment. There could be several reasons for this. Some girls may show a preference for test conditions over spontaneous conversation, working quickly and diligently to complete their tasks and certainly not sitting and chatting. There may also be a strong drive for perfection in test performance. I have seen many girls keen to achieve the highest possible scores even at the expense of their well-being. I have also worked with girls who want to dominate test conditions, removing any element of uncertainty, in some cases insisting on having all assessments explained in advance before agreeing to take part, and others who have insisted on *re-taking* test items a second time to 'improve their score'. Accurate assessment in this group can be a tough job and does require peeling away the carefully positioned layers of masking behaviour that have been used to cover up underlying difficulties. This is not always pleasant for the girl and in my experience the closer an assessment probes at the heart of the difficulty the harder they can work to cover it up. Tests on occasions have resulted in demand-avoiding behaviour, shutting down completely or diverting attention to a subject of their own choosing.

Differential decision making: autism or social communication difficulties?

Occasionally we may be seeing a girl for a supposedly isolated language or social communication disorder. However, during our intervention process wider difficulties associated with autism are noted. This is a common scenario, possibly because of the intense one-to-one time an SLT spends with a child, or the detailed observations of social interactions we have the opportunity to make, or possibly even the specific pragmatic language assessments we undertake. We are often at the forefront of identifying autism-type difficulties, and when this is the case it is our role to share information with the wider team and begin collecting evidence that will support an appropriate referral to diagnostic services.

It is important, therefore, to be familiar with the main differences between autism and language or social communication disorders. In particular we can make a note of indicators of rigid behaviour, a need for sameness, and excessive sensory activities. They may present with:

- unusually high levels of anxiety about new activities and changes to tasks

- a desire to know exactly what will happen in advance and frequent checking after completion of an assessment

- perseverance around certain topic areas during conversational activities

- repetitive or idiosyncratic vocabulary

- intrusions of seemingly copied chunks of language

- sensory behaviours.

Note: Girls may be very good at covering up sensory behaviours that they are aware will mark them as different. Despite this I have seen excessive stroking of clothing, flicking finger nails and twiddling hair during sessions. Now I always leave a basket of fidget busters in my office and give the child permission to have a look while I am 'filling in paperwork'. What I am actually doing is making observations of any sensory interests the girl shows and how easily she can break from them to come back to task. This can be useful additional information to add to a referral for autism assessment.

After therapy?

It is unlikely that the girls with autism and higher cognitive ability we have been discussing here will stay on a rolling programme of SLT provision and so, inevitably, they will be discharged from service. This can be very stressful for the child and family. Speech therapy provides a safe, often one-to-one, environment with nurturing-communication opportunities. We are trained to respond positively to interaction attempts, even when there are notable difficulties. As such, we facilitate self-advocacy and build confidence in communication. This may be a rare space for a girl with autism, and hard to move away from at the end of a programme. Normally we will provide support to transition onwards from a block of therapy. This could involve advice and work packages to be conducted in the home or school, which will cement newly learnt skills into the wider environment. It is important to note that discharge does not necessarily mean the child has no further need of therapy but may mean that the anticipated outcomes at the point of referral have been met. While it can seem scary at the time, a child who is discharged can always be re-referred when a new or changing need arises.

Final words from Etienne

I was diagnosed with autism when I was 23 after a five-year battle for a referral to the appropriate autism assessment service and two assessments. My initial assessment highlighted that I had difficulties in all of the areas necessary for a diagnosis of autism but that my difficulties with social communication and interaction were not 'severe' enough. This is because I had spent my whole life learning to mask my symptoms. Following a second opinion, involving in-depth assessment with both me and my mum, I finally received my diagnosis. For me this was a relief – I was functioning as a perfectly well-adjusted autistic adult and not a failed 'neurotypical' adult.

In primary school I made a friend on the first day and she has remained my closest friend to this day. I have been able to observe her and mimic socially appropriate behaviours – for example, I can observe her in conversation and transfer this 'script' to other situations. I also know that if I say or do the wrong thing she will tell me in a gentle and caring way so that I don't make the same mistake twice!

My friend went to a different high school and this is where I really started to realise that I was different to my peers – I had nobody in school to take the lead for me, and friendships were now heavily based on social skills – i.e. knowing what to wear, who was 'cool'. I found it incredibly difficult to make small talk with my peers and I found myself isolated and alone most of the time. I no longer had somebody to rely on when I did not understand what the teacher expected of me or what I should say in conversation.

I think that what would have really helped me, more than anything, would be to have a learning mentor at high school who I could quietly approach to talk through any difficulties I may have been having. I have always been articulate and I am able to explain my wants/needs with another in great detail – once I feel that I have been given permission to do so. I am unlikely to approach somebody for help with a problem unless I have explicitly been told that it is okay. This means that until I was older nobody really knew of my internal struggle. I was a 'good' girl at school and therefore went largely unnoticed by the staff.

Another thing that I feel would have been really beneficial to my communication skills would be specific social skills training. I learn best through explicitly being told how to do something as well as observing it in action. There are a number of packages available for schools with detailed information on how to run social skills development groups in both primary- and secondary-aged pupils. This would not only have given me clear guidance on how to interact with others and learn to read their non-verbal signals, but it would have also given me the opportunity to meet other students with similar needs and validate the fact that I struggled to communicate effectively – this could have potentially prevented the severe social anxiety that I developed during my teenage years.

I now work as a speech and language therapist with children with autism. I chose to be a speech and language therapist as I feel that I can bring empathy to the job that can only come from having first-hand experience of communication difficulties. I also feel that being able to be open with parents of newly diagnosed children about my diagnosis is proof that autism is not a predictor of either success or failure in life. I work with a team who have a fantastic understanding of my needs and support me in a number of ways. For example, I now always receive a written summary of any discussions I have with my manager, and she has made it clear to me that it is absolutely fine for me to go to her with any concerns that I may have and I will not be judged. I am also given regular opportunities to shadow my colleagues so that I have models of appropriate interactions with clients, their parents and other professionals.

References

Baron-Cohen, S. (2004) *Mind Reading Emotions Library*. London: Jessica Kingsley Publishers.

Bouchard, C., Trudeau, N., Sutton, A., Boudreault, M. C. and Deneault, J. (2009) 'Gender differences in language development in French Canadian children between 8 and 30 months of age.' *Applied Psycholinguistics, 30*, 4, 685–707.

Bowler, D. M., Gaigg, S. B. and Gardiner, J. M. (2008) 'Subjective organisation in the free recall learning of adults with Asperger's syndrome.' *Journal of Autism and Developmental Disorders, 38*, 1, 104–113.

Dean, M., Adams, G. F. and Kasari, C. (2013) 'How narrative difficulties build peer rejection: A discourse analysis of a girl with autism and her female peers.' *Discourse Studies, 15*, 2, 147–166.

Dunn, M. A. and Bates, J. C. (2005) 'Developmental change in neutral processing of words by children with autism.' *Journal of Autism and Developmental Disorders, 35*, 3, 361–376.

Dunn, W. (2002) *Adolescent/Adult Sensory Profile*. Oxford: Pearson Education Ltd.

Eigsti, I. M., de Marchena, A. B., Schuh, J. M. and Kelley, E. (2011) 'Language acquisition in autism spectrum disorders: A developmental review.' *Research in Autism Spectrum Disorders, 5*, 2, 681–691.

Enderby, P., Pickstone, C., John, A., Cantrell, A. and Papaioannou, D. (2009) *Resource Manual for Commissioning and Planning Services for SLCN*. London: RCSLT.

Eriksson, M., Marschik, P. B., Tulviste, T., Almgren, M. *et al.* (2012) 'Differences between girls and boys in emerging language skills: Evidence from 10 language communities.' *British Journal of Developmental Psychology, 30*, 2, 326–343.

Fipp-Rosenfield, H. L., Dowd, A. C., Davidson, B. G. and Neal-Beevers, A. R. (2018) *Synchrony at 15 Months, Children's Risk Status, and the Relationship to Later Language Ability at 24 Months*. Oral presentation: Early Language Development. International Society for Autism Research, de Doelen, Rotterdam, May (2018).

Goddard, L., Dritschel, B., Robinson, S. and Howlin, P. (2014) 'Development of autobiographical memory in children with autism spectrum disorders: Deficits, gains, and predictors of performance.' *Development and Psychopathology, 26*, 1, 215–228.

Hiller, R. M., Young, R. L. and Weber, N. (2014) 'Sex differences in autism spectrum disorder based on DSM-5 criteria: Evidence from clinician and teacher reporting.' *Journal of Abnormal Child Psychology, 42*, 1381–1393.

Holtmann, M., Bölte, S. and Poustka, F. (2007) 'Autism spectrum disorders: Sex differences in autistic behaviour domains and coexisting psychopathology.' *Developmental Medicine and Child Neurology, 49*, 5, 361–366.

Kozlowski, A. M., Matson, J. L., Horovitz, M., Worley J. A. and Neal, D. (2011) 'Parents' first concerns of their child's development in toddlers with autism spectrum disorders.' *Developmental Neurorehabilitation, 14*, 2, 72–78.

Lai, M. C., Lombardo, M. V., Pasco, G., Ruigrok, A. N. *et al.* (2011) 'A behavioral comparison of male and female adults with high functioning autism spectrum conditions.' *PLOS One, 6,* 6, 1–10.

MacKay, G., and Shaw, A. (2004) 'A comparative study of figurative language in children with autistic spectrum disorders.' *Child Language Teaching and Therapy, 20,* 1, 13–32.

Minshew, N. J., Meyer, J. and Goldstein, G. (2002) 'Abstract reasoning in autism: A disassociation between concept formation and concept identification.' *Neuropsychology, 16,* 3, 327.

Newman, M. L., Groom, C. J., Handelman, L. D., and Pennebaker, J. W. (2008) 'Gender differences in language use: An analysis of 14,000 text samples.' *Discourse Processes, 45,* 3, 211–236.

Paul, R., Orlovski, S. M., Marcinko, H. C. and Volkmar, F. (2009) 'Conversational behaviors in youth with high-functioning ASD and Asperger syndrome.' *Journal of Autism and Developmental Disorders, 39,* 1, 115–125.

Sedgewick, F., Hill, V., Yates, R., Pickering, L. and Pellicano, E. (2016) 'Gender differences in the social motivation and friendship experiences of autistic and non-autistic adolescents.' *Journal of Autism and Developmental Disorders, 46,* 1297–1306.

Sturrock, A., Yau, N., Freed, J. and Adams, C. (in preparation) 'Speaking the same language? A preliminary comparison into the communication differences between females and males with autism spectrum disorder.'

Tierney, S., Burns, J. and Kilbey, E. (2016) 'Looking behind the mask: Social coping strategies of girls on the autistic spectrum.' *Research in Autism Spectrum Disorders, 23,* 73–83.

CHAPTER 10

The Role of Educational Psychologists in Supporting Autistic Girls in Education

Siobhan O'Hagan and Caroline Bond

Educational psychologists (EPs) (known as school psychologists in the United States) have a distinct role within education which complements the work of teachers and other educationalists. EPs work with the 0–25 age range and use their skills flexibly in relation to a variety of presenting individual difficulties and systemic educational issues. Fallon, Woods and Rooney (2010) argue that:

> EPs are fundamentally scientist practitioners who utilise, for the benefit of children and young people, psychological skills, knowledge and understanding through the functions of consultation, assessment, intervention, research and training, at organisational, group and individual level across educational, care and community settings, with a variety of role partners. (p.4)

Unlike most other professionals working in education, EPs and speech and language therapists (SLTs) are registered with the Health and Care Professions Council (HCPC) which requires them to adhere to specific ethical and professional standards (Woods 2016). Standards of proficiency relevant to the EP role (HCPC 2015) include keeping up to date with current research in educational psychology, supporting others to apply psychological knowledge and skills, using evidence-based and evidence-informed practice, and evaluating interventions. These specific areas of expertise enable EPs to bring additional skills and knowledge which can enhance provision in busy educational environments where there are many competing demands on the time of education staff.

EPs spend much of their time working with individual young people and their families, and recent surveys (Robinson, Bond and Oldfield 2018; Saddredini 2017) have identified that EPs can spend around 25–30 per cent of their time working with autistic children and young people as well as their schools and families. A similar trend has also been identified in the United States with over 50 per cent of school psychologists reporting that they engage in autism assessments and intervention 'frequently' or 'very frequently' (Sansosti and Sansosti 2013). Work with autistic children and young people appears to be on the rise, with school psychologists identifying a 32 per cent increase in autism cases over a five-year period (Sansosti and Sansosti 2013).

This chapter begins by discussing when an autistic girl may be referred to an EP and how EP support may be accessed. Following this, the chapter explores the five predominant areas of EP work outlined above by Fallon *et al.* (2010) and how they relate to working with autistic girls. Each section includes the experiences and opinions of three EPs who took part in a focus group specifically exploring this topic.

The focus group took place in an educational psychology service in the north of England and explored the experiences of EPs whose role included assessing and providing intervention for autistic girls or girls whose difficulties are consistent with the autism spectrum. Three EPs with varying experience volunteered to take part in the group and share their thoughts. Sarah,[1] who has been an EP for 15 years and has worked in several services, is particularly interested in autism and had been trained to administer the Autism Diagnostic Observation Schedule – General (ADOS-G; Lord *et al.* 2002). She had worked in different autism resource bases and had also worked on the autism pathway for her previous local authority. Harriet has been an EP within one local authority for 13 years and had previously been the lead on anti-bullying and early years work. Liz is a newly qualified EP and is particularly interested in emotional wellbeing and mental health.

EP referrals

EP work usually begins with a referral, often from a school. An example is provided below:

Laura

Laura is currently in Year 8 at high school. Her primary school reported that she was a shy girl who received some additional support with writing, but that she generally coped well and achieved academically within the average range. Since coming to high school, Laura's form tutor has been concerned that her attendance has been dropping and at parents' evening Laura's parents reported that Laura often says she is unwell and she is increasingly reluctant to come to school or socialise outside school. Laura's friend, who she transferred to high school with, also moved to another part of the country three months ago and Laura now spends her break times reading in the library.

---

1 Pseudonyms have been used for each participant.

This is a familiar referral for EPs but for high school staff the needs of girls like Laura can be puzzling and there are many potential reasons why Laura might be experiencing difficulties. These difficulties might be transient or possibly indicative of a more pervasive difficulty such as being on the autism spectrum. The focus group EPs reported that they rarely receive referrals from schools in regard to girls with suspected autism but that referrals were more likely to be centred on concerns around mental health and school refusal. Harriet explained how in her work with secondary age girls, autism might present:

> as anxiety and other sorts of tendencies. One particular case that I remember, she had kind of deteriorated in her attendance and stopped going to school altogether but it had been gradual. They had tried to bring her in and just come in for things that she enjoyed, and she had a reduced timetable since she had come into Year 7. I became involved towards the end of Year 9, [or the] beginning of Year 10 when she just stopped going to school altogether.

One of the most salient findings from the focus group was that autism in girls was going undetected by schools, who were referring pupils to the EP due to their concerns regarding mental health and difficulties with school refusal behaviour; through further investigation it transpired in many of these cases that the difficulties were a result of unidentified autism. Referrals such as these tended to be for secondary-age girls whose behaviour had become quite extreme. As Sarah reported, 'Girls internalise and that leads to the anxiety element and I suppose they don't get noticed; and when they do get noticed it's pretty extreme behaviour where they are refusing to leave the house or other things.'

This difference in girls internalising their anxiety until they are no longer able to cope with school (compared to boys who tend to exhibit more externalising behaviours such as aggression) led the EPs in this exploratory research to feel it contributed to the later diagnosis for girls in two ways. First, due to girls internalising their feelings they appear to be able to manage within the learning environment, and therefore their difficulties can go unnoticed by school staff until behaviours such as school refusal arise. Second, with limited EP time, it was felt that the more disruptive and challenging boys would be referred to the EP before the less disruptive girls. Due to the relative subtleties in the presentation of female autism, the EPs felt that the most valuable method of investigating autism in girls was through observation in different contexts and over time. EPs then support schools in understanding the needs of their pupils and considering how best to meet their needs.

However, there can be some difficulties in accessing EP support. In the summer of 2010, with the aim of reducing national spending and in turn the national deficit, the new coalition government published their spending review (HM Treasury 2010). The focus on budget cuts and 'value for money' paved the way for a shift from public services to 'traded' services. This has meant that many EP services have become traded or partially traded services, and schools and local authorities need to buy in EP time. This has resulted in EPs and EP services developing a portfolio of services for schools to buy into (Fallon *et al.* 2010). Although the move to traded services has broadly been perceived positively by EPs and commissioners, there are some potential challenges relating to equality of access (Lee and Woods 2017) for autistic girls and many other children with special educational needs. First, it means that schools need to decide which pupils they will allocate their limited EP time to and then decide if they have enough in their school budget to buy in further time. This means it may be difficult for pupils such as autistic girls who internalise their anxiety and follow school rules to be referred and have access to the EP until they present extreme behaviour such as school refusal. Second, it has meant that schools who buy in EP time have more influence and control over the work EPs provide, which may lead to EPs providing more reactive work rather than preventative work that promotes student wellbeing. Third, the new traded model of service delivery potentially moves away from the earlier Every Child Matters legislation (DfES 2004), which emphasised a joined-up approach, with all services having responsibility for working together to achieve key outcomes for children.

Once referred, though, there are key aspects of work EPs may undertake, with consultation being a key starting point.

Consultation

Consultation is heavily embedded within EP practice and is therefore a predominant part of EP work. Consultation can be described as 'a conversation which aims to bring about some change in the completion of a task, or in the fulfilment of a work relationship' (Macready 1997). Through the consultation process, EPs aim to work with teachers to find solutions to school-based concerns on the individual, group or organisational level. Parents are often invited to have a three-way consultation with the school or to have a separate meeting with the EP. Gathering the perspectives of school staff and parents enables the EP to have a full picture of the child, which is particularly important for autistic girls. This was illustrated by the focus group EPs, who each gave examples of how autistic girls often appeared to cope at school and so the school were not concerned about them, yet at home their parents were seeing very different behaviours and were therefore highly concerned about their daughters:

> With parent drop-in, there was a parent who videoed their child because she felt that nobody understood how severe this behaviour was, as it was being held and brought back to the home. Watching it was difficult; it was related to sensory-seeking behaviour, and so it was like frantic movement in the bed to almost sensory seek but that wasn't seen anywhere else. (Sarah)

This discrepancy between home and school behaviour can be an important feature of how autistic girls present and is also highlighted in Chapter 4 on transition from primary to secondary school. It was felt by the EPs that girls can often mask their difficulties during the school day but when they are back at home in their secure base their true anguish shows. This has led to conflict between families and schools, as schools can be reluctant to use their allocated EP time on children who seem to be coping well at school.

> It's difficult then because the school are saying it's not a school issue because the behaviour's happening at home; but actually the behaviour is happening at home because school aren't recognising it, and are perhaps not giving the child an outlet because they haven't recognised it. So the school almost wash their hands of it because it's not a school issue. But the school should actually be doing more to meet those needs on site. (Liz)

However, there was not a clear consensus on whether working with children and young people who are having difficulties at home but not in school is part of the EP role: 'I mean, what is our role? Are we educational psychologists that are school based or are we now moving into supporting in the home?' (Sarah). Nonetheless, in cases where school and families have differing perspectives on the needs of a child and how best to support them, the consultation process provides a space for EPs to ensure all perspectives are heard and worked through with the needs of the child at the centre of any decisions.

Assessment

EPs assess children to ascertain what the needs of the child are and how best to support them, and they also play an important role in Education Health and Care Plan (EHCP) assessments which may enable young people to access additional resources to support their education (Department for Education/Department of Health 2015).

EPs adopt an approach to assessment which aims to understand how different systems in the young person's life such as school and home influence that young person. A recent survey (Saddredini 2017) found that the most commonly used autism assessment tools included consultation with the key adults around the young person and eliciting the views of the young person. EP assessments focus on educational needs rather than diagnosis (Saddredini 2017), and are driven by the initial questions posed by referrers. EPs use a range of evidence-based assessment tools and approaches which focus on the individual and their context to assist in answering referral questions in an informative way. For girls, their presentation may lead them to be identified as having less severe difficulties in school, which may contribute to under-diagnosis (Mandy *et al.* 2012; Moyse and Porter 2015).

Teachers' potential lack of understanding of how autistic girls present can also lead to reduced access to appropriate support (Moyse and Porter 2015). Although boys are more likely to have identified academic, behavioural and social difficulties, both boys and girls experience more peer problems as they get older (Hsiao *et al.* 2013), and the mental health needs of girls may also go unrecognised. Using the most appropriate assessment methods therefore needs to be considered to ensure the needs of girls are not missed and specific areas of need are also identified. Dean, Harwood and Kasari (2017) point out that if observational methods are being used in the playground, girls are less likely to be identified as they tend to stay close to peers and move in and out of peer groups in a similar way to typically developing girls. This fits with the camouflage or masking hypotheses and illustrates the need for assessment measures that are sensitive to the social acceptance and friendship difficulties that autistic girls are likely to experience, even at primary school (Dean *et al.* 2014). An ethnographic study by Moyes and Porter (2015) focused on the hidden curriculum, which is the implicit process of communicating norms and expectations in school. They illustrated how three autistic girls in primary school adapted to the implicit nature of the hidden curriculum by strategies such as withdrawing or controlling space and routines, thereby masking their difficulties and potentially contributing to their underachievement. These subtleties in presentation need to be taken into consideration when assessing girls.

The focus group EPs felt that the most valuable method of assessing autistic girls was through careful observation over time, as they felt that the difficulties that girls have are more subtle than those found in boys and need to be understood within the context of the environment. Liz explained:

> It's the behaviours that are not the typical ones you would expect from a boy, and not disruptive in the autism-type sense. There's a little girl at the minute and school are insistent that it is a behavioural issue but the paediatrician questioned if it was autism. The school were very much: 'We can't see it.' I feel what I've done in terms of my observation has been helpful because it's given more evidence for the paediatricians on that pathway to look at, in the sense that she's really capable of holding a reciprocal conversation and you think that she's got all this language and these lovely social cues and almost empathy – but really she is almost one step behind. I picked up that she was copying a lot of it when I was with her.

EPs need to play a role in highlighting how autism differs between boys and girls. In addition to showing fewer externalising behaviours, girls may also show more surface-level social skills than boys, such as being more likely to engage in two-way interaction and sharing of activities. Research suggests that autistic girls are more likely to use social imitation, which can mask their difficulties, especially for younger girls when social interactions are more straightforward (Attwood 2006). Girls are more likely than boys to have at least one close friend and may be perceived as shy by those around them rather than as having social difficulties (Kreiser and White 2014).

Evidence suggests that girls tend to have more developed linguistic skills than boys and have less restricted and repetitive patterns of interest (Kirkovski, Enticott and Fitzgerald 2013), which may also contribute to reduced identification. The interests of autistic girls are more likely to be related to people or animals, so interests might include soap operas, celebrities or horses, which are often less associated with autism (Kreiser and White 2014). Perfectionism, determination, eating disorders and fluidity of gender identity have also been associated with autistic girls and women (Kirkovski *et al.* 2013). As mentioned earlier in the chapter, girls may present differently at home and at school, making it important to include parent and pupil voice in any assessments undertaken (Moyse and Porter 2015). Being aware of these differences between girls and boys in how autism presents is important to ensure that girls do not go unrecognised by schools.

The focus group EPs all agreed that in their experience girls are more able and driven than boys to copy and mimic social behaviour, which can mask the difficulties they have and lead schools and other professionals not to consider autism or to dismiss it. Therefore, the EPs were in agreement that observation was vital for identifying more subtle obsessions. For example, a girl's obsession:

> can become almost a bit like the obsession with Thomas the Tank Engine but it can become almost an obsession of modelling and copying. I've worked with a young girl and [her obsession] was about copying the teacher and it was only from observing the context [that it became obvious that] the teacher had a habit of straightening her hair with her hands and she would copy that – she was beginning to copy and mimic the mannerisms of the teacher which appeared like social skills but with little understanding behind it. (Sarah)

As well as observation, Harriet and Sarah reported that they frequently use formal and informal scaling methods such as the Resiliency Scales for Children and Adolescents (Prince-Embury 2006) and a five-point scale (Dunn Buron and Curtis 2008). However, none of the EPs had used a formal assessment tool such as the ADOS-G (Lord *et al.* 2002) or a developmental neuropsychological assessment (Korkman, Kirk and Kemp 1998) with a girl as these tools do not facilitate understanding of the context in which the behaviour takes place. The EPs were all in agreement that if these tools were to be used then triangulation of information would be needed. The EPs discussed whether a new assessment tool designed specifically for girls would be beneficial. Opinions ranged from a checklist assessment tool not being useful as it would not incorporate environmental, family and background context, to a new tool based specifically on the female phenotype, suggesting that this could have some value.

In regards to the national context of diagnosing autism, the National Institute for Health and Care Excellence (NICE) provides guidelines which should be adhered to by all professionals working with autistic children and young people (NICE 2011). The guidelines provide a structure for how local authorities should organise their services and how to set up a local diagnostic pathway. The pathway should involve a multi-agency autism team whose core membership ought to include a paediatrician and/or child and adolescent psychiatrist, a speech and language therapist, and a clinical and/or educational psychologist whose work is overseen by a partnership board or local planning group (NICE 2011). Not all multi-agency autism teams will involve EPs, but irrespective of the local diagnostic process, EPs as scientist practitioners will be aware of some of the challenges around diagnosis for girls. These include later diagnosis and girls being less likely to be diagnosed if they do not have an additional learning difficulty or tending to be misdiagnosed if they do not show externalising behaviour difficulties. This is significant as early diagnosis can lead to better outcomes for the young person through early intervention, placement in an appropriate educational setting and support for the family to relieve pressure at home (Baird, Douglas and Murphy 2011).

The autism diagnostic pathway in the local authority where the focus group EPs worked did not involve EPs, but they felt the pathway would be more efficient with their involvement. The EPs felt that contextual evidence may be missed in a clinical setting and that the use of assessment checklists is not reliable without observation across time and in different situations. It was suggested by the EPs that the current practice in their service of assessment through the autism pathway was leading to some level of misdiagnosis or missed diagnosis. It was also suggested that with autism being less frequently identified in females, schools have less experience in identifying it, which is compounded by the difficulty of identifying some of the female-specific symptomology.

It was also suggested that EPs are in a unique position in regard to the relationships that they can have with schools, which means that they are in a position to collect contextual evidence that could support the diagnostic team. It was agreed that a more collaborative way of assessing children and young people for autism would lead to a quicker diagnostic process.

Intervention

Following on from individual assessments EPs will be involved in intervention planning. EPs work with key adults and young people to select and implement a range of evidence-based and evidence-informed interventions and strategies (Robinson *et al.* 2018). Important considerations for EPs in developing intervention plans include addressing intervention priorities for young people and those around them; tailoring interventions to suit the needs of the individual and their context; and using best-evidence interventions (Robinson *et al.* 2018). Through their direct work in schools, EPs are aware of the challenges of ensuring interventions in schools are feasible and offer meaningful outcomes. Wilkinson (2005) provides an example of how an evidence-based self-management intervention was successfully tailored to the needs of a young person in school to help increase on-task behaviour.

Interventions used by the focus group EPs included: a solution-focused approach through the use of a five-point scale in a backwards chaining approach; mindfulness and relaxation techniques; a desensitisation approach; routine and structure through techniques such as a now and then board; zones of regulation; Social Stories™ (Grey 2015; see also https://carolgraysocialstories.com); social and emotional aspects of learning; down time; and reframing. The ways in which the EPs described working with children and young people highlighted that the approaches they take tend to be tailored to meet the needs of each individual child rather than through the use of structured intervention programmes. For example, to help a sixth-form girl who was school refusing to understand that everything is not either brilliant or awful and that there are ways of moving between the two, Sarah described how she and the girl scaled from 1 to 10 all of the characters' outfits from the young person's favourite TV show. This solution-focused approach enabled Sarah to use the girl's personal interests to address her needs, and she felt that an assessment tool or intervention programme would not have given her this opportunity.

Another example described how a girl in Year 9 had school refused for a year before she was referred to the EP service and by this point the girl rarely left her bedroom. The EP suggested a desensitisation approach where the teaching assistant would visit her at home to form a relationship with her through walks together.

When providing intervention to promote the mental health of autistic girls, it is important to ascertain their viewpoint and listen to their voice. As Sarah explained:

> There was this one girl who felt like she was being forced to break rules that she had been taught she shouldn't break. Students weren't allowed to go through the reception room to get to another room. But a teacher had brought her through the reception room and so she had broken the rules. This caused her an enormous amount of anxiety and worry that the next day it would happen again. She was refusing

and struggling to get into school the next day over this tiny thing that could be prevented to reduce her anxiety. It's about asking the pupil about the things that are causing the anxiety.

EPs may also support autistic young people through group work or therapeutic work. This might include group work to develop social skills or therapeutic interventions such as cognitive behaviour therapy to help young people develop their skills in managing anxiety or to improve their social competence. Grieg and McKay (2005) provide an example of how cognitive behaviour therapy can be adapted to support autistic young people by using visuals to support reflection on how autism affects thoughts, feelings and behaviours.

EPs also need to be aware of how interventions for autism may need to be adapted or altered specifically for girls. The focus group EPs discussed that with the majority of students diagnosed with autism being male, intervention groups and resource bases tend to be male dominated, which can deter girls from utilising them. This highlights the importance of balancing groups so there is a feeling of inclusion and integration.

All the EPs agreed that the social rules for adolescent girls are more complex than for boys and, as such, autistic girls need down time and time to engage in sensory activities or specific interests:

The girl went and did rowing because rowing again is very active, and less conversational than being in the yard. Her respite time was very sensory, rowing back and forth, and school bought a rowing machine for her and that was her bit of sensory time and then she could socially interact – it worked wonders. Her little obsession was learning number plates and so to give her a bit of respite she would go into the car park and learn some number plates. I didn't come up with these; the school came up with them so very astute really, and she was a happy kid because of it. (Sarah)

This was supported by Harriet, who also felt that part of the EP role was to encourage a balance of respite and other types of intervention for autistic girls:

> I think sometimes that is missed. I think that these children need that down time because we're always on so much about let's support social interaction but sometimes they need that down time from it because it's a lot of work for them.

Training

EPs can also support schools in developing more autism-friendly systems and approaches. This might be through disseminating best practice or assisting schools to audit their provision using tools such as those developed by the Autism Education Trust (Daly, English and O'Brien 2016). The outcomes of such audits can then be used to plan how schools develop their autism-friendly approaches at classroom and whole-school levels. EPs are often involved in providing general autism training for school staff (Barrett 2006), which might also include more tailored training to develop the skills of specialist staff or link to the professionals and resources in the local context (Bond, Hebron and Oldfield 2017). Training in general strategies is a worthwhile investment as these strategies are often effective for a range of pupils including autistic girls. However, as recognised by the participants in the current study, there is a lack of training specific to the needs of girls:

> **Liz:** I'm just thinking that when we do any sort of training around ASC [autism spectrum conditions] there's nothing specifically for girls.
>
> **Sarah:** There should be.
>
> **Liz:** Yes, there's just not a lot of literature on it.

It is a positive development that the National Autistic Society has recently developed an online module aimed at diagnosticians which can also help school staff develop their skills in working with autistic girls (National Autistic Society 2018). Alongside this there is also a need for other training providers such as EPs to ensure that their training reflects the needs and voices of a range of autistic people, including girls.

Research

Although research into autism interventions has increased significantly in the past decade, with several significant systematic reviews being undertaken to synthesise the evidence (e.g. Bond *et al.* 2016; Wong *et al.* 2015), it is impossible to evaluate the extent to which these interventions are applicable to girls. The majority of intervention research has used male samples, or mixed male and female samples with only small numbers of female participants, making it difficult to draw specific conclusions about what works for girls and how similar or different this needs to be to generic autism interventions. Adaptations of existing interventions might include taking into account the importance of verbal interaction in female relationships or providing opportunities to learn through social modelling. A useful example is provided by McMahon, Vismara and Solomon (2013), who evaluated the differential effects of a social skills training programme. Fourteen young people aged 10–16 years participated in a weekly group; five participants were girls. The participants' behaviour was observed during each session. The researchers found girls interacted more than boys at the beginning of the intervention but – for both boys and girls – group interaction increased throughout the study. This fits with previous research which has shown that autistic girls tend to engage in more interactive activities but also highlights the importance of investigating the effects of interventions for different participant groups. This could also be extended to evaluating which aspects of an intervention are most beneficial for girls.

Jamison and Schuttler (2017) developed an intervention focusing specifically on the needs of autistic girls aged 13–18 years, called

Girls Night Out. This peer-mediated intervention took place in the community and focused on the development of social skills, self-determination and self-care through observation and practice of skills in the session and homework. Data from 34 female participants showed positive benefits in social competence and quality of life, and decreases in self-reported internalising symptoms. However, parent ratings did not show a similar pattern of improvements; this could be researched further as it may reflect that fewer parents responded or that there was less generalisation of skills. Although this study is promising, it also highlighted girls' vulnerability to anxiety and depression and the need for interventions tailored to girls' needs.

A further study by Ranson and Byrne (2014) looked at the broader school context and considered how a classroom intervention targeting the peer group could promote more positive peer attitudes towards autistic girls in a mainstream school. They compared the effects of an eight-session anti-stigma intervention for 12–13-year-olds with no intervention. Improvements in peer attitudes were found following the programme in both the intervention and non-intervention groups but fewer improvements in how peers reported that they would behave towards peers with autism were noted in either group. This study illustrates that effective systemic approaches which extend beyond a classroom intervention and directly support pupils to interact with each other are complex but warrant further investigation.

The studies outlined demonstrate the limited amount and sometimes inconclusive outcomes of research focusing specifically on autistic girls. This lack of research limits the evidence base available to EPs supporting schools; however, EPs are also able to flexibly apply a number of generic skills which inform their work with autistic girls. Further research would help to provide an evidence base for how generic autism interventions might be adapted to more effectively support this group. There is also a need for interventions that address specific areas (e.g. self-care, managing emotions, school refusal, reintegration, and planning for the future) and are aimed specifically at autistic girls. The EPs in this case study were frustrated by the lack of relevant literature but reported using their psychological knowledge to adapt a wide range of theories and interventions to address the specific needs of the child/young person. However, as not all educators working with this group would have this breadth of knowledge and resources, it would be beneficial to increase the evidence base of interventions that can be implemented by schools.

To conclude, for autistic girls education can present many challenges. Although there is growing awareness of autism among professionals working in education, it is only relatively recently that the specific needs of girls have been highlighted (Nasen 2016). Given the perception that autism is predominantly experienced by boys (Werling and Geschwind 2013) and the relative lack of knowledge regarding the needs of autistic girls, it is possible that their needs could be missed by education staff. EPs can play a key role in raising awareness of this group through their knowledge of child development and work with staff in a variety of education settings. Although little has been written to date about education provision for girls, this chapter has illustrated how EPs can be involved in supporting autistic girls, their families and schools through assessment and intervention at the individual and whole-school level. EPs can have an important role in: working jointly with home and school to understand the needs of individual autistic girls; conveying the impact of a diagnosis of autism on a young person's education to others; providing training for staff; developing individualised plans to facilitate the transition to adulthood; and assisting schools to implement and evaluate specific interventions for autistic girls. As highlighted in the examples above, EPs have a role to play in multi-agency working, which has the potential to speed up the referral, diagnostic and EHCP processes and lead to more timely intervention. The direct work EPs do with schools also enables them to promote greater awareness of the mental health difficulties that autistic girls are at risk of experiencing and which may enable educators to intervene before anxiety leads to school refusal or difficult behaviour at home.

References

Attwood, T. (2006) *Asperger's and Girls*. London: Jessica Kingsley Publishers.

Baird, G., Douglas, H. R. and Murphy, M. S. (2011) 'Recognising and diagnosing autism in children and young people: Summary of NICE guidance.' *British Medical Journal, 343*, d6360.

Barrett, M. (2006) 'Like dynamite going off in my ears: Using autobiographical accounts of autism with teaching professionals.' *Educational Psychology in Practice, 22*, 2, 95–110.

Bond, C., Hebron, J. and Oldfield, J. (2017) 'Professional learning among specialist staff in resourced mainstream schools for pupils with ASD and SLI.' *Educational Psychology in Practice, 33*, 4, 341–355.

Bond, C., Symes, W., Hebron, J., Humphrey, N. and Morewood, G. (2016) *Educating Persons with Autism Spectrum Disorder. A Systematic Literature Review.* Trim: National Council for Special Education.

Daly, M., English, A. and O'Brien, A. (2016) *AET Schools Autism Standards*. London: Autism Education Trust.

Dean, M., Harwood, R. and Kasari, C. (2017) 'The art of camouflage: Gender differences in the social behaviours of girls and boys with autism spectrum disorder.' *Autism, 21*, 6, 679–689.

Dean, M., Kasari, C., Shih, W., Frankel, F. *et al.* (2014) 'The peer relationships of girls with ASD at school: Comparison to boys and girls with and without ASD.' *Journal of Child Psychology and Psychiatry, 55*, 11, 1218–1225.

Department for Education/Department of Health (2015) *Special Educational Needs and Disabilities Code of Practice: 0–25 Years*. London: Crown Copyright.

Department for Education and Skills (DfES) (2004) *Every Child Matters: Change for Children in Schools*. Nottingham: DfES.

Dunn Buron, L. and Curtis, M. (2008) *The Incredible 5-Point Scale*. London: National Autistic Society.

Fallon, K., Woods, K. and Rooney, S. (2010) 'A discussion of the developing role of educational psychologists within children's services.' *Educational Psychology in Practice, 26*, 1, 1–24.

Grey, C. (2015) *The New Social Story Book*. Arlington, TX: Future Horizons.

Grieg, A. and MacKay, T. (2005) 'Asperger's syndrome and cognitive behaviour therapy: New applications for educational psychologists.' *Educational and Child Psychology 2*, 4, 4–15.

HCPC (2015) *Standards of Conduct, Performance and Ethics*. London: Health Professions Council.

HM Treasury (2010) *Spending Review 2010*. Accessed on 7/1/19 at https://assets. publishing.service.gov.uk/government/uploads/system/uploads/attachment_data/file/203826/Spending_review_2010.pdf

Hsiao, M.-N., Tseng, W.-L., Huang, H.-Y. and Gau, S. S.-F. (2013) 'Effects of autistic traits on social and school adjustment in children and adolescents: The moderating roles of age and gender.' *Research in Developmental Disabilities, 34*, 254–265.

Jamison, T. R. and Schuttler, J. O. (2017) 'Overview and preliminary evidence for a social skills and self-care curriculum for adolescent females with autism: The girls night out model.' *Journal of Autism and Developmental Disorders, 47*, 1, 110–125.

Kirkovski, M., Enticott, P. G. and Fitzgerald, P. B. (2013) 'A review of the role of female gender in autism spectrum disorders.' *Journal of Autism and Developmental Disorders, 43*, 11, 2584–2603.

Korkman, M., Kirk, U. and Kemp, S. (1998) *NEPSY: A Developmental Neuropsychological Assessment.* San Antonio, TX: Psychological Corporation.

Kreiser, N. L. and White, S. W. (2014) 'ASD in females: Are we overstating the gender difference in diagnosis?' *Clinical Child and Family Psychology Review, 17*, 67–84.

Lee, K. and Woods, K. (2017) 'Exploration of the developing role of the educational psychologist within the context of "traded" psychological services.' *Educational Psychology in Practice, 33*, 2, 111–125.

Lord, C., Rutter, M., DiLavore, P. C. and Risi, S. (2002) *Autism Diagnostic Observation Schedule Manual.* Los Angeles, CA: Western Psychological Services.

Macready, T. (1997) 'Conversations for change: Counselling and consultation from a social constructivist perspective.' *Educational Psychology in Practice, 13*, 2, 130–134.

Mandy, W., Chilvers, R., Chowdhury, U., Salter, G., Seigal, A. and Skuse, D. (2012) 'Sex differences in autism spectrum disorder: Evidence from a large sample of children and adolescents.' *Journal of Autism and Developmental Disorders, 42*, 7, 1304–1313.

McMahon, C., Vismara, L. A. and Solomon, M. (2013) 'Measuring changes in social behaviour during a social skills intervention for higher-functioning children and adolescents with autism spectrum disorder.' *Journal of Autism and Developmental Disorders, 43*, 8, 1843–1856.

Moyse, R. and Porter, J. (2015) 'The experience of the hidden curriculum for autistic girls at mainstream primary schools.' *European Journal of Special Needs Education, 30*, 187–201.

Nasen (2016) *Girls and Autism: Flying Under the Radar.* Tamworth: Nasen.

National Autistic Society (2018) 'Women and Girls.' Accessed on 8/7/18 at www.autism.org.uk/professionals/training-consultancy/online/women-and-girls.aspx

National Institute for Health and Care Excellence (NICE) (2011) *Autism Diagnosis in Children and Young People. Recognition, Referral and Diagnosis of Children and Young People on the Autism Spectrum.* Accessed on 4/1/19 at www.nice.org.uk/guidance/cg128

Prince-Embury, S. (2006) *Resiliency Scales for Children and Adolescents: Profiles of Personal Strengths.* San Antonio, TX: Harcourt Assessments.

Ranson, N. J. and Byrne, M. K. (2014) 'Promoting peer acceptance of females with higher-functioning autism in a mainstream education setting: A replication and extension of the effects of an autism anti-stigma program.' *Journal of Autism and Developmental Disorders, 44*, 11, 2778–2796.

Robinson, R., Bond, C. and Oldfield, J. (2018) 'A UK and Ireland survey of educational psychologists' intervention practices for students with autism spectrum disorder.' *Educational Psychology in Practice, 34*, 1, 58–72.

Sadreddini, S. (2017) *Educational psychologists' assessment practices for children with autism spectrum disorder.* Doctoral thesis, University of Manchester.

Sansosti, F. J. and Sansosti, J. M. (2013) 'Effective school-based service delivery for students with autism spectrum disorders: Where we are and where we need to go.' *Psychology in School, 50*, 3, 229–244.

Werling, D. M. and Geschwind, D. H. (2013) 'Sex differences in autism spectrum disorders.' *Current Opinion in Neurology, 26*, 2, 146–153.

Wilkinson, L. (2005) 'Supporting the inclusion of a student with Asperger syndrome: A case study using conjoint behavioural consultation and self-management.' *Educational Psychology in Practice, 21*, 307–326.

Wong, C., Odom, S. L., Hume, K. A., Cox, A. W. *et al.* (2015) 'Evidence-based practices for children, youth, and young adults with autism spectrum disorder: A comprehensive review.' *Journal of Autism and Developmental Disorders, 45*, 7, 1–16.

Woods, K. (2016) 'The Role and Perspectives of Practitioner Educational Psychologists.' In L. Peer and G. Reid (eds) *Special Educational Needs: A Guide for Inclusive Practice* (2nd edn). London: Sage Publications.

CHAPTER 11

Conclusion

Caroline Bond and Judith Hebron

In this final chapter we aim to draw together what we currently know about educational experiences and supports for autistic girls, as explored and discussed in the preceding chapters. In doing so, we summarise the themes that emerged across the chapters using the model proposed in the Introduction as an overarching explanatory framework (see Figure 11.1). This model, we believe, permits a more integrated understanding of the challenges as well as opportunities that autistic girls encounter during their educational years. The chapter concludes by highlighting future opportunities for research and practice as this important area expands and develops.

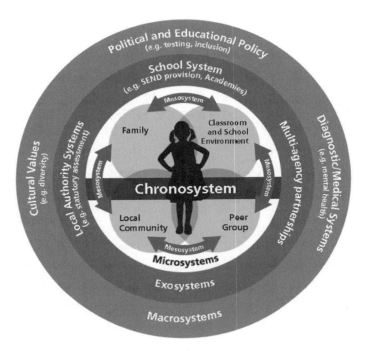

Figure 11.1 An integrated approach to understanding the educational experiences of autistic girls (adapted from Bronfenbrenner 2005)

The individual level

Starting at the individual level, a key theme throughout the book has been adopting a more sophisticated approach to identification by evaluating autistic girls' skills in relation to other girls rather than in comparison to autistic boys. Following on from this is the importance of personalised planning. In the chapters by Rachael Salter and Sarah-Jane and Elizabeth Critchley, case studies have illustrated that autistic girls, like autistic boys, will each have their own individual profile of strengths and difficulties which need to be understood and planned for in order to ensure they are able to access education and achieve. These examples also highlight how needs change over time and how strategies and interventions will require adaptation in order to accommodate challenges such as adolescence and transitions. One of the key individual issues that comes through strongly across the chapters relates to the particularly high levels of anxiety experienced by autistic girls which are often masked at school. How anxiety presents generally in these girls and at particular points such as transition are considered particularly by Judy Eaton, Sarah Wild and Judith Hebron, while the individual experiences of general anxiety and exams are powerfully communicated by Sarah-Jane and Elizabeth Critchley and Rachael Salter. This pattern of internalising anxiety appears to be somewhat more typical of autistic girls than autistic boys (Mandy *et al.* 2012) and, as discussed by Judy Eaton and Christopher Gillberg, might initially lead to diagnosis of a mental health difficulty such as an eating disorder or self-harm rather than autism. The potential issue of misdiagnosis in autistic girls is an important one for school staff to be aware of.

As individuals are part of and interact with wider social systems, Bronfenbrenner's ecosystemic model provides a framework for capturing the complex interplay of factors that impact on autistic girls from within and between wider educational and social systems. We start off by considering the microsystems which are closest to the individual (see Figure 11.1).

The microsystem

The family is a key microsystem and the role of parents and families in supporting and advocating for their autistic children has frequently been mentioned in the literature. Historically, parents of autistic children have faced challenges, including: systems that are difficult to navigate (Tissot 2011); teachers and professionals questioning their understanding of the perspectives of their child; and sometimes a lack of home–school collaboration (Lindsay *et al.* 2016), although there are some indications that this may be changing (Lindsay *et al.* 2016). This theme of parental advocacy and support comes across as important for girls in Part 1, particularly with Sarah-Jane and Elizabeth Critchley highlighting that schools and professionals may often not understand the specific needs of autistic girls, resulting in parents needing to take an active role in pursuing diagnosis and support. The differences in how girls might present at home and at school, and the impact of this upon the family, are evident in many chapters, especially those by Sarah-Jane and Elizabeth Critchley, Judy Eaton, and Siobhan O'Hagan and Caroline Bond. This is an important consideration for school staff and professionals when working with families.

Access to a local and/or wider community has received relatively little attention in academic research, although this is a priority for parents of autistic children (Pellicano, Dinsmore and Charman 2013). While not a primary focus of this book, it is promising to note that schools can – and often do – play a part in enabling girls to access different communities, perhaps around a particular area of interest such as music, as illustrated by Rachael Salter, or by facilitating access to a community of other autistic girls, as described by Sarah Wild, and Gareth Morewood and colleagues. As highlighted by Judy Eaton, schools can also have an important role to play in working with parents to support autistic pupils learn how to safely access online communities and social media platforms.

At the school and classroom level there are numerous factors to be considered. As discussed by Morewood and colleagues, there are many facets to an inclusive whole-school approach which have benefits for both autistic boys and girls, and even for the broader school population. Staff awareness and understanding are crucial and have been highlighted in most of the chapters. As illustrated poignantly by Rachael Salter, this can be a particular issue at secondary school where pupils come into contact with many different teachers. Although organisations such as the Autism Education Trust in the UK have been effective in providing autism training, which has reached many teachers (Cullen *et al.* 2013), there continues to be a lack of training that addresses the needs of autistic girls specifically. Lynn McCann highlights how training is crucial to make school staff aware of how autistic traits present in girls, often as internalising, how these traits might be masked through observing others, superficial sociability, and the challenges presented by late diagnosis or misdiagnosis. Training focusing specifically on autistic girls will help to counter misconceptions of autism and gender.

In addition to staff training, wider school systems are also important. Having systems to help manage sensory demands (such as a quiet place pupils can go to, clear routines, effective communication between staff, and a shared and inclusive ethos) is vital to ensure a consistency of approach for all pupils with and without additional needs such as autism (Bond and Hebron 2016).

There are many classroom and individual adaptations mentioned in the chapters which are equally applicable to autistic boys and girls. These include: carefully considering the language demands of tasks and providing supports such as visuals; managing the sensory environment; and supporting the child to understand and regulate their emotions. There may also be a need for more tailored interventions to enable girls to understand how to navigate female social relationships. Examples of these in the book relate to: girls' groups and explicit teaching about how to manage puberty (discussed by Alexandra Sturrock and Etienne Goldsack); developing self-awareness and anxiety management through therapeutic work (discussed by Morewood and colleagues); and keeping safe (discussed by Sarah Wild).

Peers are a final crucial part of the microsystem. Rachael Salter explains how peer relationships can be particularly challenging, and there is evidence that autistic girls may be at risk of subtle forms of bullying or reduced social acceptance, as described by Judith Hebron and Dean *et al.* (2014). However, the peer group can also be an important protective factor. Morewood and colleagues emphasise the importance of actively promoting autism awareness so that peers understand autism in girls, enabling the peer group to be a resource for friendship (Kendrick, Jutengren and Stattin 2012), social learning, and the development of a sense of school belonging.

The mesosystem

Although we have discussed the microsystems individually, it is also important to stress that these different systems interact with each other, particularly through social relationships. A crucial dimension is the active participation of autistic girls in their education. As emphasised by Morewood and colleagues, autistic girls are often keen to be involved in co-producing plans and negotiating outcomes. Sarah Wild's examples of the videos produced by the girls at Limpsfield Grange are also excellent illustrations of this active engagement in understanding autism and communicating this to others. Autistic pupils have also reported that they value teachers who actively facilitate their social relationships with peers (McLaughlin and Rafferty 2014), and the social groups described in Part 2 provide examples of this. For all autistic pupils, active collaboration between school staff (Bond and Hebron 2016), and between school staff and parents, are other key dimensions linking the microsystems and potentially leading to improved outcomes (Lindsay *et al.* 2016).

The exosystem

While the exosystem may appear more distant from the day-to-day experiences of autistic girls, there are many ways in which this can shape their educational experiences. As discussed by Caroline Bond and Siobhan O'Hagan, multi-agency partnerships between schools and educational psychologists can play an important role in enabling schools to identify autistic girls and meet their need more effectively. This can particularly be the case when other presenting difficulties such as school refusal may mask underlying autism and a change of approach is needed. Although the social communication skills of autistic girls compared to autistic boys may at first sight appear less of a concern for teachers (Hillier, Young and Weber 2014), Alexandra Sturrock and Etienne Goldsack provide a more detailed account of how autism may affect girls' language and communication skills more subtly yet still profoundly. A detailed speech and language profile can be crucial in understanding why communication breakdowns occur and assist in identifying effective strategies for supporting individual girls.

Wider local authority systems can also have an impact upon autistic girls, particularly in the context of spending cuts and the decreasing role of local authorities (Smith 2015). Sarah-Jane and Elizabeth Critchley describe how access to different support services and funding can be time-consuming, and what is offered may not be as individualised as might be hoped (this is similar to the concerns reported by parents in Tissot 2011). Given that autistic girls' difficulties may be perceived as milder than those of boys (Hillier *et al.* 2014), Siobhan O'Hagan and Caroline Bond point out that this can potentially make it more difficult for girls to be referred to specialist support services, such as educational psychology or clinical psychology, and possibly reduce the likelihood of receiving early intervention.

Linked to the local authority systems are also issues of how schools are organised and managed within a local area. In the UK there is considerable variation in the types of school, such as local authority-maintained schools, academies and independent schools, all of which may have different rules, expectations and admission criteria. Although it is generally accepted that there should be a continuum of provision for autistic pupils (Batten *et al.* 2006), the way in which this continuum is enacted locally will vary (Jones 2015). For instance, Limpsfield Grange, as described in the chapter by Sarah Wild, is unique in that it is the only state-funded residential school for autistic girls in the UK. It offers a broadly mainstream curriculum, providing more inclusive access (as well as high levels of personal support) to autistic girls for whom a mainstream setting is not currently manageable. Limpsfield Grange is therefore able to offer a bespoke approach for a group of autistic girls which provides access to a female peer group. However, in other parts of the country provision is quite different for autistic girls. The appropriateness of local provision is also highlighted by Sarah-Jane and Elizabeth Critchley who, after much persistence,

were eventually able to negotiate an online education package which
enabled Elizabeth to manage her anxiety and return to learning
while at home. Similar issues are also highlighted in Judith Hebron's
chapter, which describes the challenges faced by Lucy and her family
in finding the most appropriate specialist secondary provision to meet
her needs. Although Lucy was eventually able to make a successful
transition, her case study highlights the importance of taking social
as well as academic skills into consideration. This is also a point
made by Rachael Salter in her chapter where she describes how her
university provided a high level of sensitive support from the outset
which enabled her to successfully complete her degree and go on to
further study.

The macrosystem

The macrosystem is the most distal of the systems in our adaptation
of Bronfenbrenner's model. However, the ongoing development of
diagnostic criteria and systems can be seen to have a significant
impact throughout the chapters. The chapter by Christopher Gillberg
outlines the many challenges faced by clinicians in making a diagnosis
of autism in girls, and is mirrored in Elizabeth Critchley's and
Rachael Salter's lived experiences of the process of receiving an autism
diagnosis.

A second macrosystem factor concerns political and educational
philosophies. The impact of wider political changes in education
structures and funding at the exosystem level have been described
above. In addition to this, the positive benefits of inclusive education
approaches and strategies have been described in many of the chapters.
In particular the chapter by Morewood and colleagues locates inclusive
strategies within a clearly articulated whole-school 'saturation'
approach. However, increased pressures to 'achieve' in education,
such as the emphasis upon testing and the consequent anxiety created
by exams, are highlighted by both Sarah-Jane and Elizabeth Critchley
and Rachael Salter. This is a particular point of concern in terms of

access to higher education, as A levels return to a more examination-based approach that may impact negatively and disproportionately upon certain groups of learners, including autistic girls.

A final macrosystem consideration is the impact of wider culture. This includes values and attitudes such as awareness of disability and constructions of gender. The issue of awareness of autism in girls is highlighted throughout the book. For instance, in Sarah-Jane and Elizabeth Critchley's chapter, professionals decided that Elizabeth did not meet criteria for diagnosis as she made eye contact and participated in conversations, despite meeting many other key criteria. Similarly, in Sarah Wild's chapter she describes a senior local authority officer stating that girls could not have autism, while in Judith Hebron's chapter parents of peers openly questioned Rose's diagnosis, given her 'normal' appearance. Understanding of autism in girls is a key challenge for everyone working in education and supporting schools in order that autistic girls are no longer 'twice excluded' (Shefcyk 2015), and receive the intervention they need in order to succeed in education.

A further linked cultural issue is construction of gender. As Christopher Gillberg outlines in his chapter, autism has been viewed predominantly through 'a masculine lens' (Krahn and Fenton 2012) but there is increasing evidence for a female phenotype (Mandy *et al.* 2012). It is therefore important to consider how constructions of gender influence how autism presents in girls. As Risman (2004) argues, gender is socially constructed, constantly reconstructed over time, and intersectional in that it is embedded at the individual level and across the systems identified in Bronfenbrenner's model. This has important implications for autistic girls, as their socialisation into cultural gender roles will influence how their autism is expressed, with girls often being more likely to internalise and camouflage their difficulties (Lai *et al.* 2015). Kanfiszer, Davies and Collins (2017) also describe how autistic women in their sample reflected on feeling different from peers, particularly at secondary school when there was increased and conflicting pressure to conform to feminine stereotypes.

Concluding thoughts

In this book, we have aimed to illuminate for the first time the complexity of education for autistic girls, and in doing so have revealed how this experience cannot be isolated from the wider social context. We have illustrated that there are many similarities between autistic boys and girls, and since they have the same diagnosis, we would anticipate a high degree of similarity in core symptoms (Mussey, Ginn and Klinger 2017). Given the many similarities between autistic boys and girls, it is unsurprising that many of the educational strategies identified (such as visual timetables, structure and emotional regulation interventions) are effective for both groups. As pointed out by Simpson, Mundschenk and Heflin (2011), many interventions used to support autistic pupils, particularly in mainstream education settings, are often quite generic and effective for a range of children (i.e. not just those with autism) (Bond and Hebron 2016). A key principle for autistic boys and girls is adopting a personalised and collaborative approach which values the insights and priorities of young people themselves and their parents (Pellicano et al. 2013).

However, it is evident from the chapters in this book, as well as recent research, that there are subtle differences between boys and girls in their presentation of autism. These are likely to have a significant impact upon timely and accurate diagnosis and in turn how girls' needs are met in educational settings. These subtle differences include greater likelihood of masking of symptoms and imitating others in order to try to fit in. This can lead to developing compensatory strategies such as flitting in and out of playground games, an interest in social relationships and development of self-awareness, appearing bossy in an attempt to control the environment around them, avoiding demands, and a tendency to internalise rather than externalise difficulties. These factors contribute to autistic girls often presenting initially with mental health or eating difficulties.

Throughout this book we have identified many gaps in our current knowledge and the need for further development of research and practice. A key priority is to increase awareness of autistic girls among staff in schools, support professionals, clinicians and the wider community. Increased awareness of how autism presents in girls will help families and school staff to refer girls with social communication difficulties earlier, hopefully leading to more timely diagnosis and intervention. Irrespective of diagnosis, an understanding of social communication difficulties in autistic girls will enable schools to collaboratively develop and evaluate plans for meeting their individual needs. Further research is also needed to understand: what effective provision looks like for autistic girls in different educational settings (i.e. mainstream and special); how this is perceived by girls themselves; evaluation of interventions which are more specific to the needs of autistic girls, such as girls' groups and peer support; how generic interventions such as anxiety management can be tailored more effectively to girls; and how girls with multiple needs such as autism and mental health problems can be met. With the majority of autistic girls receiving mainstream provision, many examples in this book have focused on girls in these settings. However, this does not diminish the requirement for further research to understand the experiences and needs of girls in specialist provision, especially given their minority status in these settings. Despite the significant challenges faced by many autistic girls, it is hoped that an optimistic message can emerge from the chapters within this book: positive outcomes are not only possible for autistic girls but should become embedded within the broader drive towards a truly inclusive education for all young people.

References

Batten, A., Corbett, C., Rosenblatt, M., Withers, L. and Yuille, R. (2006) *Make School Make Sense. Autism and Education: The Reality for Families Today.* London: National Autistic Society.

Bond, C. and Hebron, J. (2016) 'Developing mainstream resource provision for pupils with autism spectrum disorder: Staff perceptions and satisfaction.' *European Journal of Special Needs Education, 31,* 2, 250–263.

Bronfenbrenner, U. (2005) *Making Human Beings Human: Bioecological Perspectives on Human Development.* London: Sage Publications.

Cullen, M. A., Cullen, S., Lindsay, G. and Arweck, E. (2013) *Evaluation of Autism Education Trust Training Hubs Programme, 2011–13: Final Report.* Warwick: Centre for Educational Development, Appraisal and Research. Accessed on 28/9/18 at https://warwick.ac.uk/fac/soc/cedar/projects/completed2013/autismeducationtrust/aet_-_final_report1_pdf.pdf

Dean, M., Kasari, C., Shih, W., Frankel, F. *et al.* (2014) 'The peer relationships of girls with ASD at school: Comparison of boys and girls with and without ASD.' *Journal of Child Psychology and Psychiatry, 55*, 1218–1225.

Hillier, R. M., Young, R. L. and Weber, N. (2014) 'Sex differences in autism spectrum disorder based on DSM-5 criteria: Evidence from clinician and teacher reporting.' *Journal of Abnormal Child Psychology, 42*, 1381–1393.

Jones, G. (2015) 'Autism: Enhancing whole school practice and the skills and understanding of the workforce.' *Journal of Research in Special Educational Needs, 15*, 2, 154–160.

Kanfiszer, L., Davies, F., and Collins, S. (2017) '"I was just so different": The experiences of women diagnosed with an autism spectrum disorder in adulthood in relation to gender and social relationships.' *Autism, 21*, 6, 661–669.

Kendrick, K., Jutengren, G. and Stattin, H. (2012) 'The protective role of supportive friends against bullying perpetration and victimization.' *Journal of Adolescence, 35*, 4, 1069–1080.

Krahn, T. M. and Fenton, A. (2012) 'The extreme male brain theory of autism and the potential adverse effects for boys and girls with autism.' *Journal of Bioethical Inquiry, 9*, 1, 93–103.

Lai, M. C., Lombardo, M. V., Auyeung, B., Chakrabarti, B. and Baron-Cohen, S. (2015) 'Sex/gender differences and autism: Setting the scene for future research.' *Journal of the American Academy of Child and Adolescent Psychiatry, 54*, 1, 11–24.

Lindsay, G., Ricketts, J., Peacey, L. V., Dockrell, J. E. and Charman, T. (2016) 'Meeting the educational and social needs of children with language impairment or autism spectrum disorder: The parents' perspectives.' *International Journal of Language and Communication Disorders, 51*, 5, 495–507.

Mandy, W., Chilvers, R., Chowdhury, U., Salter, G., Seigal, A. and Skuse, D. (2012) 'Sex differences in autism spectrum disorder: Evidence from a large sample of children and adolescents.' *Journal of Autism and Developmental Disorders, 42*, 7, 1304–1313.

McLaughlin, S. and Rafferty, H. (2014) 'Me and "It": Seven young people given a diagnosis of Asperger's syndrome.' *Educational and Child Psychology, 32*, 1, 63–78.

Mussey, J. L., Ginn, N. C. and Klinger, L. G. (2017) 'Are males and females with autism spectrum disorder more similar than we thought?' *Autism, 21*, 6, 733–737.

Pellicano, L., Dinsmore, A. and Charman, T. (2013) *A Future Made Together: Shaping Autism Research in the UK.* London: Institute of Education.

Risman, B. J. (2004) 'Gender as a social structure: Theory wrestling with activism.' *Gender and Society, 18*, 4, 429–450.

Shefcyk, A. (2015) 'Count us in: Addressing gender disparities in autism research.' *Autism, 19*, 2, 131–132.

Simpson, R. L., Mundschenk, N. A. and Heflin, J. L. (2011) 'Issues, policies, and recommendations for improving the education of learners with autism spectrum disorders.' *Journal of Disability Policy Studies, 22*, 1, 3–17.

Smith, N. (2015) 'The changing scene – Local authority support for SEND and inclusion matters: A case study of schools led partnership.' *Journal of Research in Special Educational Needs, 15*, 2, 141–146.

Tissot, C. (2011) 'Working together? Parent and local authority views on the process of obtaining appropriate educational provision for children with autism spectrum disorders.' *Educational Research, 53*, 1, 1–15.

Author Biographies

Caroline Bond is placement director for the Doctorate in Education and Child Psychology, which is an initial educational psychology training programme at the University of Manchester. She also practises as an educational psychologist with Catalyst Psychology, Manchester. Caroline's research focuses on meeting the needs of autistic learners in education and professional practice in educational psychology. She has published extensively in these areas. She has also been a member of the Autism Education Trust's Expert Reference group and is a member of autism@manchester, a collaborative research group involving autistic people, parents, professionals and academics.

Elizabeth Critchley was diagnosed with autism in March 2016 at the age of 16. She drew the illustrations for *A Different Joy* by Sarah-Jane Critchley over the course of a year and is currently studying for A levels, encouraged by her cats who sit with her for lessons (the perks of home-schooling!). She has an online shop selling products featuring her designs on Red Bubble (www.redbubble.com/people/elizabethcritch?asc=uk).

Sarah-Jane Critchley is the founder of the Different Joy Partnership. She is the internationally recognised author of *A Different Joy: The Parents' Guide to Living Better with Autism, Dyslexia, ADHD and More...*, has presented on autism education in China and Scotland, and has written for Charity Finance and ICSA. Sarah-Jane worked with colleagues in the UK, Italy and Greece on Transforming Autism Education, a project funded by the EU ERASMUS programme.

She spent ten years with the Autism Education Trust working to improve educational provision for young people with autism. She has been instrumental in the development, monitoring and management of workforce development programmes including training supported by the UK Department for Education that has reached over 180,000 education-based staff in England since 2012. Sarah-Jane holds an MBA from CASS Business School in London. She is a mother to two autistic teenagers (a late-diagnosed girl and a boy) and her husband is on the autism spectrum.

Judy Eaton is a consultant clinical psychologist currently working in independent practice. She worked within the UK National Health Service for ten years as the lead clinician within an autism diagnostic team. Subsequently she worked in low and medium secure in-patient services as lead consultant clinical psychologist for autism. A period of time working in an inpatient Child and Adolescent Mental Health Service with young people sectioned under the Mental Health Act led to a growing interest in the mental health challenges faced by young women with autism. She has recently been appointed as a research associate in the MRC Social, Genetic and Developmental Psychiatry Centre at the Institute of Psychiatry, King's College, London.

Christopher Gillberg is a professor of child and adolescent psychiatry at the University of Gothenburg, Sweden, and head of the Gillberg Neuropsychiatry Centre. He is one of the world's most experienced, clinically active child and adolescent psychiatrists, with 45 years of clinical work in treatment of patients and families with complex psychiatric and neurodevelopmental problems. His research ranges from genetics and basic neuroscience through epidemiology and clinical phenomenology to treatments/interventions and outcome. Christopher is a highly published and cited author in the autism field and is on Thomson Reuter's 2014 list of the world's most influential researchers.

Etienne Goldsack is a speech and language therapist working with children with a range of speech, language and communication needs. She was diagnosed with autism at 23 years old and following this has developed a strong interest in working with pre-school children with social communication difficulties. Etienne has provided training to professional groups about the presentation of autism in girls, including how it affected her life growing up.

Judith Hebron is a researcher and programme leader for the BSc Psychology with Education at the University of Leeds. She originally trained as a secondary school teacher and spent over a decade teaching French and also managing a languages department. A growing interest in understanding and addressing the needs of young people with special educational needs, and in particular autistic students, led to her returning to higher education, completing her PhD in Education and Psychology. Her research has focused on how to understand and promote positive learning experiences among young autistic people, including the importance of peer relationships and friendship, bullying, well-being, risk and resilience.

Lynn McCann has been an autism specialist teacher for over 12 years and is the author of *How to Support Children with Autism Spectrum Condition in Primary School*, *How to Support Students with Autism Spectrum Condition in Secondary School*, and *Stories that Explain* (a book of social stories), published by LDA. She works with autistic children and their teaching staff to make school successful. Communication, social interaction, sensory needs and access to learning are supported by many practical strategies and resources that she provides. Lynn also writes and delivers autism training and is an assessor for the National Autistic Society's Autism Accreditation scheme.

Gareth D. Morewood started teaching in the mid-1990s and has been the Director of Curriculum Support (SENCO) at Priestnall School in Stockport since September 2002. At the start of his SENCO career Gareth volunteered for the charity IPSEA (Independent Parental Special Education Advice) supporting families with tribunal preparation and appeals, and has recently been appointed a trustee. Over the last 20 years Gareth has helped shape provision in a number of schools, multi-academy trusts and local authorities across the UK, Ireland and Chile through support, research, training and consultancy and continues to regularly support parents/carers with special educational needs and disabilities (SEND) legislation and provision, as part of his wider interests in equality and opportunity for all. Gareth is an Honorary Research Fellow in Education at the University of Manchester. He is education advisor to Studio III, which provides training and advice to education settings on low arousal approaches. He is also vice chair of the online special needs and disabilities forum 'senco-forum'. Gareth has written and published extensively on SEND issues and his main areas of interest are autism and emotional regulation. Gareth tweets @gdmorewood, and his website can be found at www.gdmorewood.com

Siobhan O'Hagan is a trainee educational psychologist on the Doctorate in Educational and Child Psychology at the University of Manchester. Siobhan's previous research has explored the role and nature of friendships for children with autism, as well as educational psychologists' experiences of assessing girls with autism. Her current research is looking at autism and home education and how girls with autism who school refuse can be supported to return and thrive in mainstream education.

Rachael Salter is a talented young musician who has performed in orchestras and ensembles nationally and internationally. She received a diagnosis of Asperger's syndrome at the age of 11. Rachael has previously completed a BA Music and an MA Applied Psychology of Music. She is currently studying towards an MA in Social Research (Interdisciplinary), with her dissertation project focusing on the impact and role of music in the lives of young people on the autism spectrum. Following this, she plans to fulfil her ambition of training as a secondary school teacher.

Alexandra Sturrock is a highly specialist speech and language therapist working with autistic client groups since 2009. During this time she has specialised in autism with minimal or no additional learning difficulties (so called 'high-functioning' and Asperger's groups). This has involved providing assessment and therapeutic support in school services and leading on complex cases in adult diagnosis. During this time she developed a particular interest in understanding the female phenotype, initially to improve diagnostic accuracy for clients, but ultimately it became her area of research focus. Since 2014 she has been studying communication and gender differences in 'high-functioning' autistic children and has presented her work to professional and charitable groups across the UK. Together with Etienne Goldsack and Etienne's mother Lynn she established and still runs the Aspire: Female Autism Network, an online community group sharing resources and advice. She is a clinical lecturer at the University of Manchester, lecturing in developmental language disorder and autism spectrum condition. Since 2015 she has also been part of autism@manchester.

Carla Tomlinson is a trainee educational psychologist on the Doctorate in Educational and Child Psychology at the University of Manchester. A former teacher of A level psychology, Carla is researching the school experiences of adolescent females on the autism spectrum for her doctoral thesis. Alongside her research, she is currently practising as a trainee educational psychologist with Salford Educational Psychology Service.

Sarah Wild is the headteacher of Limpsfield Grange School in Surrey, a state-funded residential special school for girls with communication and interaction difficulties including autism. She is interested in how autism impacts on and manifests in girls and women, and in raising awareness of how autism in girls can present differently to autism in boys. Sarah is also interested in promoting and sustaining positive mental health and resilience in young people with special needs through education. She has the privilege of being a headteacher who works with a school full of curious, kind, compassionate teenage girls who will one day change the way we see the world, and a reflective and energetic staff team who have the capacity to teach her new things every day.

Subject Index

Author Index